Writing the Black Diasporic City in the Age of Globalization

Writing the Black Diasporic City in the Age of Globalization

CAROL BAILEY

Rutgers University Press

New Brunswick, Camden, and Newark, New Jersey, and London

Names: Bailey, Carol, author.
Title: Writing the Black diasporic city in the age of globalization / Carol Bailey.
Description: New Brunswick, New Jersey : Rutgers University Press, [2023] |
    Includes bibliographical references and index.
Identifiers: LCCN 2022010240 | ISBN 9781978829664 (paperback) |
    ISBN 9781978829671 (hardcover) | ISBN 9781978829688 (epub) |
    ISBN 9781978829695 (pdf)
Subjects: LCSH: Urban Black people—Social conditions. | City and town life |
    African diaspora. | Globalization. | BISAC: SOCIAL SCIENCE / Black Studies (Global) |
    LITERARY CRITICISM / African
Classification: LCC HT128.A2 B35 2023 | DDC 307.7608996—dc23/eng/20220825
LC record available at https://lccn.loc.gov/2022010240

A British Cataloging-in-Publication record for this book is available from the British Library.

www.rutgersuniversitypress.org

Manufactured in the United States of America

For my family and friends and for all minoritized people whose struggles and triumphs drive these creative accounts and sustain these critical engagements

Contents

Writing the Black Diasporic City in the Age of Globalization

Introduction

∎∎∎∎∎∎∎∎∎∎∎∎∎∎∎∎∎∎∎∎∎

Readers enter Ama Ata Aidoo's short story "In the Cutting of a Drink" in medias res to hear the narrator paint a picture of the city of Accra, to which he has recently traveled in search of his sister, Mansa. The shocking elements of city culture that he relates include the following observations: "I was dizzy from the number of cars which were passing. And I could not stand still. If I did, I felt as if the whole world was made up of cars in motion" (*No Sweetness Here* 30); "A woman prepares a meal for a man and eats it with him. Yes, they do so often" (33); "I sat with my mouth open and watched the daughter of a woman cut beer like a man" (34); "In the city, no one cares if you dance well or not" (34); and "any kind of work is work" (37). Each of the foregoing quotes highlights features of not just the city described in this story but cities in general; these quotes shape my theorization of modern global cities as ostensibly open, complicated, limber, and semicircular spaces, as well as locations of constantly shifting possibilities. The speaker's observations about women's apparent parity with men—"the woman eats with a man" and "cuts beer like a man"—mark clear departures from Eurocentric and some Global South "traditional" gender expectations. The pace of the city that the speaker describes, "cars and motion," for example, highlights movement, change, and the spirit and energy of cities. "In the city, no one cares if you dance well or not" captures the well-understood anonymity, freedom, and possibilities for self-making and remaking that cities are reputed to offer. The final quote, "any kind of work is work," leaves much open for conversations about opportunity and questionable agency. "Any kind of work is work" articulates the city as a site of trade, of commodification, where any skill or possession is available and accessible for trade. Work, in the context of the story, is in a bar, and the ready availability of women suggests sex work or exotic dancing—occupations in which women are often vulnerable victims. This range of city characteristics indicates just some ways in which cities function as sites of simultaneous opportunity and marginalization. They illustrate the unique position of cities as locations of change, newness, difference, and most significantly, complication. Over three decades after the publication of "In the Cutting of a Drink," Aidoo's fictional portrayal of the city still resonates in these current times of significant social change and amid ongoing challenges.

A comment made by Steve Fletcher—a city council member for Minneapolis, where George Floyd was killed—provides an example of the pivotal role of cities and makes visible the complex global exigencies of the twenty-first century. In a conversation about specific proposals to defund the police and the more general conversations about police reform, Fletcher contended, "Cities are the laboratories of democracy, and we are also the employers of police departments, and we are the ones who need to lead in this conversation" ("Politics with Amy Walter" 34:17–34:25). Fletcher's assertation is one more of observation than prescription, not so much suggesting what cities should do but recognizing how cities have been functioning and how that demonstrated vibrancy should translate into cities being increasingly visible in advancing social-justice work.

Aidoo's late-twentieth-century artistic representation and Fletcher's more recent sociopolitical observation also illustrate the synergy among creative, scholarly, and performative engagements with cities. For example, in *The Postcolonial City and Its Subjects* (2014), Rashmi Varma argues that "the urban space of the colonized city is wrenched from being an instrument of the colonialists into the very space of rebellion and self-making for the colonized" (13). This defensible point notwithstanding, the expectation that cities would provide a fuller sense of agency for former colonized peoples, immigrants, women, and other marginalized groups has not been fully or even sufficiently actualized. In depictions of the city experiences of peoples of African descent, writers and other creative artists offer a complex set of renditions of late-twentieth- and twenty-first-century Black urban citizens' experience in European or Euro-dominated cities—such as Boston, London, New York, and Toronto, as well as Global South cities such as Accra, Kingston, and Lagos—that emerged out of colonial domination.

To think of the city as a purely or even predominantly disempowering space would be to render the city circular, a proverbial "vicious circle," a space in which the already disenfranchised—immigrants, people of color, women, and others who move from rural areas to cities, as well as marginalized people born in these cities—simply give up one kind of marginality for another or live in an unchanged, tenuous state of stasis. Similarly, to see movement to cities entirely as promise for positive self-fashioning, material prosperity, and freedom would be to overlook the contemporary experiences that the creators of the works under consideration in this book recover. Yet it is difficult to ignore or deny

Monica Smith's observation that "a city—however small it was at the beginning or however large it may grow to be—feels like a place in which many aspects of life hold open the possibility of choice among a variety of potential actions" (*Cities*, 13). It is this inherent "openness" of cities that drives the creative accounts that, in turn, propel the theorization of Black diasporic cities in this book.[1]

The creative output from writers of the African diaspora has been consistently attentive to the complexity of city experiences for individuals for whom the city was not meant to be home. My study of such works has led me to ponder the status of Black bodies and Black embodied experiences in cities in both geographical and sociohistorical terms. This book theorizes the city as what I call a generative, "semicircular" social space, where the vicissitudes of globalization are most profoundly experienced. That is to say, taking seriously the seemingly competing narratives about cities—they are both sites of liberation and locations of marginality—I suggest that the fictive accounts offered in the works under consideration here configure cities as spaces where movement is simultaneously restrictive and liberating and where life prospects are at once promising and daunting. A semicircle is simply, and literally, half a circle; it is open in a way that the circle is not and is potentially less restrictive of movement than the circle, and it allows for movement to an end point. The presence of an end point along the contours of the semicircle therefore mitigates return to the point of origin, unless the individual makes the choice to return to where they started.

In choosing the semicircle as a visual and conceptual representation of city experiences, I seek to capture the city as a generative space of openness, movement, multiplicity, and flow in order to underscore my attention to the literal spatial considerations of these conversations as well as their ideological, socioeconomic, and cultural meanings. I take into account movement in and out of the city, especially when inward flows are grounded in a search for more—more freedoms, more and better jobs, and in general more access to modern capitalism. Semicircularity allows us to think about movement within the city, both in terms of physical location—bodies in places and spaces—and in more abstract terms, such as socioeconomic mobility. To say that the city is a semicircular space is also to admit its inherent openness and to acknowledge its promises and possibilities, because even as it restricts and marginalizes many people, the city very rarely excludes—even when we adjust our understanding of inclusion-exclusion to mean more than simply being allowed to exist in the space. My figure of the semicircle stands in contrast to the closedness of a circle, which would imply that city residents would be locked into unchanged circumstances—the aforementioned vicious circle.

Semicircularity is therefore the central theoretical axis for the wide-ranging and intersecting portrayals of cities in these creative works. For example, in

Marlon James's depiction of an inner-city culture of violence and underground economic systems in *A Brief History of Seven Killings*, we observe the incompleteness and thwarted possibilities that semicircularity conveys in the transnational urban sprawl; here, characters are ultimately unable to fully escape the debilitating conditions of postcolonial and postindependence urban communities. In the works of Michael Thomas and Zadie Smith, the city emerges as a space of historical trauma in which education facilitates some freedom from the socioeconomic marginalizations; notably, however, this socioeconomic marginalization is merely exchanged for other traumas, such as psychic dislocations. In Cecil Foster's portrayal of Toronto, the city is a site of cultural continuity, even as it operates as a latent space of displacement and exclusion. In these instances, the notion of semicircularity affords cohesiveness to my attempts at theorizing the multiple examples of openness, challenge, and possibility that each of these works highlights.

This book grounds its theorization in works set in urban locations; cities are particularly important sites of global intersections and naturally the centers of the ever-increasing scope of globalization. In arguing for the significance of a discussion of place, particularly cities, in conversations on globalization, Saskia Sassen connects cities with "Postcolonial forms of empire" ("Whose City" 314). Overall, though, as the fictional works on which this book bases its argument illustrate, and as Sassen also suggests, cities are complicated spaces: "The city has indeed emerged as a site of new claims: by global capital, which uses the city as an 'organizational commodity,' but also by disadvantaged sectors of the urban population, frequently as much an internationalized presence in large cities as capital. The denationalizing of urban space and the transformation of new claims by transnational actors raise the question, whose city is it?" (309). The notion that the city is "up for grabs" for both the ostensibly privileged and marginalized is tantalizing because of the provocatively disruptive possibilities that being "up for grabs" implies. In characterizing the city in this way, Sassen also speaks to an ongoing struggle for control, space, or dominance, as well as to the infinite possibilities that city spaces continue to offer.

The nexus of city exigencies, imperial (colonial) legacies, and global capitalism is notable because these three factors, which often combine, overlap, and intersect, repeatedly emerge as the primary complicating factors in the representations of African diasporic writers. Varma suggests that the postcolonial city (and, I would argue, cities in general) "is riddled simultaneously with imperial legacies and nationalist re-inscriptions of spatial practices, as well as with the complexity of representing 'difference' within the city, situated as it is within the global capitalist order" (1).[2] Varma also refers to the city as the "natural home" of capitalist cultures (3). This book further contemplates how the interactions among these interrelated factors are mediated and further complicated by gender (both the African American male body, as portrayed in Michael

Thomas's *Man Gone Down*, and Black female immigrant, fictionalized in Zadie Smith's *NW* or Chika Unigwe's *On Black Sisters Street*); by the opportunities and barriers of immigrant experiences explored in *Sleep On, Beloved* and *Call the Midwife*; by the flow of cultures that diasporas have engendered; and, perhaps most disruptively, by the unintended and unexpected consequences of the "free market," which Marlon James's *A Brief History of Seven Killings* helps us to understand.

An examination of creative works that allow us to think about the city space and its current challenges through a global perspective, and with the critical tools of globalization studies, takes us even further than postcolonial criticism, which, despite the valuable conceptual map it has afforded us, still centers primarily on the colonizer-colonized dyad/dialectic. The critical apparatus of globalization studies helps us to get at the more nuanced and multilayered systems of power and marginalizations in twentieth- and twenty-first-century cities. The fictional accounts that detail these experiences offer imagined, but context-driven, renditions of mostly colonially derived, but differently manifested, power imbalances. In other words, these works help us to understand the ongoing impact of the long arc of imperialism through their (re)newed enactments of social inequalities, labor exploitation, gender and sex discrimination, racism, xenophobia, and hegemonic practices. Sassen's observation that the city serves as an "organizational commodity" ("Whose City" 309) for global capital further highlights the value of thinking about the deep imprints of globalization on cities. Furthermore, Sassen's claim that the presence of disadvantaged groups, immigrants, the urban poor, and others in cities highlights the ravages of imperialism—which as Justin Edwards reminds us Edward Said has argued was not just "a moment in history" but rather a "continuing interdependent discourse between subject peoples and the dominant discourses of those in power" highlights how conditions in modern cities reflect past colonial atrocities (Edwards, *Postcolonial Literature*, p. 161)

This book is also concerned with representation, particularly with fiction writing and the unique place of the novel as a genre in which writers have historically confronted, in significant detail, the shifting landscape of imperialism in its various iterations. Given the consistent self-reflexivity of creative artists, this book examines writers' depictions of the challenges and opportunities of writing and of representing city experiences within a global matrix. For example, given the now vast discursive legacies in literary and other rhetorical-performative modes, this book explores how writers locate themselves in current global discursive and creative context. How are long-standing questions about representation, which have taken on new forms in a global context, worked out stylistically, thematically, and ideologically? These questions are also on the mind of the contemporary author-critic Patrick Chamoiseau, who—having represented cities himself and having remained keenly interested in the implications of global exigencies for writers—is particularly relevant to this book. In his essay "Globalization, Globality, Globe-Stone," Chamoiseau argues that the writer, whom he characterizes as a wayfarer, is today thrust into a global context—the landscape of "globalization." He names "the temple sanctuary of the market" as a "totalitarian regime" (3, 8) within which all contemporary writers must create their art. Chamoiseau's somber characterization of the urgencies that today's creative writers must confront instantiates the importance of taking questions about representation, including craft, into account in theorizations of creative renditions in the twenty-first century. He writes, "Never before has humanity found itself in so global, total, totalitarian, and totalizing system. . . . Economic globalization is a loose, baggy system that no longer affords the slightest prospect of elevation. It threatens the fundamental equilibrium of the planet, indeed the survival of the species, while telling stories of 'sustainable development' in an effort to persist with and conceal its folly" (5).

Chamoiseau, though realistically somber, still sees in this totalitarian system a place for the writer: "I can imagine no true wayfaring toward art that ignores the urgency, dominations, and impossibilities of its time" (5). Like Sylvia Wynter, who argues, as does Goldmann, that the novel "among all literary forms [is] the most immediately and directly linked to the structure of exchange and production for the market" (97), Chamoiseau considers creative writers to be vital in helping both to make sense of the shifting global scene and to expose its fissures. Chamoiseau sees the plot of the novel as a potentially empowering space where the plantation, in all its lingering forms, can be challenged and where freedoms can at least be imagined. Wynter asserts, "The novel form reflects [a] critical and oppositional stance to a process of alienation" (97). Particularly when we turn our attention to how writers engage cities—which, as I highlighted earlier, also presents a continuum of opportunities—this "oppositional stance" that many writers offer in their depictions, with its possibilities for interrogation, is central to this inquiry. Wynter's further insight that "instead of expressing the values of the market society, [the novel] develops and expands as a form of resistance to this very market society" (97) makes clear the interconnected stakes of examining representations of cities in a global and globalizing age primarily through novelistic representations that are timely and well warranted. Turning in the same direction that Wynter did over four decades ago, Chamoiseau makes the case for the relevance of art in general, and writing in particular, for its disruptive potential and as a means of breaking through this ostensibly impermeable, totalitarian global economic system.

The combined focus on cites and globalization necessarily implies recourse to postcolonial conversations that engage similar questions. This is the kind of work Varma engages in *The Postcolonial City and Its Subjects*, which examines fictional representation of three imperial-colonial cities. Along similar lines, I theorize the Black diasporic city as an entangled, contested, and contestable social and discursive space in a way that takes the colonial-postcolonial history of each fictional locale into account and recognizes how these contexts embed imperialist worldviews and mechanisms. Furthermore, because of the longer view of cities that it opens up, placing the analysis of these works in the twin colonial-globalization critical framework advances the notion of openness—if even partial—that I suggest characterizes the cities represented in these works.[3] Varma's assertion that "the postcolonial city is transformed into a site of the politics of liberation of women in particular, and the colonized in general" (13–14) is particularly valuable for engaging how cities function both historically and in today's modern global context. This book engages such transformations and offers analyses that mark moments of transformation within unfinished, complicated contexts.[4]

Part of the contribution that this study aims to make to critical engagements with cities, particularly their intersection with globalization, is an expansion of conversations beyond the plight of the much discussed "urban poor." *Writing the City* engages this question in, for example, the examination of the partial social mobility of gang leaders in *A Brief History of Seven Killings*. However, the majority of the fictional characters, for example, Ishmael in *Man Gone Down* or Keisha-Natalie in *NW*, are living middle-class lives, or they straddle urban-suburban spaces and experiences. Such creative accounts and the analyses they generate deepen our understandings of cities as spaces with more complicated experiences, which in turn offer even more potential for productive chaos, resistance, and regeneration. The range of representations highlighted in this study affirms and expands Jeremy Seabrook's observation that "cities are made up of worlds within worlds, often not touching each other and unaware of each other's existence" (17). Yet, even in what appears to be unawareness of each other, there are clear synergies across the representations of cities in the range of creative works under consideration in this book. And the patterns that writers and other creative artists make visible in their work provide the groundwork for theorizations, such as semicircularity, that appear in diverse ways in each set of representations.

Therefore, as I attend to the particularity of each city, part of what makes this study—which theorizes the city, with its shared but not uniform features, as a concept—viable, is the identifiable, even predictable, patterns that allow us to characterize a space as a city. Monica Smith begins her archeological study of *Cities* by offering a profile of two seemingly different cities, Rome and Tokyo, to establish the inherent and sustained similarities among cities and to show how cities are, by their very nature, sites of commonality. She writes, "Ancient Rome and modern Tokyo are literally a world apart, but if we stand back and look at them as cities, they have identical characteristics" (*Cities*, 2–3).[5] Of course, these "identical characteristics" that create the city's reverberations in turn produce simultaneous shared and distinctive features that connect and distinguish creative accounts. But even more importantly, and pertinent to the intersecting considerations of this study, is Smith's further insight: "The vast majority of the world's first cities are still right underfoot in the biggest metropolitan areas today: not only Rome and Xi'an, but also London, Paris, Guangzhou, Mexico City, Tokyo, Baghdad, Cuzco, Cairo . . . And those cities became interconnected with other cities that sprang up alongside them, growing into a global phenomenon that dominates the planet" (4–5).

The long-standing interconnectedness of cities, and Smith's characterization of them as constituting a "global phenomenon," is precisely what makes critical inquiry of creative representations that address some standard themes in globalization studies especially timely. Placing the works under consideration here in dialogue with each other both allows for a sense of continuity, where patterns emerge and converge, and also reveals the multiple, contextually driven tributaries of these patterns. Even as we ask similar questions of the various fictionalized cities, the continuum of responses to these questions illustrates the very complexity that also defines cities—the cityness of cities, so to speak.

The Case for Globalization Studies

Anne McClintock's important essay "The Angel of Progress: Pitfalls of the Term 'Post-Colonialism'" and several others challenge the use of the nomenclature *postcolonial* to name the field of study that has now become established among many others *posts*. McClintock and other scholars question the usefulness of *postcolonial* because of the way the term reinscribes linear progression, one of the key dogmas of colonial discourses, and also because *postcolonial* privileges the colonial era as a "marker of history" and measure of "development." McClintock's explication of multiple forms of colonization, particularly recent and present-day examples, makes her discomfort with the term even more reasonable (84). I have thought about this important rebuttal for a long time, wrestling with the need to account for a break in some parts of the colonial enterprise, most obviously the end to control of territory, while also acknowledging the persistence of colonial forms, ideologies, and practices. I have been especially compelled by McClintock's closing sentences: "Asking what *single* term might adequately replace 'post-colonialism' . . . begs the question of rethinking the global situation as a *multiplicity* of powers and histories, which cannot be marshalled obediently under one flag of one single theoretical term. . . . A *proliferation* of historically nuanced theories and strategies is called for, which enable us to engage more effectively in the politics of affiliation and the currently calamitous dispensations of power" (97).

McClintock is by no means alone in the questions she has raised about the field of postcolonial studies. David Scott's similar pondering, in "The Social Construction of Postcolonial Studies" (2005), and Sankaran Krishna's *Globalization and Postcolonialism* (2009) exemplify the sustained and varied ways that scholars have contemplated the question of where to turn for methods and language to address what Scott refers to as the "postcolonial present" (399).[6] Contemplating, the issue in "Postcolonial Remains" (2012), Robert Young argues forcefully for the continued usefulness of postcolonial studies as a toolbox for critical inquiry.[7]

McClintock's acknowledgment of the usefulness of *postcolonial* is indicative of, among other things, the value (inadequacy notwithstanding) of nomenclature to capture phenomena, in particular the scope, impact, and persistence of colonization. Despite the three-decade life of McClintock's 1992 essay, I find its urgings to be still relevant. Indeed, they resonated as I turned to creative works set in the late twentieth and early twenty-first centuries and as I searched for a term and a field of study that captures, even if it falls short of fully doing so, the spectrum of city experiences that the writers examine. Logically, in my own wrestling with this persistent and pertinent question and with the increasing presence of globalization studies—which I consider an arm of postcolonial studies—questions about the usefulness and adequacy of the term *globalization* and the field of globalization studies and theories also emerge.

For the purposes of this book, I have opted for *globalization studies*, not with a view to submit it as a replacement for *postcolonial studies*, since obviously such a move would take us back to the conceptual cul-de-sac that scholars have appropriately highlighted. Instead, my choice of *globalization* is more responsive to McClintock's call for multiple "historically nuanced theories" and to Jennifer Wenzel's question, "What is the relation between the state of the field [of postcolonial studies] and the state of the world?" (Agnani 633). In dialogue with these two pertinent reflections and because the texts I analyze in this book compel us to engage the current "state of the world" and the historical forces that have shaped current conditions, I embrace *globalization studies* as one critical tributary because of the way its questions and methods inevitably proceed from, and overlap with, classical postcolonial studies. *Globalization studies* helps me to get at a shared set of city-specific constraints that are indeed mostly offshoots of colonial hegemonic ideologies and practices in their manifold forms. For example, the proclaimed free movement of goods, people, and ideas that is so central to globalization links Amma Darko's and Chika Unigwe's treatment of the illegal transportation of women's bodies to the flow of drugs and violence between Kingston, Medellin, and New York City in another iteration of a triangular trade of roughly the late sixteenth to nineteenth centuries. These works contextualize the current challenges they creatively examine in ways that insist on engagement with the past, as well as the (re)newed challenges of global contexts. The critical tools and vocabulary of globalization studies facilitate both the historicizing of the creative representations and the understanding of their present-day intersections.

Globalization studies logically embeds, amplifies, and makes current the core critical principles of postcolonial studies. Justin Edwards's characterization of the grievances of protestors involved in the 1999 globalization protests that began in Seattle, Washington, illustrates the multilayered and intersecting consequences of global capitalism, thereby making visible the genealogy of oppression with which globalization studies concerns itself.[8] Edwards suggests that globalization constitutes "a set of multiple processes that impact the relationship between the local and the global, between historical ruptures and continuities and the construction of new global subjects and identities" (161).[9] Pramod K. Nayar's lament, "As the world map is being redrawn after 1989, postcolonial studies has done little to keep pace with the changing forms of imperialism as an actual set of strategies and developments," in tandem with his suggestion that globalization studies are among the "key elements in a re-orientation of postcolonial thought" (191), illustrates the broader necessary inclusion of other critical tools for making sense of currents iterations of the reaches of Western powers.[10] A logical question that arises then is what critical globalization studies or theory might most usefully look like if it is to expand and interrogate the work of postcolonial studies. It is worth reiterating that the obvious areas of commonality between colonization and globalization do not constitute or justify seeing or employing globalization studies as a replacement for postcolonial studies, nor is it an answer to the critical conundrum that postcolonial studies both addressed and created. Rather, as I aim to demonstrate in this study, the critical apparatuses of globalization studies offer us another set of tools, vocabulary, and areas of emphasis that expand and complicate what postcolonial studies has helped us to accomplish, while also extending analyses of the accounts that straddle these intersecting critical approaches.

At the heart of the examination of creative representations of cities that I undertake in this book is an engagement with the city as the hub of the modern state and, therefore, as a hotbed for the manifold ways in which empire has morphed into global systems of power. In this regard, another useful way to see the intersection between postcolonial and globalization studies is to consider this kind of work as ongoing engagement with, and interrogation of, empire. This is what Michelle Stephens suggests when she outlines the value of a return to the work of Black intellectuals in *Black Empire*. Stephens writes, "The work of Garvey, McKay, and James forces us to place notions of diaspora, nationhood, transnationalism, and even the status of the modern state within the context of empire and coloniality," and "we need to add back to our discussion of nationalism the work of Black intellectuals who specifically theorize and engage with colonial space" (9). Stephens's inclusion of "the status of the modern state" encapsulates that combination of relevant aspects of postcolonial studies and fresh critical perspectives that most usefully address the current moment. This book reads the portrayal of cities in the works it analyzes as depictions of colonial spaces, as versions of empire that, as Stephens argues, are characterized by "multiplicity and hybridity" (9). The varied forms of oppression and exclusions, as well as the subversive and deliberate push against these systems, illustrate the genealogy of both colonial hegemony and resistance.[11]

Centering the City

Scholars, creative artists, and observers from multiple fields of study concur on recent and ongoing demographic trends as well as the increasing significance of cities in world affairs. For example, among the notable statistics on the growth of urban populations highlighted by Mike Davis is that 90 percent of population growth will be in what he characterizes as "less-developed regions" (11).[12] Similarly, Monica Smith notes that "more than 50 percent of the world's people live in cities, and their percentage will soon be larger" (5).[13] Saskia Sassen also reminds us that "a growing number of cities today play an increasingly important role in directly linking their national economies with global circuits." One consequence that Sassen names is "the formation of new geographies of centrality in which cities are the key articulators" ("Introduction" 2). And with regard to their potential geopolitical power, Sassen also identifies cities as one of the "spatial units" that result from "the partial unbundling or at least weakening of the nation as a spatial unit" (1).[14] Evidently, in light of the current and predicted rate of growth, cities will continue to be perhaps the most critical economic, social, and ideological sites; significantly, they will also continue to be locations to which creative writers and other artists will turn, in perhaps larger numbers, for the settings of their creative accounts.[15]

The demographic, economic, and other realities of cities therefore compel and generate creative and scholarly contemplations not only of what these spatial shifts mean for conversations about the most urgent issues of the twenty-first century but also of what the centrality of cities makes possible in the cities themselves, in creative accounts, and in critical debates and theorizations. The inherent global nature of cities also necessarily implies that cities continue to be shaped (deliberately and inadvertently) by dynamic global vagaries. To speak of cities is necessarily to engage with the global, a point I take up in greater detail later in this introduction.

The constant and ever-increasing flow of diverse people into cities not only changes the constitution of these spaces but, more importantly, greatly impacts how the social and demographic architecture of the cities unsettles and disrupts power dynamics, or what Varma refers to as the "troubling of old binaries" (3); Varma also argues for an "imperial genealogy" that connects the "modernist" and "imperial" and that can be placed within the project of "resistance to impe-rialism" (3). The connection that Varma makes between the "modernist" and "postcolonial" city resonates with the conceptualization of the city as dynamic and incomplete; I read the global city as yet another step in this genealogy. This is not to say that there is a forward and/or linear march from one phase to the next. In fact, part of the value of genealogy is its attentiveness to continuity and overlay, a view that Nayar expresses in his assertion that globalization is marked by Euro-Americanization—evidence of repetition of old systems of mar-ginalization overlaid with new mechanisms. In exploring the portrayal of cit-ies as part of an extended colonial-imperial affliction, this book identifies virtual through lines in how these systems have stymied possibilities for full integration of peoples of African descent into these cities, even as they continue to find spaces of agency through mostly subversive acts of contestation. For example, an examination of the imperial city of London in *Call the Midwife* highlights how the presence of the colonized Black female body in a professional space—even a female-dominated one such as nursing—exposes the persisting colonial fissures in the London body politic. *Writing the City* reads this retro-spective dramatic portrayal alongside Zadie Smith's contemporary novelistic depiction of a woman with a similar, though not identical, immigrant back-ground who confronts similar challenges; the juxtaposition of these two por-trayals highlights the ongoing challenges, rooted in the same colonially grounded prejudices and exclusions, that Black women experience in their ostensibly suc-cessful professional lives.

I argue further that this genealogy necessarily carries with it the impulse toward resistance that has always been part of the responses of colonized people, as well as of people who have lived and continue to live under different kinds of imperialist power structures. Part of what makes this "genealogy of resis-tance" inevitable is the urbanization of world poverty—what Davis notes as "the new urban poor" and "a surplus humanity." Perhaps most relevant here is Davis's assertion that "the new urban poor will not go gently into this dark night" and that "their resistance . . . becomes the principal condition for the survival of the unity of the human race against the implicit triage of the new global order" (13). This impulse toward resistance found in contemporary cities—with their larger and constant inflows of some of the world's most marginalized people—is among the most vibrant components of multidisciplinary conversa-tions about cities.[16] In arguing for the city as a semicircular limber space, I am exploring, in large part, the extent of this resistance, how much it is enacted and impacted, and how it is constrained and contained by the very conditions that both necessitate and facilitate resistance. If, as Varma suggests, we can imagine contemporary global cities "in terms of an imperial genealogy . . . of resistance to imperialism," what do these creative accounts tell us about the reaches of such resistance? As I demonstrate in the analysis of James's *A Brief History of Seven*

Killings, even the partial and temporary shift, or if we prefer, the unsettling of power dynamics, that the transnational city-to-city drug trade makes possible instantiates the possibilities for agency that urban locations allow for some of the most marginalized and exploited groups.

The Necessity (and Limits) of "Black" and "Diaspora"

In mobilizing *diaspora, diasporic*, and their variations as a cultural, spatial, and conceptual axis for analysis, this book necessarily acknowledges and engages with the etymology, usefulness, and limits of diaspora as a concept and structuring idea. The efforts to organize Africans and dispersed peoples of African descent have been ongoing; they began as early as the nineteenth century but picked up momentum that continues to shape scholarly conversations today in the early twenty-first century. I will not recount the multiple iterations of these attempts here but instead offer a brief sketch of a few key moments that I find especially relevant to the way I employ the term in this book.[17] Among the best known efforts are those of the early-twentieth-century thinkers and activists C.L.R. James, Marcus Garvey, and Claude McKay, which received comprehensive treatment in Stephens's *Black Empire*.[18] At the center of these (and other) attempts at theorizing diasporic formations was the identity formation and group affinity grounded in a shared politics of Black affirmation and resistance to ongoing colonial-imperialist dominations.[19] That is to say, these efforts at identity formation highlight both the recognition of and need for something shared. This book also explores this question through its examination of Black masculinity in *Man Gone Down*, which I argue finds its possibility for affirmation and agency in a diasporically grounded musical culture.

In its examination of works by Black writers from a range of backgrounds and works set in multiple national locations, *Writing the City* explores the value of diasporic conversations that address the following questions: What areas of commonality and points of departure might be evident in the way writers and other creative artists represent colonially derived modes of oppression? And, relatedly, how do they portray and engage with strategies for resistance and renewal? What is the role of shared African-based cultures, particularly performative modes, both in shaping these texts stylistically and in providing spaces of regeneration? This book therefore submits and affirms that there are characteristics shared across the African diaspora and that such shared contexts and experiences shape creative engagements with cities. This notion of a shared something (somethings) has stirred critical debates over the past century and is the critical-theoretical grounding of Catherine John's *Clear Word and Third Sight: Folk Groundings and Diasporic Consciousness in African Caribbean Writing*.[20] Two aspects of John's engagement with diaspora are useful for the way I activate the term in this book. The focus on diasporic consciousness informs the reading of texts included in this study, which engage with different ways out of colonially derived, traumatic Black experiences, demonstrated in Michael Thomas's *Man Gone Down*; this reading of Thomas's novel addresses the way the novel represents music as an example of this shared diasporic consciousness.[21]

In choosing to focus so specifically on representations of Black experiences in this work, I have contemplated the ongoing, often-heated debate about Black essentialism, the basis on which multiple scholars have dismissed African cultural continuities in the diaspora.[22] This rejection, even fear, of essentialist ideas is at the heart of John's diasporic inquiry. Brent Hayes Edwards's work in *The Practice of Diaspora* (2003) offers a useful map for navigating the diverse views on diaspora that John and others have sought to reconcile. I find Edwards's detailed treatment of the extensive and meandering genealogy of diaspora useful in clearing a pathway that acknowledges the usefulness and limits of diaspora as a concept and critical tool.[23] For example, in his discussion of W.E.B. Du Bois's framing of racism (the color line) as a modern world problem, Edwards calls attention to how a globally impacted imperialism has created what Stephens characterizes as "the material conditions for Black solidarities to emerge" (5). This is the system that prompts Du Bois to place the race or color problem in a global framework because empire, with its racist and capitalist pursuits, was a world system on which the sun was never able to set. This book is most interested in how the "material conditions" created by long empire impact Black subjectivity and, in turn, how writers have harnessed artistic expression to expose these conditions and offer fictional accounts, grounded in verisimilitude, as part of the ongoing attentiveness to the equally persistent and amorphous empire, understood this time as globalization.[24]

Any conceptual use of *Black* must acknowledge and engage with the fraught genealogy of the term as well as its multiple, politically charged usages. In contemplating the high-stakes historical burden that the term *Black* carries and the necessity of critical engagement with its use, I draw on Carole Boyce Davies's detailed delineation of the term in the introduction to *Black Women, Writing and Identity: Migrations of the Subjects* for the way I mobilize "Black" as one of the conceptual cornerstones of this book. In the following quote, Davies captures both the value of *Black* and its limitations against the backdrop of its meandering and still-diverse usages and possibilities: "I want to activate the term 'Black' relationally, provisionally and based on location or position. The term 'Black,' oppositional, resisting, necessarily emerges as whiteness seeks to depoliticize and normalize itself. Still, 'Black' is only provisionally used as we continue to interrogate its meaning and in the ongoing search to find the language to articulate ourselves" (8).

I too use the construction *Black* provisionally, with a recognition of its inadequacy in naming and fully conveying the breadth of historical, cultural, and spatial ground we often use it to cover. I also use the term with a recognition of its essentializing potential, but I lean more toward its unifying potentialities because of its usefulness in helping us to get at the kind of relationality that Davies includes. Such an understanding of *Black* is central to the diasporic, transnational experiences and cultural reverberation that the creative works in this study make visible. In this book, then, *Black* refers to peoples and cultures of African descent located in and moving into and out of settings in which whiteness, through historical colonialism and its current offshoots—most notably globalization—has sought to assert itself vis-à-vis this necessary foil. Most importantly, continuing along the lines of Pan-Africanism and transnationalism, this book offers *Black* as a term reclaimed, removed from white-supremacist usages that embedded inferiority and pathology in Blackness and reduced it to be understood always as the "B side" of the normalized or unmarked whiteness (Kernicky).

My writing of this book coincides with renewed, perhaps unprecedented attention to the unfortunate ongoing assault on Black lives, as well as to the centrality of African American experiences, activism, and history to diasporic relationships; I think it logical, then, that this book begins its critical analysis with Michael Thomas's *Man Gone Down*. Chapter 1 initiates the inquiry into creative renditions of cities through a reading of Thomas's portrayal of New York and Boston as traumatic locales for Black people and people of color. The inquiry begins with an exploration of a question: What does it mean to be Black, male, and educated in a modern city space in one of the most global cities of the world? Yet a second question emanates from Thomas's representation of a wounded African American man, which has led me to Tommy Curry's definition of Black male vulnerability as the most useful point of departure for the argument that this chapter pursues. I therefore examine Thomas's navigation of this vulnerability, taking into account Rachel Griffin's assertion that "Black males of all ages are not hopeless. They are not irreparably damaged" (172). The central question that this chapter poses and seeks to answer is, How does Thomas reconcile "vulnerability" and redemption? I argue that what Thomas offers as the path to wholeness, regeneration, and affirmation is a turn to community—both a located African American and an expansive Black diasporic community—grounded in an embrace of a shared and intrinsically defined Blackness through agency and resistance.

One can imagine exploring the same question about Black female subjectivity along the lines of vulnerability that I pursue in chapter 1, while it may be in some instances different in its manifestation. I therefore extend that conversation about gendered experiences in modern cities by investigating creative accounts of female experience in chapters 2 and 3. These chapters take up questions about the representation of women who have moved, or have been moved, and who occupy city spaces in which they navigate the intersection of multiple historical mechanisms of marginalization. For each of these chapters, I have chosen to look beyond novelistic accounts, beyond writing, to explore the continuities across different genres and creative modalities. This exploration is grounded primarily in the notion of the migrating female subject, for which Carole Boyce Davies has offered a formative theoretical map that enables critical navigation of earlier and subsequent treatments of related themes. I also consider Kimberly Juanita Brown's assertion that Black women's vulnerability is often elided by the age-old configuration of them as strong. Brown insists that we examine the totality of Black women's lives by "remember[ing] everything," (4) including their often-ignored vulnerability. Bringing together these two ideas— the "migrating subject" and the importance of "remembering everything"— this book investigates the continuities of female experiences, with particular attention to how these texts allow for consideration of wide-ranging and complex understandings and depictions of women in urban spaces.

Chapter 2 examines both Zadie Smith's treatment of Black female vulnerability in *NW* and the representation of Lucille, the Black Jamaican nurse in the BBC television series *Call the Midwife*. I explore how Smith's crafting of the professionally successful character Keisha, the daughter of Jamaican immigrants who renames herself Natalie, tackles and problematizes notions of success in modern racist and sexist London. Similarly, Lucille—whose experiences are set in mid-twentieth-century London, during the Windrush era—is forced to assert a kind of strength that is not required of her white female colleagues; Lucille must therefore cast aside vulnerability. I place these two works in conversation with each other to extend the theorization, begun in chapter 1, of the city as a traumatic space and site of wounding. I read Keisha-Natalie's anguished subjectivity as part of a twentieth-century historical arc, which the portrayal of Lucille's experiences in the later seasons of *Call the Midwife* helps to illuminate. Part of the value of including this television series in the analyses is that *Call the Midwife* offers a visual view of the city that literally maps the changes that a section of the imperial city of London undergoes as a result of movement, including that of the migrating female subject. Drawing on Brown's call to "remember everything," this chapter explores in detail what "everything"—or at least multiple dimensions of Black women's experiences—looks like as the characters live as "successful" professional women. Most significantly, the chapter examines what is often masked or obscured by women's success and socioeconomic mobility.

One of the most significant aspects of globalization that I engage in this book—and one in which cities have consistently played a significant role—is in the area of trade. Chapter 3 examines two novels, Amma Darko's *Beyond the Horizon* and Chika Unigwe's *On Black Sisters' Street*, to explore sex trafficking, the experiences of (forced) female migrating subjects as a commodity that harkens back, in perhaps the most vulgar and stark ways, to the transatlantic slave trade. This illicit trading of bodies was central to the early wave of global capitalist enterprise—the triangular trade in which the capture, purchase, and sale of Black bodies was central. This book takes notice of the fact that the source of traded bodies in both novels is West African cities and that the destinations are European cities, in order to extend and complicate the theorization of the modern city as space of (economic) colonial haunting.

Chapter 4 reads the illicit drug trade depicted in Marlon James's *A Brief History of Seven Killings* as a subversive act of agency, whereby the mechanisms put in place to continue the economic hegemony of Euro-Americans are disrupted by inner-city gang leaders. These working-class leaders, taken from among the poorest of postcolonial, postindependence Jamaica, harness the skills that the ruling class afforded them through intended exploitation of these inner-city residents to create an underground economic system that shakes the foundations of modern capitalist structures. Here I mobilize the term *urban sprawl* to account for the way that the city extends beyond the geopolitical boundaries of inner-city Kingston. The chapter also addresses the unintended socioeconomic mobility of poor urban residents who emerge as leaders but whose "progress" is contained, interrupted, and therefore only fleeting because of the city's neocolonial base of violence and destruction, which makes their mobility possible in the first place. This chapter also tackles, in the most explicit and extensive way, the inclusion of *writing* in the title of this book in order to explore what James's overt treatment of writing tells us about the place of the creative arts in the current global landscape.

In chapter 5, I return to a number of the key themes addressed in earlier chapters. This chapter examines female migrant experiences represented in the city of Toronto. Exploring the classical alienation and displacement that have been extensively addressed as a distinctive feature of migrant experiences, this chapter returns to the role of Black diasporic culture as a basis for regeneration for excluded immigrants. I place in dialogue Cecil Foster's *Sleep On, Beloved* and the well-known Caribbean festival formerly named Caribana to theorize the city as a door ajar and also as a source of cultural opiate. Through Foster's portrayal of dancehall and Caribana, which has become an integral part of the Toronto summer experience, the city of Toronto offers Caribbean immigrants respite from their everyday experiences of exclusion and well-concealed marginalization in what appears to be a model immigration city. The chapter also engages briefly with the historical context of Caribana and examines its decades-long shifts, including its complicated place in the Toronto imaginary as both a site of reconciliation and an occasion for perpetuating racial stereotypes and aggressive policing of Black bodies.

The book then offers a concluding chapter that returns to the intersection of the key structuring ideas of the book: the challenges and opportunities that people of African descent encounter in modern, global cites. The conclusion revisits some of the key concepts explored in the book through a brief discussion of three texts: Frantz Fanon's *The Wretched of the Earth*, where Fanon characterizes the postcolonial city as a Manichean city; Caryl Phillips's *Color Me English*, which enables a return to the question of the role and limits of the creative arts in general, and writing in particular, in the current historically based and rapidly diversifying global and globalizing milieu; and Steve McQueen's 2020 film anthology *Small Axe*, which offers a historically grounded portrayal of some central issues addressed in the body of the study. Finally, I examine a few sample texts to demonstrate the points of intersection and representations of cross-racial solidarity illustrated in works by other minoritized groups or, in the case of *Small Axe*, alongside the representation of Black immigrant experiences. In this way, this book looks ahead and acknowledges other depictions of cities beyond those of people of African descent examined here.

1

"Natty Dread Rise Again"

■■■■■■■■■■■■■■■■■■■■■

The Haunting City and the
Promise of Diaspora in
Man Gone Down

As I pursue this diasporic-based study from my physical and temporal location in the United States, I feel compelled to launch the critical engagement
through analysis of a fictional work set in this important location in the
Black diaspora. The paradox inherent in the United States' successful self-
construction, particularly the irreconcilability with its fraught relationship
with race, has been well documented.[1] Yet one of many key moments in that
long and troubled history warrants recollection here. In declaring, "Be it
enacted by the Senate and House of Representatives of the United States of
America in Congress assembled, That any alien, being a free white person,
who shall have resided within the limits and under the jurisdiction of the
United States for the term of two years, may be admitted to become a citizen
thereof," the United States Naturalization Act of 1790 categorically inscribes
the "social experiment" of the United States as one specifically meant for
Europeans, for "white" people. That sentiment was resurrected in President
Donald Trump's 2018 (reported) assertion, "We should have more people
from Norway."[2] In light of this rhetorical return to the original Immigration
Naturalization Act, I am interested in examining what, if anything, this early
and recovered racial-spatial demarcation means for the experiences of a Black
person in a globalized US city in the twenty-first century.

At the time of the writing of this act, African Americans had been living in the United States as enslaved people for almost a century. In the age of globalization and Trump-related antiglobalization attitudes, this chapter considers what it means to be Black and male in a still racist, capitalist, white patriarchal space that was not intended for the Black male, a place where the Black body was never included in the imagined citizenry but, rather, was configured as chattel and a means of production to facilitate the (white) "social experiment" (to borrow a term from the novel under consideration) of democracy. *Man Gone Down*—Michael Thomas's rendition of Black male subjectivity in the United States city space—is the creative ground from which this argument proceeds, as this contemporary work, set in the live and present New York City, navigates this very question of the place of the Black male within the larger social (democratic) experiment.

In a useful chapter, "The (Im)possibilities of Writing the Black Interiority into Discursive Terrain," E. Lâle Demirtürk writes that "white supremacist practices against blacks not only entail the racialization of space and the spatialization of race, but also help us to define urban spaces such as the prison or ghetto as the most visible sites of white supremacist power." Demirtürk further suggests that "less visible racist spaces such as schools, the workplace or suburban homes provided with services and opportunities are unavailable to inner city residents" (*Contemporary African American Novel*, 160). Demirtürk's inclusion of George Lipsitz's comment about the exclusion of "non-whites" from these spaces underscores her focus on specific sites such as prisons and inner-city communities as the primary locations of exclusion. Given the well-known modern and historical role of these spaces as primary loci of exclusion, such a focus is judicious. We can also ask, though, What happens to the raced male body when the prison and ghetto are not the primary urban sites? That opportunity to consider the experiences of Black, educated, middle-class males is among the fresh perspectives that Thomas's *Man Gone Down* (2007) allows us to examine.

Throughout the novel, Ishmael—Thomas's "middle-class" protagonist—offers multiple variations of his recurrent observation that "it's a strange thing to go through life as a social experiment." This refrain, which also frames this chapter, is especially poignant because it captures the particular presumed privilege and burden that Ishmael's middle-class status engenders. Ishmael returns to this phrase as he walks the streets of Brooklyn in search of work to support his family; he is haunted by his memories, by his state of "failure" in a global capitalist economy, and even more importantly, by his resulting inability to provide for his family. While Ishmael tells the story over the few days that he is in New York looking for work and money, readers are allowed access to his memories, his failings, fears, and hauntings. The stories he tells take place in New York and Boston over the course of his thirty-five years.

Self-identifying as Black, Irish, and "Indian," Ishmael embodies the multiple cross-fertilizations—physical, cultural, geographical—that colonization has engendered. The global marketplace, initiated by the transatlantic slave trade, has now taken on renewed life in global capitalist hubs such as Boston and New York. These cities are epicenters of neoliberal capitalism in the now global framework and therefore offer writers and critics unique opportunities for exploring and revisiting questions of citizenship and belonging in the United States and, thus, for examining the debilitating impact that poverty has on a descendant of enslaved, excluded, and indentured peoples. Most significantly, Thomas allows us to contemplate Black masculinity through the not-often-considered experience of an educated, middle-class, Black male whose problem is not a lack of opportunity, education, or access to the ostensible mechanisms of social mobility. Yet, because the character Ishmael is as stymied by the burden of his Blackness as are his uneducated, working-class Black male counterparts, the fictive example that Thomas affords us simultaneously opens up and complicates our understanding of the Black male experience in a twenty-first-century global/globalized "first-world" city.[3] Thomas's representation of Ishmael dramatizes Rachel Griffin's observation that "there are distinct and unique disadvantages to being Black and male in US society" (169), irrespective of class and other standard indices of success.

This chapter focuses specifically on definitions of masculinity outside the hegemonic Western, patriarchal-capitalist model of masculinity. While I take into account alternative modes—such as the individual self-definition as theorized by Demirtürk and the "performance of Cool," as revisited and further explicated by Griffin—given Thomas's representation of a wounded African American man, I find Tommy Curry's definition of "black male vulnerability" (28) as the most useful point of departure for this study. I also take a similar view to Griffin that "Black males of all ages are not hopeless. They are not irreparably damaged" (172). Along these lines, then, I reiterate that what Thomas offers as the path to wholeness, regeneration, and affirmation emanates from a turn to community—both a located African American and an expansive Black diasporic community—grounded in an embrace of a shared and intrinsically defined Blackness through agency and resistance. *Man Gone Down* fictionalizes what Griffin refers to as the "[embodiment of] an Afrocentric worldview that positions relationships, reciprocity, interconnectedness and collectivism" (171).

Intersections of Trauma, Haunting, and the Masculine

The prism of the city that guides this study is especially useful for a consideration of Black male subjectivity and its various intersections. As has been well documented, since the late nineteenth / early twentieth century, cities have been the preferred refugee sites for African Americans seeking reprieve from Jim Crows laws, lynching, and systemic, sanctioned racism (63). This historical fact explains, in part, the high number of Black men in cities across the United States and the importance of an engagement with Black, urban, male subjectivity as part of this inquiry. A return to literary accounts of Black male experiences in urban contexts is not only timely but well warranted, given both the renewed attention to the experiences of African American men in cities such as Baltimore (Freddie Gray), New York (Eric Garner), and Ferguson (Michael Brown), to name just a few. Multiple writers, such as Claudia Rankine and Ta-Nehisi Coates, have turned their craft to addressing Black experiences in these cities and beyond.

Ishmael does not dwell for long periods on the Great Migration; but there are multiple references to that journey, and this pivotal era in African American history is a constant backdrop throughout the novel, through Ishmael's references to his parents' past, their journey to northern cities, and the subtextual resonances with his own journey. The movement of African Americans to cities is part of Ishmael's consciousness. The references to that period historicize Ishmael's presence in New York City; they situate his economic quest within a genealogy of Black men's flight to spaces where the possibilities of fulfilling the white, patriarchal, capitalist expectations are imagined to be more likely. Given how such sojourns have historically gone, and the current state of the Black male collective in cities such as New York, I theorize Ishmael's experience in the cities, New York in particular, as an experience of haunting and, relatedly, the city as a space of haunting.

I find Marisa Parham's theorization of haunting useful for thinking about Thomas's depiction of Ishmael and his circumstances. "Haunting," Parham writes, is compelling "because it is appropriate to a sense of what it means to live in between things—in between cultures, in between times, in between spaces—to live with various kinds of double consciousness" (3). Haunting, then, occurs in the space between the past and present, between self and community, between the lived and the vicarious. Given the choice of narrative strategy (which I address later in the chapter) and the way memory functions both structurally and thematically, Ishmael is a useful fictional example of the kind of haunting that Parham theorizes. Parham's observation about the role of memory in African American literature is also instructive: "Memory—conscious or unconscious, individual and collective—drives African-American cultural production in significant ways" (2). It is true: to represent an African American experience is necessarily to engage in an act of recovery, of looking back, to place experience in the interstice between then and now. Surely, one could make the argument that this is true for human experiences in general and for creative renditions of such experiences. But Black-embodied experiences in the New World are unique because they express something particular, something that history has sought to erase—a corporeal disruption of the United States' self-constructed democracy. And yet the very presence of African Americans in the United States and, by extension, Black people in the diaspora compels society to notice and to remember. This is why Parham's assertion rings true. In constructing a character who is so obviously preoccupied with and pursued by the past, Thomas engages in a conscious recognition of the weight of the past in African American experiences of the present.

I also want to expand the standard, perhaps more common, understanding of haunting by returning to its early usage. Joseph Shipley points out that "*haunt* from Fr. *hanter*, (to frequent) first meant doing something frequently; then going somewhere frequently" (176). I want to stay with that initial and generic meaning of *haunt*—even as the melancholic and potentially debilitating connotations of haunting remain central to this discussion—because I want to suggest that haunting, in the way that Thomas configures it in this novel, is not entirely malevolent. I refer to haunting in its generic meaning of preoccupation with the past, to go to the past frequently. Additionally, although this usage also takes into account hauntings that are unsettling—that is, in this context, haunting as in remembering, ruminating, frequently returning to the past—it also functions as the foundation of regeneration. This is because it is Ishmael's virtual obsession with the past—with its memories, the unearthing of multiple "consciousnesses," and the way he makes connections—that takes him to the sites of diasporic memory and connection that I am arguing imply a different, perhaps more manageable path for Ishmael, despite an unclear economic future. In other words, it is because Ishmael allows himself to exist in the liminal space between the past and present—in a word, to be haunted—that he is able to find space for the potentially regenerative pieces of the past that become available to him.

That Thomas does not resolve the novel's main conflict—the weight of a version of manhood that configures man as provider and grounds self-worth in a man's ability to provide—is significant. By the novel's end, Ishmael is still without a job yet manages, through a counterfeit job letter, to secure his children's reentry into a private school, but there is currently no money to suggest that there will be sustained tuition payments. Securing an apartment for the children to live in is even more uncertain. It is because of the lack of clarity about Ishmael's economic situation (which seems to drive the novel) that I am suggesting that what this novel ultimately projects as a way out of the grip of a patriarchal-capitalist definition of masculinity is a recourse to community and the adoption of a Black diasporic sensibility grounded in resistance. In this way, then, Ishmael's story can be justifiably located within the African American tradition of redemptive stories, as the "rise" that is suggested is grounded in the opportunities for diasporic and ancestral affinity that cities (New York City in particular) make feasible. Theorized through this analysis of *Man Gone Down*, the city's semicircularity manifests itself in the way New York allows Ishmael, a fictional and representative Black male subject initially constrained by the historical weight of the city, access to a multiethnic and African-inspired Black resiliency.

As Matthew Kernicky, Demirtürk, and others have pointed out, Ishmael grapples with one of the most persistent and debilitating issues that has historically plagued Black men—that is, the expectation, instituted by patriarchy, to be the head of household and provider for the family. This expectation and the way it further and specifically marginalizes African American men has been repeatedly addressed by scholars across multiple disciplines since the abolition of slavery and, most consistently, since the middle of the twentieth century.[4] bell hooks's treatment of the pernicious issue is especially relevant to the argument I seek to make here about the intersection between Black masculinity, twenty-first-century capitalist demands, and the special meaning these take on when the subject is the educated Black male. Hooks consistently uses the term "White-supremacist capitalist patriarchy" to characterize the system within which Black men have been forced to define their masculinity, and it is this characterization that is at the heart of what Thomas grapples with in this novel (*Real Cool* p.x). Patriarchy, as hooks has repeatedly underscored, is the version of masculinity that has debilitated Black men and from which they must extricate themselves if they are to establish wholesome relationships with Black women and women in general and, more importantly, to achieve a level of self-community that is defined independently from Euro-patriarchy. For hooks and other gender theorists, the patriarchal racist construction of masculinity that has functioned as what Curdella Forbes refers to as "iconic masculinity" (184) must be disavowed and replaced by versions of masculinity that are not only independent of Euro-American patriarchy but also, most importantly, self- and community-affirming. Black men's most productive way out of what Tommy Curry defines as "black male vulnerability" is a self-community-generated, rather than a white-patriarchal, definition of masculinity. Vulnerability, and the weakened state of Black men that the term connotes, is precisely the result of a vision of masculinity that emanates from oppressors and from a historical context of exclusions. Therefore, as I show through this examination of Thomas's treatment of Black male subjectivity, a reorientation—away from Euro-based patriarchy—of the way masculinity is understood, performed, and realized is the way out of vulnerability. Despite the challenges it presents, part of what Ishmael's experience in the city offers him is the possibility for such a self-community definition of Black masculinity, grounded in a diasporic tradition of resistance and marked by a turn to African-inspired culture.

As the trigger for Ishmael's journey to New York City, money—the lack of it and all it can bring him for his family—tortures, temporarily frees, and entraps him, all at the same time. It is money—his need and quest for it and the possibilities that New York City holds in these aims—that sends

Ismael back into his opaque and wounded past. This chapter therefore unfolds with an examination of the intersection of money and the centrality of the city experience in shaping the main character's memories. Overlaid with and intersecting with the economic demands and made more poignant in the urban space are Ismael's hauntings, which instantiate the fashioning of selfhood, more particularly an African American masculine self, in a global, capitalist milieu. Returning to this theme of haunting, I suggest that, in *Man Gone Down*, to be haunted is not to be defeated; haunting, in this context, is potentially regenerative, and further, this possibility of regeneration occurs in the opaque space between self and community, between the (Black) nation and the Black diaspora.

Literary Hauntings

A necessarily haunting endeavor, writing, and specifically writing African American experiences, draws attention to a novel such as *Man Gone Down* as a self-referential inscription of textual interaction. Because this novel structurally engages with literary hauntings—that is to say, it includes explicit moments of intertextuality and deeper resonances of other texts—literary haunting is one of this novel's most prominent subjects. *Man Gone Down* exemplifies the African American double or multilayered cultural wealth in which orature-performance—blues, spirituals, gospel, R&B, rap—is as available to writers as Euro-based traditions of the likes of Emerson, Shakespeare, and Whitman. Thus, the narrative strategies and diverse modes of representation on which Thomas draws reflect and fittingly portray the conflation of diverse and globally inspired literary traditions. Parham suggests that "in literary and cultural texts, haunting often appears as allegory, doubling, and irony" (3). Engaged in what I argue is an *active*, conscious conversation with other texts, *Man Gone Down* fashions literary haunting as an instance of generative intertextuality. By this I mean that earlier texts speak into and reverberate in this novel, that they are interwoven in its fabric with a view at once to demonstrate the inevitability of the past and also to engage with the past as a way out of the debilitating effects of the personal and collective past.

Given the vast and varying traditions available to African American writers in the twentieth and twenty-first centuries, the question of how to write about, treat, and theorize African American literature has been part of critical conversations for decades. And central to these conversations is the question of the usefulness of literary, Western-derived theories such as "modernist," "postmodernist," and other critical-theoretical approaches under the broader "poststructuralist" rubric that has been central among these critical deliberations. As Winston Napier has outlined, "By the middle to late 1980s, African American literary theorists had begun incorporating the poststructuralist assumptions of

French thinkers such as Jacques Derrida and Michel Foucault" (5). At the center of these critical debates was the importance of centering modes of representation grounded in African American vernacular traditions, even as critics drew on the commonalities between these grounded aesthetics and prominent poststructuralist theories. Citing Houston Baker and Henry Louis Gates Jr. among the prominent voices of the 1980s, Napier suggests, "Poststructuralism provided both Baker and Gates the philosophical support for the vernacular theories they developed to study black literary culture" (6). I too approach my reading of Thomas's poetics and its significance for my investigation of a literary haunting as a hybrid of aesthetic modes grounded in African American culture and Western-derived modernist and poststructuralist modes.

Thomas declares his comfort in and affinity with a decidedly modernist literary tradition in, among others, two ways that I would like to highlight here. All of Thomas's epigraphs are from T. S. Eliot, a striking choice that not only signals this writer's modernist inclinations but also illustrates his attentiveness to the past and to the centrality of memory, hauntings, and the relationships between the past and present. For example, the novel's penultimate epigraph brings into focus the novel's and its main character's wrestling with temporality, with that space that Ishmael necessarily occupies as a twenty-first-century educated African American man who carries the weight of the past and that of his forebears, who are also part of his present:

> And right action is freedom
> From past and future also.
> For most of us, this is the aim
> Never here to be realised;
> Who are only undefeated
> Because we have gone on trying
> —T. S. Eliot, "The Dry Salvages" (353)

Even more striking is Thomas's choice to craft Ishmael's story and develop his character over the course of a few days and mostly as he walks and runs on the streets of Brooklyn, which makes connection between this current century's African American novel and Virginia Woolf's 1922 *Mrs. Dalloway* inevitable. An equally striking textual resonance is the deep and troubled psychological profile of Ishmael that is the centerpiece of the novel. So, while Ishmael tells his own story, the fact that so much of that story emanates from his memories, that the novel is a montage of past and present, mostly past, makes Thomas's modernist inclinations in this work notable. For example, Thomas's recurrent use of associational loops, a stock modernist writer's technique, is the primary way in which the haunting, the way the past presses on the present, is made visible: scenes and experiences in New York over the course of the four days (the novel's present) that Ishmael roams the city and ponders his failing open multiple windows, introducing key moments that have shaped the person we meet. In one striking example, the presence of a young white woman and a young Black man sends him and the novel's readers to one of his primary hauntings: his life with his white wife and, more broadly, Black-white relations: "The girl who is lovely is joined by a black boy. . . . They truly believe they care—for one another, for everyone else." Then Ishmael returns to the past, merging his private and public hauntings:

> I know what day it is . . . August twenty-second. One day after my birthday, six days before our anniversary and the march on Washington. . . . We ask everyone to hold hands—the bridal party, the congregation—a ridiculous mélange of the American gene pool, . . . and the congregation said "Amen" on this historic day. And they *"reckoned that she would sivilize me."* . . . And in the receiving line people blessed us. And her aunt, whoever she was, took her by the hand, smiling, but speaking with gravity reserved for funerals, said, *"Beautiful, just beautiful. The day, the music."* Then to me, *"Congratulations. Welcome to the family."* Then back to Claire, *"We'll teach him about classical music now."* And then she was gone. And Claire looked at me with two eyes: one as though I had an open head wound, the other as though I had just stepped onto the line. (229–230)

Even as he marries the woman he calls "my Claire," Ishmael is haunted by the colonial past, this history of prescribed Black inferiority being recalled by one who simultaneously welcomes him to the family and characterizes him as a "social experiment," one who needs to be taught the "classics," a recast "noble savage." Thus, in crafting this contemporary, colonially laden Black, urban, male predicament as unbelonging to a world in which his character lives most intimately, Thomas creatively exploits the now familiar modernist strategy even as he grounds this story in a (re)newed racialized context.

The story of literary haunting—meaning here the lingering presence of specific works that, in turn, make even more visible the pressing urgency of engaging Black urban experiences—calls to mind Gates's theorization of the talking text, "how black texts 'talk' to other black texts" (xxvi). In establishing the context and stakes of "speakerly texts," Gates returns to Ralph Ellison's observation that in literature by Black writers about Black experiences, there is "a sharing of that 'concord of sensibilities which the group expresses.'" Expanding Ellison's characterization of tradition, Gates contends, "Texts written over two centuries ago address what we might call common subjects of condition that continue to be strangely resonant as we approach the twenty-first century" (128). Napier suggests that "the development of [African Americans'] artistic culture should be understood as deriving significantly from this reformative spirit and, accordingly, as regulated by a need to engage expressive culture as a form of protest" (1). If the writing of African Americans was birthed in and remained committed to "reform" and "protest," then these works also necessarily address the conditions that warrant a need for such change. Therefore, because of clear imprints of past literature in Thomas's novel, I propose haunting as a way of situating *Man Gone Down* in a literary tradition engaged in the kind of reformatory work that Napier articulates. Furthermore, because Thomas visibly locates his "individual talent" within a specifically Black literary "tradition" and engages particular literary works, the resonances that Gates suggests continue into the twenty-first century.[5] That is to say that the hauntings being addressed here shed light specifically on the ongoing challenges of Black, urban, male experiences that other writers address, as Coates does in *Between the World and Me.*

Even as we are compelled to notice the modernist Woolfian hauntings in the structure and thematic thrust of this work, even more present is the homage to Ralph Ellison's *Invisible Man* (1952). Set in a time when Black invisibility has been repeatedly revisited in scholarly and public discourses, this particular literary conversation makes the fashioning of the city as a locus of past colonial and present global capitalist unease poignantly relevant. The parallels between the two works are remarkable: Ishmael is, like Ellison's character, almost unnamed. For over 400 pages, we hear his name only once. Both characters are based in New York City, and though Ishmael himself did not move from the South to the North the way Ellison's character did, Ishmael's parents' south-north drift is a constant presence and reference point over the course of the novel. Furthermore, the characters' shared quest for visibility is perhaps the most obvious through line between these two works. It also seems fair to suggest an allusion to Herman Melville's portrayal of Ishmael, the seafaring narrator in *Moby Dick.*

The reverberations of past African American works, and even more specifically works located in urban spaces that detail urban experiences, extend beyond *The Invisible Man.* For example, it is to the writings of James Baldwin that Ishmael turns as he recovers one moment in in his youth and as he tries to make sense of his brokenness, "I wonder if I'm too damaged" (9). Ishmael recalls, "[Baldwin] once wrote somewhere about someone who had *a wound that he would never recover from,* but I don't remember where. He also wrote about a missing member that was lost but still aching. Maybe something inside me was no longer intact" (9). The allusions to Baldwin's mid-twentieth-century embedded protest, his direct reference to trauma, and the physicality of racial trauma that bleeds into Thomas's twenty-first-century representation extend beyond intertextuality or even homage to a literary forebear. It is both a deliberate and inevitable signal of a man being pursued by a generational trauma and an expressive system that simultaneously acknowledges and documents that trauma, engages in protest, and lays the foundations for regeneration or the hope of it. Thomas's usage here, therefore, adds to the mosaic of literary recordings of sustained Black protest and the insistence on reform within the urban context that he also shares with Baldwin.

As an embodiment of the ongoing dialogue among Black texts, *Man Gone Down* is also the text that haunts later works. Preempting Coates's *Between the World and Me*, Thomas provides a shared picture of the anxiety of Black parenthood in New York City, a place Ishmael's wife believes to be more welcoming to her brown children.

> *Stand up straight* I say. *Enunciate*, I say. *Dignity*, I say—the preparation for life is more daunting than life itself. I'm too hard on my boy. I wish I could take it all back, but I fear already that my boy is too damaged. I've tried to cram what I have learned into his little body before he's experienced it himself. What else is a father to do? They tried to make me ready, but I never was ready. What am I supposed to do? Perhaps a brown father needs only be a safe place for his brown boy, where he can come to be afraid, to fall apart and cry. (249)

Among the multiple Black texts in conversation here is Thomas's early reference to Baldwin's use of the Black man having a "wound"; the experience of being permanently damaged is shown here to be mapped onto the body of Ishmael and his wounded son, who is not yet aware of the generational injury that he too has inherited. As if in response to Thomas's 2007 fictive account, Coates's contribution to this man-to-man, man-to-boy conversation similarly calls to mind Curry's theorization of Black male vulnerability.[6]

The access to an even more expansive Black expressive system that a global city such as New York makes possible allows Thomas to extend the intertextual conversation to other works of art, this time with a diasporic reach to Trench Town, where Bob Marley's globally resonant music first emerged. Trench Town is another city, the inner city to be more precise, where Black men—whose particular experience with neocolonial global capitalism I address more extensively in chapter 4, on Marlon James's *A Brief History of Seven Killings*—encounter extraordinary pressures resulting from the inequities of global-Western capitalism.

> I remember moving day. [. . .] The boys were confused and moping among the stacked boxes. I put the stereo on. [. . .] The boys jump to their feet ready to dance and sing "*. . . the stone that the builder refused . . .*" sings Bob "*. . . shall be the head corner stone . . .*" I bend down low. "Fire!" Bob and I cry. "Fire! [. . .]" Teaching my boys, right in front of their Brahmin mother, to hold the burning spear, [. . .] Whipping them into righteous rage and indignation—the young lions, [. . .] the griot enchanter. (295; bracketed ellipses added)

Ishmael is listening to Marley's "Ride Natty Ride" in the present, and this song loops him back to Marley in another moment, a moment when he, and by extension the readers, shared an artistic impulse toward protest; that Black diasporic resonance, the common pursuit of racial justice, and the protest that Napier reminds us has always undergirded African American literature moves Ishmael from a place of vulnerability to one of strength. The seamless integration of "holding the burning spear," an obvious reference to Burning Spear, another Black-diasporic, revolutionary protest singer, underscores the focus on Black-diasporic protest-oriented art that offers succor for Ishmael. The distance that Ishmael establishes between himself and his "Black" children and his wife "right in front of their Brahmin mother" in the remembered moment is a subtle but clearly perceived instance of the microcosmic racial divide of this family, a point that I return to in greater detail later in the chapter.

The presence of Marley and Burning Spear in *Man Gone Down* not only offers instances of "talking Black texts" but also illustrates the complexity of the city experience for a tormented and vulnerable city resident such as Ishmael. As a nexus of multiple peoples and cultures—even as a hotbed of racial oppression, violence against Blacks, and a plethora of other historically grounded social ills—cities, because of their constant flow of people, are also loci of a multiplicity of Black ethnicities and historical and ongoing sites of racial solidarity. Thus, part of what makes Ismael's journey to New York and his experiences there semicircular—that is, not a full return to his diminished self—is the cultural wealth of New York City as a "contact zone," to borrow a term from Mary Louise Pratt, where hearing Marley is as likely for this character as it would have been for an urban citizen in Kingston. Such an overt instantiation of Black-diasporic relationship extends beyond the provision of evidence of the shared history, the shared sense of protest in Black cultural production. Of equal significance is the way these moments of cultural contact locate Ishmael himself, the individual, and also the racialized social being as part of a larger Black male community connected not only through the shared experience of ongoing racism but more importantly as part of a collective engaged in protest.

The Black Male Body, the City Space, and Capitalist Hauntings

This double-edged characteristic of United States cities—New York in particular—for Blacks is captured in James Baldwin's suggestion that Baldwin's character was part of a "Southern community . . . violently driven north" (*Collected Essays*, 773). More recently, Evan Hughes makes a similar observation about Brooklyn, the setting of Thomas's novel, noting that Thomas's main character and narrator "embodies . . . the push-and-pull beneath the languid, happy surface of a Brooklyn environment that sometimes 'feels like a giant set for a sitcom about trendy young people' . . . and gives us a greater insight into American life" (280). The violence that accompanied this journey to New York marks this city space as a particular kind of complicated and multilayered memory site, which explains the similarities in Baldwin's mid-twentieth-century observation and Hughes's twenty-first-century characterization of Thomas's fictive account of this space.

A turn to Pierre Nora's much-contemplated "site of memory" is a useful but, as Melvin Dixon has shown, somewhat limited way of thinking about African Americans in the context of this analysis of Ishmael as representative of the Black male experience. Nora's suggestion about the status of "memory" is useful for thinking about Thomas's work within the African American tradition of a preoccupation with memory: Nora writes that "memory has been torn . . . in such a way as to pose a problem of embodiment of memory in certain sites where a sense of historical continuity persists. There are *lieux de mémoire*, sites of memory, because there are no longer *milieu de mémoire*, real environments of memory" (284). The rupture of colonization and displacement from Africa, from the origins so to speak, is not in dispute. Nora's view regarding "sites and real environments of memory" (284) does not fully capture memory sites in African American cities and in New York City in particular. I want to argue that there are *milieu de mémoire*—real environments of memory, if we define *real* as sites where ancestral presence is tangible—where history is being both revisited and made. In this way, then, New York is a memory site where Ishmael finds the memories of reprieve for his Black southern ancestors, a space of current displacement/dislocation but also a site of African American and African-diasporic cultural regeneration—what New York has been and is for African Americans. The presence of African Americans in northern neighborhoods such as Harlem in New York marks the creation of new histories. Dixon notes the presence of street names such as "Malcom X Boulevard, . . . Frederick Douglas Boulevard, Johnny Hartman Plaza, Marcus Garvey Park, and Adam Clayton Powell Boulevard" (20). Dixon rightfully points out, "What you may gather from these places is a sense of changes within history, for these people were important to Harlem's past. . . . Not only do the names celebrate and commemorate great figures in Black culture, they provoke our participation in the history" (20). The case that Dixon makes here is for these places to be understood as historical sites—what I would suggest are *milieu de mémoire*, "real environments of memory." They mark and write into history places that African Americans have been and, more importantly, places they have "created." Black people have marked these spaces and in that way have reinscribed spatial history. What Thomas offers us, then, is the possibility of a more layered understanding of memory sites: in other words, for African Americans, in northern cities, there is both *milieu de mémoire* and *lieux de mémoire*.

To reiterate, the significance of thinking about Blackness and Black experiences through an examination of depictions of cities takes on another dimension because of the specific focus on Black male experiences. As historical bastions of trade, financial institutions, manufacturing, and so forth, cities have unique relationships with neo-Western expansion in the form of globalization; as a result, cities continue to be destinations for people seeking necessary economic viability. Part of the irony and complexity of cities and their specific relationship to African Americans is that these spaces where Black experiences have been especially fraught with danger and Black bodies especially vulnerable were also locations of their refuge in the early twentieth century. In light of the construct of American iconic masculinity and associated links between patriarchal power and materialism, cities are at once attractive and debilitating memory sites for the Black male collective, a view that is embodied in the fictional Ishmael. As Marcy Sacks has noted, "many southern Black men looked to New York City as an escape from the emasculation they encountered under the South's Jim Crow system" (42). Thus, with its allure of opportunities, New York in particular has been a logical destination for men who seek to fulfill the imperative of breadwinner and provider. Yet, in the case of Black men, this understanding, of New York in particular and of Western or Westernized cities in general, must be positioned vis-à-vis redlining, white flight, and structural racism that deliberately and calculatedly deny Black men access to the very thing—money and its corollaries—that is supposed to define them as men. bell hooks reminds us of the refusal of the "white-supremacist capitalist patriarchy to allow Black males full access to employment" (8). These expectations about what the fulfillment of manhood is based on—being a provider, having feelings of self-worth, being validated, to name a few—have necessarily been bought into the dominant discourses about the male's role and not only have been instituted by the white patriarchal system but often have been uncritically embraced by the broader society and even by some Black people. The absence of meaningful interrogation of these expectations is itself an unavoidable function of the unavoidable capitalist system. As the work of Curry, Mark Anthony Neal, and others has demonstrated, without interrogation of the systemic failings that make Black men's abilities to actualize these expectations unlikely, the psychic and societal wounds remain, as does the limited degree of capitalist-oriented "success."

Thomas's novel engages in such an interrogation through realistic fictional portrayals that ask readers to consider the experience of one educated, twenty-first-century Black man who embodies the weight of failings based on modern and patriarchal capitalist expectations and who also carries in his body the burdens of a past so indelibly etched in his memory that it functions as a central element in the hauntings that underpin this work. Constantly contemplating his specific history and plight, Ishmael, like James Baldwin, must make sense of the understanding, "Some things happened to me because I was black and some things had happened to me because I was *me*, and I had to discover the demarcation line if, there was one" (Baldwin, *Collected Essays* 774) The portrait of Ishmael that Thomas offers illuminates the character and characterization of this wounded man and, in so doing, renders this fictional portrayal an example of the impact of the conflation of race-racism, capitalist imperatives, and a necessary wounded masculinity in the city space.

Ishmael's musings during his late-night runs offer some of the most insightful recollections and commentary on his condition and, by extension, on the condition of all of his Black male counterparts. Thomas's choice to use Ishmael as first-person narrator is especially effective because the author has crafted his character as a brilliant thinker and writer, a self-described "man of . . . talents" (400). Thomas is a creative writer, and his depiction is both artful and credible and is grounded in a multidisciplinary exploration of the Black male experience; it successfully includes its very central sociological content through the reflections of a philosophical character. Demirtürk characterizes the narrative style as autoethnographic, a fitting characterization that allows for what Demirtürk reads as an example of Damion Waymer's notion of "ongoing sense making" and, for Demirtürk, of multiple levels of consciousness. In other words, Ishmael is engaged in an ongoing self- and societal reflection and analysis of his circumstances.

Thomas's choice of New York City as the fictional setting through which to examine Ishmael's debilitating efforts to support his family and as the site and spark for his psychological explorations and hauntings embeds this story in a long history of Black male experiences in New York City and, as Hughes has pointed out, a long history of Brooklyn's "richness as a site of the literary imagination . . . , dating back centuries" (4). Here in New York City, where Black people came in multitudes decades before, Thomas places another artist, who, in the moment of the text's setting, must center his life around his economic obligations. The readers' introduction to Ishmael's plight may be understood as simultaneously haunting, emasculating, and "normal" for an adult male who is experiencing the kind of downward mobility that Ishmael perceives:

> I go into the kiddie bedroom, turn the light off, and lie down in the kiddie bed. I need to make a plan, which means I need to make a list of the things I need to do. I need to get our security deposit back from our old landlady. I need to call the English Departments I'm still welcomed in to see if there are any classes to be had. I need to call more contractors and foremen I know to see if there's any construction work. I need to call the boys' school to see if I can pay the tuition in installments. I need an installment. I try to make a complete list in my head. It doesn't work. . . . Claire has always been good at making lists—to do lists, grocery lists, gift lists, wish lists. (M. Thomas 26–27)

As an early window into Ishmael's "failure" and the debilitating weight of white patriarchal-inspired expectations, the image and reality of a grown man sleeping on the bed of his friend's child is as strikingly significant as is the fact that Ishmael cannot fully register all he needs to do. However, equally importantly, if less obvious, is his inclusion of his (white) wife's ability to make lists; this point of variance marks the chasm between their worlds—that of the Black man who tries but constantly fails to function in the structure that demands his compliance and one in which his wife, with *her* habits, flourishes. As Thomas does in multiple moments in the text, he uses the relationship between Claire and Ishmael as the basis for a meditation on the veil, to recover W.E.B. Du Bois's term, that separates Black and white people. And even as they share the intimacy of a marriage and what Ishmael presents as sincere love, this relationship is never disentangled from the larger structure in which it must exist and the haunting past that hovers over it. The incremental style powerfully captures the weight of the tasks and the constraints of a capitalist-driven definition of manhood into which Ismael has fallen: "I need," a phrase that recurs eight times, underscores the weight and inescapability of the responsibility to provide.

As Kernicky has pointed out, one of the most revealing moments of the confluence of economic incapacity, masculinity, and the race- and class-based gulf between Ishmael and Claire occurs early in the novel when their frustration over their financial collapse pits them against each other. This conversation, too, is extraordinarily revealing about the weight of patriarchal-capitalist masculinity. When Claire declares, "We need to make more money," Ishmael corrects with "You mean *I* need to make money" in what seems to be a way of conveying to Claire the weight of Euro-patriarchy on him (M. Thomas 67). But Claire, in unchanged oblivion, continues to advocate for the family's financial needs. In her incomprehension about the racial-gender-based economic plight they face, she suggests, "It shouldn't be so hard. You're smart. You're talented," then asks him, "Why?" And when Ishmael responds with the matter-of-fact "I don't make the rules" (68), even that is not enough to enlighten her. Her continued questioning—"Why don't you?" (68)—is left unanswered, a silence that offers readers some insight into the difficulties that the intersections of race, class, masculinity, and capitalism present. This passage so clearly addresses the extent of the illustrative Black-white disconnect: Ishmael's reference to "the rules" definitively articulates his unambiguous understanding of the dominant patriarchal structure within which he as Black man must fit in order to claim his place as the man in his family and align himself with the broader culture's definitions of manhood.

Kernicky's suggestion that "sole financial responsibility is not something that is just thrust upon [Ishmael]; it is something he takes upon himself" (214) calls to mind again Baldwin's assertion, "some things had happened to me because I was Black, and some things happened to me because I was *me*"

(*Collected Essays* 774). Kernicky's reading of this situation raises a number of questions about agency and, relatedly, the extent of the weight of Euro-capitalist patriarchy on Black men. Taking into account the obvious societal weight represented by the expectations, frustrations, and resulting demands of Ishmael's wife, Claire, it is hard to determine how much of this weight Ishmael takes upon himself. However, a reading of this moment in the novel, within the context of systemic racism and what Kernicky describes as the commingling of "race and income," (213) certainly allows for a more nuanced understanding of the difficulty of parsing what has been "thrust upon" Ishmael and what he "takes upon himself." We could therefore extend Baldwin's statement to include how much is me/personal, me/Black, or me/societal. Even more uncertain is the question of what it even means to "take" something so deeply entrenched "upon" oneself. Demirtürk's view that "it is not possible for any person to live outside of discursive regimes of power" (*Contemporary African American Novel* 167) might be helpful here, since the impossibility of functioning outside a Euro-patriarchal apparatus would neutralize the possibilities of avoiding a "taken for granted" imperative, such as taking the responsibility to provide for one's family upon oneself.

That imperative to function, even to succeed, in a defined structure such as New York, the representative of the capitalist milieu, is among Ishmael's most sustained hauntings. Its appeal, even in the face of failure, is almost comically addressed in Ishmael's own understanding of the power and necessity of self-making in even the momentary participation in this Sisyphean attempt at success. Following on the heels of a humiliating moment—"I hover over the change bowl. . . . Marco has replenished it. . . . I take a dollar seventy-five cent, enough for a slice or a sport bar"—Ishmael admits to being "ashamed" to be "excited" by Marco's note: "Meet me at 57th and 5th, 8:00. Bring the cigars. Happy Birthday. If you don't mind, would you drive the car" (M. Thomas 155). In order to measure up to the occasion, he wears a white man's suit, his father-in-law's: "three-piece, wool but thin, dark blue with pin stripes, . . . periwinkle shirt and medium blue tie tucked into it—a ready-made outfit" (157). Ishmael's assessment of himself is self-consciously revealing of the inevitability of his participation, even investment, in the world in which he has not been able to survive. The white man's suit will not really fit, because, although he says, "I hate to think it, but I look pretty good," his thoughts turn immediately to the temporary nature of this moment. "Why can't I be successful? I look successful. I leave the mirror before I change my mind" (158). And although he does not change his mind about occupying this temporary image of New York success, the hauntings, the failed social experiment, return again and again.

We may get closer to more accurately addressing questions about control and agency that Kernicky's preceding comment raises by locating this question within the context of the city experience. While this chapter has focused on

Ishmael's experiences in New York City, Thomas also includes insights of Ishmael that are grounded in his earlier childhood and adult experiences in Boston. To underscore the point that the city is being written as a location of residual and persistent racial trauma and, as such, is a project still under construction, Thomas offers Ishmael's thoughts on a part of the New York landscape, the shipyard, in what could be read as a short sociological/historical essay on the two cities of the novel's setting and of Ishmael's making. After he takes in and comments in detail about the shipyard, Ishmael asks of the city,

> I wonder what others would do. Some would move away, but where to go? New York's no damn good. It seems those born here become, ironically enough, provincial. Boston is too thick with history. . . . Claire believes she loves it here; having grown up in the country, she never wants to go back to the homogeny, the boundless whiteness, in which she believes our children could not survive. But to escape that, we've thrown them into another mess, the social experiment redux. . . . Now, however, there is at least one brown kid per class instead of per grade. It's another disaster. Brown kids are cultural experiences for white ones. (M. Thomas 248)

This passage illuminates the major argument of this chapter, that the semicircularity of the city lies mostly in its capacity to offer more—better than the tribulations of a Jim Crow South, for example, more than Claire's homogeneous white country or suburb—but not yet enough to make Blacks integral and no longer a specimen for what Thomas calls "social experiments" for white people. The "mess" that Ishmael names here is conceivably the flux of the city that makes such spaces still open—at once sites of both hope *and* despair that renders Black people such as Ishmael and his children both insiders and outsiders, therefore urging us to consider notions of citizenship, belonging, and perhaps more fittingly, unbelonging in discourses about the place of Blacks in city spaces. This instance and others like it also hark back to the previously mentioned 1790 Naturalization Act and draw attention to what Orlando Patterson refers to as "the ordeal of integration" (*Ordeal of Integration*).

This insight that Ishmael's observations provide to the reader also highlight, yet again, the divide between Ishmael and his wife, the microcosmic Black-white divergence: for Claire, New York City is diversity paradise, a far cry from the whiteness of her childhood. Yet, for Ishmael, who must navigate the city in a Black male body, this social experiment is still just that—an experiment. New York City still renders Black "citizens" as simultaneous spectators (they are not fully integrated into the performance) and specimens, useful for the dominant culture's ongoing experiments. In the end, like Boston, which haunts Ishmael with its longer "thick" history of racism, conquest, and genocide, New York is still haunted by its own, more recent racist past.

As if to confirm that Ismael's fear is not the result of what could be perceived as his psychological instability and as a way of staving off any notions of Black paranoia, Thomas provides another glimpse of New York City in the present, underscoring what it means to be Black and male in this global and diverse space:

> When I walked these streets alone, before anyone knew anything about me, I was afforded the respect reserved for large dark men: Other dark men would nod gravely; dark women would roll their eyes up or smile or just ignore; the cops would slow down but pass on, somehow discriminating between me and those men in the van, whom they would stop and question. The white people scattered—not the ones who'd been here—the old Italians and their children and pre-crack whites to whom this neighborhood belonged. . . . . It was neopioneers—a strange breed of professional liberal whites, bankers and lawyers and midlevel media folk . . . Things had changed—a restaurant, a shop, a gut renovation. They were in, cramming into the old butcher, the green grocer, the coffee roaster, perturbed by lack of service. Playgrounds were suddenly clean. Trash cans appear on corners. (M. Thomas 121)

This fictional account highlights the same dilemma that Curry raises when he asks, "What possibilities do black males have when they are reduced to their bodies and determined to be little more than the fear elicited in others?" (36) Through this novel's portrayal of Black male experience, the assumption that cities are spaces of escape, of inconspicuousness where anyone from anywhere can just be without being under scrutiny, is undermined, if not fully debunked. Instead, the hypervisibility that writers such as Claudia Rankine insist on is dramatized here: difference is noticed—the Black body is marked by a cross-section of people including other Blacks, and its perceived threat is noted: "the cops slow down . . . the white people scattered" (M. Thomas 121). The discomforts of the Black male in the city space turn historical and current characterizations of Black males as threatening and dangerous onto New York City, which in this instance is unmasked as monstrous, intrusive, and haunting—haunting because in this representation, instances of terror, such as lynching, forced labor, incarceration, and exclusions, are recuperated, not as psychological haunting of a hypersensitive Black man but as lived reality. Feeling noticed in the way Ishmael describes here is a function of the segregation cultivated in the city, where attention from the police brings to the forefront the very strong possibility of being killed. Instances such as this constitute a literal haunting and real-time surveillance that is as monstrous as the haunting memories and imaginings. Further undermining perceptions that this global space of New York City is a place of belonging for all, Thomas highlights how Blackness is mapped onto the bodies of other marginalized urban citizens of color: "young white girls scurried about, pretending the Arab and Latino boys who drank soda, leaned on mailboxes, and called each other nigger weren't there" (M. Thomas 121–122). As a space in which boys "of color" are cast as objects, ignored by the white subjects for whom the city has been cleaned up, patrolled, and kept under surveillance, any characterizations of New York as a space of equal coexistence are even more convincingly challenged.

I will not rehearse in detail here the well-documented and extensively discussed historical and contemporary experiences and representations of Black manhood, except to note that the centuries-long efforts to diminish Black men in the United States and throughout the Black diaspora continue unabated, despite some racial "progress."[7] Indeed, it is Black men's labor, and the way their bodies and the bodies of Black women were used to advance Western capitalism, that serves as the core of the dominant-culture dehumanization of Black men; money and the capitalist system are therefore central to any conversation about the state of Black manhood in the United States. In this regard, Thomas's work is central to the conversation that Curry, hooks, Robert Staples, and others engage in. Ishmael notices change in some New Yorkers' attitudes to his large Black body once he has married Claire. "They had always considered Claire as one of their own, and perhaps, after I became a father they considered me that, too. Somehow they let us in—they let me in" (M. Thomas 122). The doubt and hesitation are apparent in the way Thomas represents the change on the page: the separation between Ishmael and Claire, his most intimate relationship, painfully underscores the point that Black-white separation at the micro and macro levels remains a vexing issue in contemporary US society. Ishmael's personal feelings of uncertainty therefore speak to the persistently tenuous state of Black male subjectivity.

Thomas captures the often-illusive race-class intersection in the extensive list of criteria he includes for being let in that mirrors the way that Ishmael thought he might have been after he married a white woman and started to build the classical "American" family: "the right stroller, the right books and movies, the right politics, the right jobs" are ultimately trumped by what is really at the core of Ishmael's struggles, because as he remarks, "the only relevant divide was those who could afford to pay and those who could not—an us and a them" (M. Thomas 122). And while this recognition disrupts the aforementioned Black-white divide that purposely obfuscates the enduring presence of class, the intersection between race and class is the more important element being marked here: "I heard it in quick snatches—*they had to pull their kid out. I think they defaulted. He hasn't worked in over a year. And this one knows the best real estate broker. And that one's a trustee*" (122).

To say that an experience such as this one transcends race and therefore does not speak enough to Black male subjects' unique experiences is to elide both the history and the sustained exclusions and impediments that Blacks and other racial minorities continue to endure, even when socioeconomic realities transcend racial lines. In the world of Western capitalism, economic survival for a Black person might be termed a dilemma of survival. Work for the Black person, in this instance the Black male, is always entangled with considerations such as dignity, personhood, and perhaps most significantly, the history of racism and slavery, and often Black men, with the various pressures that accompany masculinity, must choose between dignity and survival. And as one incident in Ishmael's search for the economic viability of his family demonstrates, the options are sometimes irreconcilable. Just a few days after Ishmael finds construction work that should help him make a dent in the large sum he needs to move his family back to New York City and to restore a manhood that is so heavily reliant on his capacity to provide, he faces such a choice: he overhears the general contractor ask, "Who's the big nig on the Baker?" (M. Thomas 280). And in what appears to be racial solidary, his colleagues and another man "of color," KC, ask, "You alright wit dat, mon? . . . Mon, if I was a big boy like you, I wouldn't fear no man. No man couldn't say nothing to me" (281). This encouragement and support challenge Ishmael to defend both his manhood and his race, and in that moment, he makes a decision about his family's economic viability. His decision to retaliate with the resulting fight that sees him defeating his superior costs him this job.

Curry contends that the "overrepresentation of black men in prison" (110) is deeply intertwined with their ability to secure and keep employment. After Ishmael recovers his dignity by physically overpowering his racist employer, that possibility looms large for Ishmael, and it is left unresolved in the novel. As the racist offender is taken to the hospital, Jonny, a supervising colleague, reminds Ishmael, "You gotta watch out. He's the type that'll sue you" (M. Thomas 285). It is this reminder that brings readers back to the very real and constant possibility of incarceration; because Ishmael is already economically diminished, in the face of a lawsuit and the cost of legal representation, prison would be the most likely outcome. In this way, Thomas lays bare the haunting dilemma of Black male subjectivity and the virtual impossibility of occupying all the spaces of masculinity—physical prowess, dignity, breadwinner—that the dominant culture insists on. This example conjures up haunting in a few ways: it calls to mind a time when the line between Black men's labor and their incarceration was blurred, as these men could be returned to labor under the guise of lawbreaking. But this incident is also reminiscent of the ongoing challenge that Black men face in their encounters with law enforcement; often, their lives depend on their willingness to surrender rights and dignity. Furthermore, as an educated man, Ishmael is not immune to the precarious, vulnerable status of Black male—that at any moment, a defense of any aspect of prescribed masculinity might lead to incarceration.

Among the most important contributions that *Man Gone Down* makes to the conversation about Black masculinity is its focus on a demographic within the larger Black male population—formally educated, academically and artistically gifted men who suffer from actual underachievement but also from the psychological weight of being "social experiments." The attention to this segment of the population at once broadens conversations about the ordeals of Black men as these tend to focus on men such as Freddy Gray, Eric Garner, and other working-class men whose victimhood and diminished experiences in cities are more immediately apparent. Ishmael has attended Harvard University—he is so gifted a writer and student that despite his having dropped out of Harvard, his mentor, Professor Pincus, is able to fast track him into a graduate program. Paradoxically, as the presumed place of deviation, indeed the space that drives and allows critique of systems such as neoliberal capitalism, Thomas's representation—his crafting of a character who is entangled with academia—provides insights into the connections between academia and the economic system it sometimes critiques and in that way draws attention to the inescapability of modern modes of oppression.

As Thomas's fictional account illustrates, one casualty of the normalization of the narrow definition of masculinity is that the confines of breadwinner-provider continue to be encumbrances on Black men's self-actualization outside the patriarchal-capitalist construct; these restrictive and single-focused configurations of manhood also impede African American men's potential to contribute to their communities in other ways. With Ishmael having had to dispense with the ideas that his writing should "do things" and that it should "contain transformative powers," his desperation is, in part, the result of the failure of writing to address his deeper longing (M. Thomas 277). But even more crucial and damaging is the fact that, with the weight of the provider, his writing is now intertwined with his family's existential crisis: "A finished manuscript means a contract and a contract means a new silver minivan. So my words, in a sense, are written to that automobile, calling for it to show itself to me" (277). These words encapsulate Ishmael's inevitable entrapment in the economic scheme that he seeks to escape. Notably, early in the novel, Ishmael interprets his wife's purchase of a computer for Christmas and her whisper of anticipation, "*This is your year. . . . This is our year*," as even more suffocating pressure to provide. According to Ishmael, the computer "would help extract the last portion of whatever it was that I was working on and buff it with requisite polish to make it salable" (4). Now part of the failed "social experiment," Ishmael's failure to write his way into greatness becomes part of the economic failings and hauntings.

That Ishmael returns to meet with his old academic advisor when he feels cornered by the economic system is significant in the way this meeting further links intellectual endeavors with capitalism. Despite being a supportive professor, Pincus, the longtime civil-rights activist whose picture with Dr. King hangs in his office, could only offer Ishmael meaningful support through what might be termed the academic industrial complex. Thinking that Ishmael had recovered himself enough to make it through the formal academic system, Professor Pincus "brightens" upon hearing that Ishmael "needs a letter" and asks, "Did you finish your doctorate somewhere else and not tell me?" The answer, "No, sir, just the letter," elicits the professor's disappointment: "His face turns, and he leans back in his chair like someone slowly realizing he's been insulted. He covers his mouth with his hand and looks away from me, out the window, down Lexington" (395). Professor Pincus's unspoken but clearly conveyed dismay illustrates the wider consensus that Ishmael is a failure, that he is unable to survive within a structure that Pincus both resists and supports. "Cover[ing] his mouth with his hand," that utter disappointment is a reminder to Ishmael that any sense of himself as measuring up from the perspective of his own race—and, more so, of an activist—is impossible unless he is able to meet the expectations of the established Euro-American patriarchal capitalist-academic framework of success.

Furthermore, Ishmael's responses to two other questions make clear the conundrum he faces as an "educated" Black man in the United States. Ishmael has not finished his dissertation; for him, not finishing is not an indication of failure, nor is it the casualty of circumstances—a family to feed, adjunct teaching, lack of motivation in the conventional sense. Rather it is an absence of motivation, a choice, a sense that this work on "Eliot, Modernism and Metaphysics" was, in Ishmael's view, "archaic and therefore frivolous": "a man of my history, background, and talent should know better" (M. Thomas 400). A bit above the subtextual, this response lays out the dilemma of survival for a Black man on whom the social experiment has been enacted multiple times. Thus, the cost of Ishmael's resistance to being "*sivilised*" (399) is his semicircle; he must return to the very place he spurns so that he might survive. But that return is only partial. With the consent of his professor, he manages to undermine the system, to say he has a job he could have had but has chosen not to pursue. Yet the inescapability of Western capitalism—whether in the form of crude money or disguised and sanitized in academia—is underscored in this encounter. At the same time, the novel entertains the notion that one can indeed circumvent that system somehow, as it portrays Professor Pincus, arguably the man in the middle, as complicit in Ishmael's paradoxical exploitation of the system. I am opting to read the last question Pincus asks Ishmael—"To whom do I address this letter?" (400)—as a moment of Black male solidarity, but not just for the sake of it. I believe this gesture is a more far-reaching act of resistance to the false system of meritocracy that Professor Pincus joins Ishmael in circumventing, a system already so skewed against Black men.

Reclaiming the Self

Curry suggests that "black male vulnerability is an attempt to capture the Black male's perpetual susceptibility to the will of others, how he has no resistance to the imposition of others' fears and anxieties on him" (29). While Thomas explores and dramatizes instances of "Black male vulnerability" in many of the ways that Curry catalogues in his study, he also seems to suggest that there is some possibility for Black male resistance and self-reclamation, which is more consistent with Griffin's and hooks's theorizations. Furthermore, the tools for such resistance are drawn from an African American and larger diasporic community, what Griffin refers to as "a strategy of resistance that emerges from within . . . the black community" that helps Black men "to liberate themselves from Eurocentric notions of manhood" (172). Melvin Dixon suggests that "by calling themselves to remember Africa and/or the racial past, black Americans are actually re-membering, as in repopulating broad continuities within the African diaspora" (21). To make this point, Dixon highlights the Black remapping of the New York City space, the Black-Africanizing of this urban location as testament to African American memorializing agency. For Thomas, such a diasporic reach is the basis for self-regeneration.

Interestingly, Thomas only uses the term *diaspora* once (9), yet it is at a very important point in the novel. About this, Demirtürk writes, "Ishmael feels he may be damaged. . . . He relates his . . . emotional damage to that of living in a diaspora, 'collateral damage of the diaspora'" (*Contemporary African American Novel* 164). Demirtürk's extension of the possibilities that a diasporic connection offers aligns well with one of the central arguments of this chapter. She writes, "The term diaspora represents a contradictory site: it does not only signify 'transnational movement' because diaspora links identity to spatial location. . . . Hence, we are faced with a notion of dominated black male identity whose very site of oppression may function as a transformative site in the narrator's ordeal to allow him the space to liberate his manhood from his blackness, a stereotype in the white imaginary, to develop an individual identity outside the normative frame of recognition, and a lifestyle outside the discursive frame of the American dream" (164). Demirtürk takes us a good distance here with her suggestion that a diasporic identity offers possibilities for imagining and actualizing the self, outside Euro-patriarchy.

I want to extend Demirtürk's point along two important paths. The first is that the value of the diasporic identity lies primarily in its shift from the individual, the individuality of Western Euro-America, to a community-driven diasporic sensibility and affiliation. My second point of divergence from, or as an amendment to, Demirtürk's focus is related to the individual- community question, specifically as this relates to Blackness. Demirtürk also suggests that part of what the turn to diaspora makes possible is a definition of self outside the Blackness of the white imaginary. I can see the value of this point especially in light of the fact that African Americans' existence, self-evident in the use of the qualified ("African American") identity, is grounded in and arguably demarcated by race. Yet affinity, something shared by members of the African diaspora, also necessitates and productively allows for a claiming of that "Black" collective self that has historically been used to paralyze African American men. Here, though, Blackness is reimagined and celebrated through culture and group affinity; hence, it is not the debased Blackness. This is, therefore, one instance in which "Black" simultaneously carries but also transcends its negative colonially oriented characterization. With Ishmael's turn to diaspora then, he does not need to "liberate his manhood from his blackness," as Demirtürk suggests; instead, he is able to embrace both by shifting his understanding of Blackness away from its age-old, but specifically North American, definition to an affirming diasporic definition.

As I have argued in the introduction to this study and elsewhere in the book, all the creative works under consideration in this study validate the long-standing view that cities are spaces of opportunity. In this final turn of the chapter, I want to suggest that the semicircularity and the open possibilities for which I argue are manifested here in Ishmael's recognition of and willingness to reach for diasporic solidarity; this in turn prevents a total collapse and is the basis for the novel's open-ended semiclosure (see M. Thomas 428). Thomas's engagement with this view of the city is especially useful as it offers space for a discussion of both the role of cities in fostering diasporic, racial solidarity and the importance of a diasporic lens in reading and writing about African American literature. In this way, then, Thomas writes into and out of a tradition and a genealogy of diasporic Black activism: the artistic, cultural, and intellectual relationship of West Indians such as Claude McKay and Marcus Garvey in the Harlem Renaissance; C.L.R James's work in the 1930s and 1940s; and the connections that leaders such as Kwame Nkrumah, Jomo Kenyatta, and others established with African American and Caribbean communities, among other diasporic connections. Thomas therefore taps into a long and continuous history of solidarity and racial activism among African Americans and others from Africa, Europe, the Caribbean, and Latin America.

The tension between dignity and survival that I referenced earlier and that is so deeply interwoven with Black male vulnerability addressed earlier in this chapter highlights one of the novel's most significant engagements with racial solidarity. Ishmael's recognition of this solidarity with the men with whom he does construction work makes such alliance visible: "We're all brown and we are all, at least in part, New World Indians. We have that. That is where we begin" (M. Thomas 129). Resisting the class barriers of Western capitalism (though the other workmen refer to him as "professor"), Ishmael's choice of alliance is rewarded when KC encourages him to challenge Feeney's verbal racial violence by asking, "you alright wit dat, mon?" (281). But even more significant than simply urging Ishmael to respond, KC helps Ishmael to escape safely after the fight, urges him to leave, and even more, offers help: "You gotta number man? You in the book. . . . Like I said, I get jobs of my own. I call you next one na" (284).

Diasporic links are forged in city spaces such as the fictional and actual New York not only through interpersonal connections but also, as numerous examples of cultural connection in this novel demonstrate, through performance and cultural modes such as uplifting and resistant reggae music. Thomas establishes that connection early in the novel and goes so far as to contemplate and introduce the Black-diasporic music to which he often turns:

> Ray Charles is singing "America the Beautiful." . . . Dylan makes me feel alienated and old; hip-hop, militant. Otis Redding is too gritty and makes me think about dying young. Robert Johnson makes me feel like catching the next thing smoking and Satan. Marley makes me feel like Jesus. I thought for some reason that listening to Ray . . . would be good, or at least better than others. He's not. I'm confused. I never know what he's singing. A blind, black, R&B junkie gone country, sing an also-ran anthem—dragging it back through the tunnel of his experience. The gospel organ pulse. The backing voices, not from Nashville, not from Harlem, Mississippi, or Chicago—they float somewhere in the mix . . . *America, America* . . . It falls apart. (M. Thomas 25–26)

When Ishmael hears a Black man singing "America the Beautiful," he feels that "it falls apart"; this is in stark contrast to the diasporic music that revitalizes Ishmael. Though offered without explanation, "Marley makes me feel like Jesus" is a different cry from the observation that Ray Charles "falls apart" (26). I do not believe that Ray Charles "falls apart" because his musical talents are in any way inferior to Marley's. Instead, I think what Thomas illustrates here is the impossibility for a Black man of talent to be fully actualized in the "American" context precisely because of that dominant culture's exclusions of and cruelties toward Black men. This is why, for Ishmael, Ray Charles's beautiful voice is not enough to successfully render "America." In fact, for much of his career, this was the "America" in which Ray Charles was not allowed in some spaces unless he was entertaining white people.

Because Ishmael taps into a larger Black-diasporic artistic community—and despite the limits that US racism places on even the most talented—in the same chapter in which he confronts racism, loses his job, and in general opts for dignity over materialism, reggae provides uplift. Among his first stops after he is fired is a café where, with an "Oh yes," he accepts the offer to listen to some reggae music when the owner asks him, "Do you like reggae?" (M. Thomas 294). The song they play, "Ride Natty Ride," loops Ishmael back to moving day, when he played the same song for his children at a time when they all seemed to need a boost. And beyond that song, the integration of other reggae lyrics, "ben down low," and Ishmael's invocation of Burning Spear when he says, "teaching my boy right in front of his Brahmin mother to hold the burning spear, whipping them into righteous indignation—the young lion" (295), are obvious connections to reggae music. Ishmael chooses reggae not just for its militancy—its inherent orientations toward protest—but also for the link the musical genre provides to Rasta, a global symbol of Black affirmation. The repetition of the word *fire* in that recollected moment names one way in which Ishmael separates himself and his children (all Black or mixed raced) from his white wife, their mother—not to deny their filial connections with her but rather to acknowledge a difference that was marked from the founding of the United States and that, in his experience, persists. Ishmael and his children therefore join a virtual community of fellow Black activists; he instills in his children, and at the same time reminds himself of, the need for protest. In this moment, Thomas highlights the value of a diasporically inspired cultural tradition that creates and sustains its own system of self-definition, validation, and resistance to a mostly racially based oppression.

Although Ishmael chooses reggae music, Marley, Burning Spear, and therefore Rasta, I want to suggest that it is not to Jamaica that Thomas ultimately turns. Reggae functions instead as a diasporic rerouting to Africa. Like the place names that Dixon cites, these locations of rememory, reggae, and the voice of Rastafari, normally associated with Jamaica, become a diasporic conduit. As a spiritual-cultural point of departure from Garveyism, Rastafari is distinguished by an unapologetic, twentieth-century foregrounding of Africa as motherland, as Zion, as the ultimate place of return and redemption for Blacks in the diaspora. Returning to Ray Charles's failed rendition of "America the Beautiful," this performance does not work for Ishmael in his moments of despair because it does not reroute him to, and ground him in, Africa—in Black memory, in virtual community, history, and agency. Instead, it sings of America, a country whose formation exists, as scholars such as Nathan Huggins point out, because of the dehumanization of indigenous peoples, Africans, and peoples of African descent.

Ishmael's movement is semicircular, still open for multiple possibilities, rather than circular because of community: Pincus undermines the system established by academia and writes a letter that Ishmael is able to use to negotiate an apartment. Although he is fired, there is just enough money to shave off the deficit on the school fees and potentially allow his children to reenroll in their school. He can conceivably bring the family back to New York because he is helped by his more immediate African American community (through Pincus). His diasporic community lays the groundwork for a more sustained regeneration, survival, and agency because, through music, Ishmael is strengthened by a productive cultural haunting. Therefore, when he boards the bus to return to his family, instead of taking his own life, Ishmael in many ways emerges as the "Natty Dread" who "rise[s] again."

2

"Putting the Best Outside"

■■■■■■■■■■■■■■■■■■■

A Genealogy of
Self-Fashioning in *Call the
Midwife* and *NW*

> She had been asked to pass the entirety
> of herself through a hole that would
> accept only part. (Natalie's conclusion.)
> —Zadie Smith, *NW*

The quotation in the epigraph, from Zadie Smith's *NW*—one of many instances in the novel when the omniscient narrator provides readers access to a character's thoughts—is an astute observation that serves as the structuring idea for this chapter. It encapsulates the theorization of creative representations of Black female experiences in two low-income communities in the northwest and East End sections of the imperial city of London. The texts under consideration here are Smith's fourth novel, *NW* (2012), and the British Broadcasting Corporation (BBC) series *Call the Midwife*. Set in the mid-1990, *NW* tells multiple intersecting stories about four main characters—Keisha-Natalie, Felix, Nathan, and Leah—who are linked by, among multiple points of contact, their early lives in a housing project in northwest London and their attendance at Brayton Comprehensive School. This chapter focuses primarily on the representation of Keisha

Blake, the daughter of Jamaican immigrants who later changes her name to Natalie and who is henceforth referred to here as Keisha-Natalie. *Call the Midwife* centers on the lives of a group of nurse-midwives in a midwifery service run by a group of Anglican nuns from the Community of St. John the Divine; the nurses are constantly adjusting to a changing social and demographic landscape in and around their convent, Nonnatus House, located in the East End of London. Based on a memoir by Jennifer Louise Worth (Jenny Lee), *Call the Midwife* also includes material gleaned from historical sources. Series 1 is set in 1957, and the most recent, series 11, is set in 1967. One of the most striking features of the series is the way it tackles sociopolitical issues of the periods in which it is set. These include postwar trauma, intellectual disability, birth control, abortion, environmental concerns, urban "renewal," migration, and its concomitant challenges, such as integration and racism. In this chapter, I analyze selected scenes from series 7, when the first nurse of color, a Black Jamaican immigrant named Lucille Anderson, enters the series.

Theorizing the city of London as a dynamic semicircular space of constant movement that engenders looping and repeated agonies, in this chapter, I consider the portrayal of two professional women, one a recent immigrant and the other a child of immigrants, to examine the intersection of race, class, gender, and immigrant subjectivity across roughly four decades. Despite the decades of separation in the experiences of these two characters, the similarities between them are striking enough to allow for a theorization of female subjectivity in the city—one that represents what I term a *genealogy of anguished self-fashioning.* While I do not argue for an evolutionary progression between the representation of Lucille and Keisha-Natalie, given the patterns, the repeating experiences that define their lives as Black professional women in this imperial city, I find *genealogy* a useful term for the way it conveys the sense of something shared, of deep connection that remains with the passage of time. The core meanings—family, descent, and resemblance—of *genealogy* capture the sense of continuity that I seek to establish here. Furthermore, given the chapter's attentiveness to the characters' Black and immigrant subjectivities, *genealogy*, which also includes *ethnicity* and *race* as part of its etymology, advances the chapter's focus on the persistence of a kind of sustained assault, rooted in race and gender, on the bodies and personhood of these representative women.

While the chapter seeks to establish repeating patterns in the experiences of the two women, it is important to highlight some key differences in their backgrounds, self-presentations, and experiences. Apart from the temporal separation, Lucille and Keisha-Natalie inhabit London equipped with different cultural memories and resources. Lucille, a relatively new immigrant, has been in England for about four years, while Keisha-Natalie, the child of immigrants, is the product of a diverse corner of London at a time when ethnic and racial varieties and mixtures are mainstays. The differences in their upbringing also mean that each brings different kinds of cultural wherewithal to the experience, which in turn impacts how they engage with the challenges they encounter. These differences add nuance and complexity to the inquiry into depictions of Black professional female experiences being undertaken here. And placing a novel in conversation with a television series allows an even more expansive view of artistic representations of Black female experiences; the visual presentations of the city bring to life and concretize the urban landscape and, therefore, broaden the scope of the book and thus opens opportunities for additional critical engagements.

More specifically, because of the inherent embodied representations that dramatic performance offers, one advantage of including a film series in the study, particularly for addressing representation of Black female experiences in cities, is that we are able to see the impact, even if it is unspoken, that racial and gendered experiences of aggression have on the bodies of Black women. The wealth of interactions that audiences see provides useful insights into how race and gender-based prejudices impact Lucille. By this I mean that, while—unlike Keisha-Natalie—Lucille seems to retain her composure, viewers can see the strain that Lucille undergoes to avoid surrendering to the the race-based assaults on her personhood.

My use of *self-fashioning* to describe the characters' self-constructions and public performance of identities is drawn from Stephen Greenblatt's explication of the term in *Renaissance Self-Fashioning*, which analyzes the biographies and writing of six early-modern British writers.[1] As Greenblatt indicates in his early disclaimer, "there are always selves . . . and always elements of deliberate shaping in the formation and an expression of identity" (1). Greenblatt stresses "an increased self-consciousness" in the sixteenth-century context that his study engages. It is here in the notion of "increased self-consciousness" that I find Greenblatt's theorization useful because it provides a critical framework within which the necessity of a conscious self-construction is essential for survival in an imperial city. Even more relevant is Greenblatt's suggestion that mobility (in his case, for both his writers and the characters they create), mostly socioeconomic, is a characteristic feature of those who are engaged in these deliberate acts of self-construction. In the case of both Lucille and Keisha-Natalie, the urgency to construct acceptable selves emanates from their movements; for Lucille, these are mostly spatial and economic, while Keisha-Natalie's movements are spatial, socioeconomic, and psychological. Perhaps most relevant in Greenblatt's configuration is the suggestion that "self-fashioning . . . involves submission to an absolute power or authority situated at least partially outside the self" (9). Greenblatt's inclusion of a "colonial . . . administration" (8) as one of the likely authority figures is especially notable given both characters' location in the imperial city—a city designed as a space of exclusion and domination but one that also functions as a site of hope and prosperity. It is also noteworthy that their current unhomely home city was and continues to be a hub of the capitalist system on which the characters must rely for the economic advancement that they must seek—a set of circumstances that render self-fashioning virtually an existential necessity. Greenblatt's suggestion that "self-fashioning occurs at the point of encounter between an authority and an alien" (9) is, therefore, particularly salient; these female characters construct their identities in spaces of unbelonging, which inevitably renders their self-construction torturous.

As this chapter's epigraph, from *NW*, articulates, "the hole would accept only part" of the Black woman. This inability to bring the entire embodied self, with all its histories, joys, sorrows and scars, is the main focus of Kimberly Juanita Brown's argument in *The Repeating Body: Slavery's Visual Resonance in the Contemporary*. Brown's focus, which is primarily concerned with representations of Black women, "requires an examination of transatlantic slavery and Black women's necessary position within it. It requires a totality of vision— the image and the afterimage—in order to grapple with all the ways in which Black women fail to be seen with any clarity and insight" (3). I find these observations about the representation of Black women relevant to and resonant with the self-representations that are the subject of this chapter. What Brown refers to as "a totality of vision" translates here into a representation of the full self or, at least, of the type of complex and layered self that human beings generally include in their self-presentations. Keisha-Natalie and Lucille understand that as they move about the imperial city and into spaces where visible and invisible, colonially derived authority prevails, the presentation of a totality of self, or of anything other than the self that performs for the power structure, renders them unworthy of occupying these spaces. These two female characters are therefore embodiments of Brown's "after-image"—what is left over after slavery and, I would add, after immigration, after life in an urban housing project, and after living in a necessarily anxiety-ridden immigrant family.

Change, Continuity, and Creative Recuperations in London's Urban Landscape

It is useful to return briefly here to the earlier discussion of the significance of London, the historical epicenter of colonization, in this inquiry into creative accounts of the interplay between global capitalism and experiences of marginalized urban communities. As a city at the forefront of far-reaching capitalist exploitation, London has its own genealogy of global capital, which has in turn made the city a hub for immigration, diversity, class distinction, spatial exclusion, and the accompanying personal-social characteristics, including the quest for personhood and self-definition, that are central to the experiences of the characters in the texts under consideration here.² It is hard to overstate the significance of London as an instantiation of colonization and the ripples of dislocations, exclusions, and unintended disruption of British homogeneity that have necessarily become part of the city's character. It is no wonder that, as Magali Cornier Michael has noted, "this particular history of Britain . . . has created literature that treats the city in distinctive ways. . . . Britain's experiences with industrialization, colonialism, postcolonialism and global capitalism . . . have had marked influence . . . [on] British literature's depiction of the city and urban contexts" (1). Smith's writing has, as John Hadlock has noted "attend[ed] to the realities of urban experiences of the environment, especially those experiences of marginalized urban dwellers" (161). Similarly, *Midwife* depicts the experiences of the increasingly diverse population of London's East End—an area that Rashmi Varma has described as representing the "simultaneously intriguing and repellent scenes of poverty and chaos" (41).

Although the settings of series 7 of *Call the Midwife* and *NW* are separated by about four decades, when the landscape of London underwent significant changes, the repeating patterns of simultaneous racial-cultural expansion and exclusion portrayed in both texts is remarkable. Lucille enters the series in 1963, well into a decade of the Windrush era, a period that saw droves of West Indians heading to the United Kingdom, and mainly London, to supply labor that was in high demand at that time. During this same period, the former British territories of the Caribbean were experiencing economic stagnation due, in large part, to the departure of an empire that left a very shaky economic foundation for the majority-Black populations of former enslaved peoples.

As is the case in other series of the show, series 7 of *Midwife* opens with a panoramic view of London's East End, replete with high-rise buildings that appear to house factories, offices, and homes. Careful cinematographic attention has obviously been paid to highlighting the changing social landscape, particularly the racial composition of the city. One of the first glimpses of the people in the city is of a group of exclusively white women and their babies socializing; another quick glimpse shows women, but only white women, at work inside a factory. Most other images and scenes, however, include at least one person of color. These include a still image of two white children and one Black child playing; two white children and a Black child are also among the children seen at the door of Nonnatus House, greeting Sister Monica Joan at Christmas time. Later in the episode, there is a quick shot of a couple of color (probably Asian) walking along the street and an even quicker shot of a Black man in a club. The latter scenes are so brief that I had to replay them multiple times to ensure that these people of color were actually in view. Perhaps the most striking intimation of a budding multicultural and internally globalizing London is the song Nurse Franklin finds on the radio after remarking, "The water is out in Lisbon buildings again. That's enough gloom and doom for the day." She then turns on the radio, and the song being played is "He's So Fine" by The Chiffons, a 1960s US group consisting of four Black women. The women dance and smile, and as the scene shifts to the Turner family in their car, the same song is heard; the Turners' teenage son, Timothy, asks for the volume to be turned up, while his stepmother comments, "I don't know about these American pop groups. There's a lot of slang in their songs, and their diction leaves a lot to be desired" (series 7, episode 1, 1:00–1:35). Both scenes indicate not only the gradual and steady globalizing of London but also the first inklings of the mixed responses to the changing racial and cultural composition of the city.

Around four decades later, the London—more precisely northwest (NW) London—that Keisha-Natalie inhabits, circles around, and is held captive in, in *NW*, is by all indications a much-expanded version of the burgeoning racial, ethnic, and cultural diversity evident in series 7 of *Midwives*. Capturing the global diversity of the novel's setting, Smith provides a snapshot of the route, with a focus on the array of countries and cultures that have claimed this space as home—"Polish paper, Turkish paper, Irish, Arabic, French, Russian, Spanish, *News of the World*"—and emphasizes as well the global (street version) commercial hub that is now part of the landscape. This is where Londoners can "unlock [their] (stolen) phone, buy a battery pack, a lighter pack, a perfume pack.... Deal or no deal? TV screen in the TV shop . . . Call abroad 4 less.... Bank of Iraq, Bank of Egypt, Bank of Libya" (Smith 42–43). At the same time, the narrator calls the readers' attention to other examples of global capitalism, gentrification, and exclusions that are also highly visible in the space: "Watch the money pile up. Holla! Security lights, security gates, security walls, security trees, Tudor, Modernist, prewar, postwar, stone pineapples, stone lions, stone eagles. Face east and dream of Regent's Park, of St. John's Wood. The Arabs, the Israelis, the Russians, the Americans: here united by the furnished penthouse, the private clinic. If we pay enough, if we squint, Kilburn need not exist" (43). Through Pauline's—the mother of Leah, with whom Keisha-Natalie grew up—narrative perspective, readers get a view of an urban space from which Keisha-Natalie's family and other working-class and immigrant families are excluded, locations that are in stark contrast to the scenes of long-neglected Kilburn where these families live.

> Pauline turns the page with violence. The window logs Kilburn's skyline. Ungentrified, ungentrifiable. Boom and bust never come here. Here bust is permanent. Empty State Empire. Empty Odeon, graffiti streaked sidings rise and fall like rickety roller coaster. Higgledy piggledy rooftops and chimneys, some high, some low, packed tightly, shaken fags in a box. Behind the opposite window, retreating Willesden. Number 37. In the 1880s or thereabouts the whole thing went up at once—houses, churches, schools, cemeteries—an optimistic vision of Metroland. . . . All the mod cons! Indoor toilet, hot water.

Well-appointed country living for those tired of the city. Fast forward.
Disappointed city living for those tired of their country. (52)

Kilburn, a diverse neighborhood populated primarily by immigrants, and
mostly people of color, is a microcosm of modern global cities, not only because
of the racial, ethnic, and cultural diversity it represents but also for the way it
highlights the development of historical and growing inequities that cities make
so apparent. "Disappointed city living for those tired of their country" centers
attention on phenomena such as "white flight." Neglect marks Kilburn as a
location of disappointment for immigrants, a place where dreams are mostly
deferred. The placement of this description of Kilburn—just a few pages after
the section on global capitalism, quoted earlier—brings into focus the economic
unevenness that is a seemingly "natural" part of city experiences. Kilburn's
"ungentrified" status underscores the significant extent of neglect, since
gentrification—well understood to be a mechanism of displacement—is not
even under consideration for this derelict urban space.[3]

This is the kind of neighborhood that, over a few decades, transitioned from
a predominantly white, working-class one, such as that depicted in *Midwife*,
to a cosmopolitan and decaying urban location where Keisha-Natalie's
family, like numerous other immigrants, tried to fashion different, hopefully
better, economic circumstances for their families. Despite its glaring and
ostensibly inhospitable conditions, the space described was a space of possibility for advancement within the capitalist matrix, as well as one of security
for spatially excluded and economically marginalized residents. *Midwife* presents an early example of this hope in series 7. As soon as Nurses Dyer and
Franklyn leave Lucille's bedroom, Lucille rises from her bed, kneels, looks
lovingly up at her uniform with its nurses' watch and other professional
emblems, smiles, and clasps her hand in prayer (series 7, episode 1, 22:53).
Audiences do not hear Lucille's prayer, but even a cursory reading of her
body language will convey the satisfaction, the hope, and the gratitude for
everything that her new life as a professional promises. And on the morning
she is scheduled to begin her work, in the quiet solitary moment before her
colleagues arrive in the dining areas, she looks at her nurses' bag in a similar
way. She positions her body in a way that suggests anticipation and even a little
nervousness; she eyes her bag, caresses it, picks up the envelope containing her
assignment, and gives a wider, longer smile. Here the camera's focus on Lucille is
closer and sharper, making the significance of the hopeful moment readily
apparent. This scene also brings into clear view the writing on the envelope:
"Miss Lucille Anderson, SRN, SCM." When the other nurses enter the room,
she quickly closes and turns her back to the bag, suggesting that this is meant to
be a scene of private recognition and excitement (23:50–24:00). Undoubtedly,
this scene is a moment in Lucille's journey that performs immigrants'

expectation that the tales of socioeconomic and professional success that the imperial city promises can be realized.

NW explicitly highlights that, for immigrants, the working class, and people of color, safety and safe spaces in urban spaces take on different and more complicated meanings. This is especially apparent when Keisha-Natalie and Rodney (also the child of immigrants) have the opportunity to attend university, their first step toward social mobility. Despite the assurances that "there is a church, the train goes straight there, she'll be safe, she won't be the only one, . . . Keisha did not expect these campaigns to succeed. Marcia had been to the 'countryside' and did not consider it a safe environment, preferring London, where at least you knew what you were up against" (Smith 228). This report about Keisha-Natalie's mother Marcia's fear of the "countryside" is followed by a recollection of the real-life murder of Stephen Lawrence, whom Marcia refers to as a "poor defenseless boy" in Eltham, a suburb of London.[4] Marcia's belief that London—and, most likely, other ungentrifiable inner-city spaces that are home to many immigrants and people of color—is safer than the countryside highlights a persistent color line in Britain. The taken-for-granted safety of the suburbs constitutes an existential threat for Black people, an idea made even more poignant by the use of quotation marks for the inscribing "countryside."

Lucille and Keisha-Natalie: Profiles of Performers

For the ensuing analytical profiles of the two characters under consideration here, I return briefly to the structuring concept of genealogy to address the way I read Smith's more comprehensive portrait of Keisha-Natalie and, in a sense, to fill in some gaps in the mostly public professional performance that audiences see from Lucille. In a recent class discussion of *Midwife*, one of my students made an insightful point: while she appreciated the show's positive portrayal of Lucille, she also found her depiction as a "squeaky clean," always-perfect professional to be its own commentary on the unreasonable expectations placed on Black women. Lucille's consistently professional, strong, and steely deportment in the face of racism and other pressures exemplifies the compulsion that Black professional women feel: that they must sacrifice or mask natural human shortcomings and frustrations just to be considered worthy or competent. Conversely, readers encounter Keisha-Natalie in a variety of contexts and in many social, family, and other informal settings. Because of this fuller picture, readers have access to more of Keisha-Natalie's insecurities and therefore see the impact that the necessity of public performance has on her psyche and her relationships; this view, in turn, fosters a deeper understanding of her ultimate breakdown. What I suggest here, then, is that establishing an intertextual relationship between *Midwife* and *NW* allows us to approach a response to the question, What might happen to Black women who are models of professional success, who move, or whose families' move, to a city, and who show tangible evidence of success? To use a version of Brown's term, what do we witness when we remember or include multiple layers and experiences to access a fuller version of self? The fuller profile of Keisha-Natalie makes clear the costs of social mobility that is made possible by professional and material success. This more expansive picture makes the inadvertent trade-offs of success within the context of modern, Western-centered capitalism more visible, which then calls into question the very notion of success for Black, immigrant, working-class women.

In the discussion of *Midwife* that follows, I engage two broad levels of analysis: I address the performance, image, or experiences that the audience sees in scenes and interactions and through body language. I also offer a kind of metacinematic analysis. By this, I mean that I also engage what appears to be the creators'/directors' choices to represent certain scenes, characterizations, and experiences in ways that highlight the challenges of diversity in the historical moment (1960s London) being represented. Attention to these two components of the series allows both for recognition of the historically grounded, recuperated experiences being depicted and for attentiveness to the kind of critical engagement that a twenty-first-century production reflects.

Sister Julienne's initial mention of Lucille's arrival is presented as neutral and enthusiastic. She tells the other nurses at breakfast, "As it happens, a new midwife is on her way to join us. Our burdens will be eased immediately.... Fortunately a new class just qualified from a teaching hospital in Somerset" (*Midwife*, series 7, episode 1, 6:25–6:43). Lucille excelled there. The next thing the audience learns about Lucille is from Nurse Crane's remark that "she is a young girl traveling alone" (18:18–18:20). And even when she is being reported missing, after not showing up at the expected time, the descriptions are vague and race-neutral; we hear, "Nurse Lucille Anderson, SRN, SCM. Age twenty-five. Not likely to be in uniform. Height unknown. Hair color unspecified. Eye color a matter of conjecture" (18:43–18:45). Race is not mentioned in any of these interactions, omissions that may be read in a few ways: it could be about the "progressive" and open-minded orientations of her prospective colleagues, or it could perhaps mean that they do not know her race. Or this could be one example of the series calling our attention to the erasure of race as a problem of the time; in other words, these opening scenes may represent a critique of the pretense that bodies are racially unmarked in London. Read yet another way, the neutrality of these opening scenes may also be reflective of a scaffolding of the racialization of Lucille. I am inclined to read these opening scenes as both a critique of the prevailing attitudes toward race (the marking of racial difference and attitudes toward them) and also as scaffolding (a gradual unveiling of the mixed, but partly hostile, context of a space in which she will always be called on to affirm her legitimacy). These representations, then, call attention to the fact that the social and professional space in which Lucille will live and work will be neither completely friendly nor neutral.

Lucille's arrival at Nonnatus House is eventful, if not dramatic. Among the early signs of the challenging social and professional contexts within which she must carve out her space are the hostile weather conditions that precede her arrival. Early on in the scene, a radio announcement states, "The winter of 1962–63 is now known to be the coldest in almost three hundred years" (1:02–1:06). Audiences first glimpse Lucille from behind, trudging through the snow and bitter cold, and as soon as we get a frontal view, she falls, with only a flashlight in hand. Lucille's literal fall and rise capture the path of constant hurdles that will define her life and work in Poplar, the community where Nonnatus House is located. And although she is mentally ready to work the next day, she faints just before she can even decide whether to have breakfast. Soon after she receives her assignment, she is diagnosed with a bladder infection, and along with "lemon water and antibiotics," Dr. Turner orders "no work for at least a week" (24:00). This early setback, then, sets up the East End of London as a location where Lucille will be tested and where she can only experience professional success by overcoming setbacks.

Lucille's eventual arrival at Nonnatus House offers some intimation of the nature of her experiences in this new assignment: Nurse Dyer welcomes her warmly, "Come in, quick! Out of the snow," and her first question, "Do you need to see a midwife?" illustrates simultaneous compassion and even racial blindness. But this question may also embed a possibly different set of assumptions. At this point, the entire staff at Nonnatus House is eagerly, and with some consternation, awaiting the arrival of the new nurse. Yet it does not occur to Nurse Dyer that Lucille could be that nurse. While it is easy to understand why there could be some error in judgment here, the error that Nurse Dyer makes is not on the side of assuming that this Black woman might be the nurse they are all expecting. Nurse Dyer's body language is especially helpful here. When Lucille responds, "I am a midwife," Nurse Dyer is obviously taken aback. She blinks quickly and leans in closer as if to say, "Did I hear you correctly?" Lucille's "I am Nurse Anderson. Lucille Anderson" elicits, from Nurse Dyer, "Ah, of course you are!" As a sign of Nurse Dyer's warm embrace of Lucille, and the latter's resilience, the brief moment of misunderstanding turns to mutual apology: Nurse Dyer's "I am sorry we're in the middle of a power cut" and Lucille's "I'm sorry I'm late." They quickly bond; Nurse Dyer tends Lucille's wounds, and Nurse Franklin brings her warm tea with brandy and a candle. So here the scene is set for a work space of openness, acceptance, and professionalism without regard for the obvious racial difference that Lucille's entry brings to Nonnatus House.

The thread of commonality that defines Lucille's life and work experience between series 7 and series 10 points to the expectation of strength that many writers, particularly scholars who address Black female experiences in the United States context, have addressed. The way that Lucille begins the actual work in her profession is another striking depiction of the landscape she has to occupy and of how she will be asked to exceed expectations. Before she is able to complete the week of rest that Dr. Turner had ordered, she is asked to assist in a difficult birth. Nurse Dyer remarks, "I'm sorry, Lucille. I know you're not well, but this is like when Churchill had every plane in the in the battle of Britain" (31:31–31:38). Lucille's enthusiastic acceptance of the task is notable. In the middle of taking a pill, perhaps to dull pain, she responds, breathless with enthusiasm, "Just give me a bicycle and a map." And she is more than ready to assist in a breech birth:

NURSE FRANKLYN: How many breech births have you seen?
NURSE ANDERSON: Three. Two complete breech during hospital training and one frank on the district. Everything else is in my head fresh as paint from my final exams (32:48-32:59).

Further playing up Lucille's brilliance and readiness, when the more experienced Nurse Franklyn declares that she "can feel a foot or a hand," Lucille recites, "Toes are all the same length, and the great toe cannot be abducted. The os calcis bone has no equivalent on the hand." This provides exactly the information Nurse Franklyn needs to maneuver this difficult delivery. "It's a foot," she declares. In addition to Lucille's academic competence, her bedside manner and empathy are remarkable, as is her constant encouragement: "Motherhood starts here, with a vengeance" and "You're a natural-born deliverer of babies!" (33:46-34:35)In Lucille's first assignment, coming off her own convalescence, she is not just competent but supercompetent, showing knowledge and skill up to or beyond that of her much more experienced colleague; this depiction demonstrates the "ten times better" that is believed to be expected of Black people in any Euro-dominated workspace. Later, even before the more experienced nurse recognizes it, Lucille diagnoses a stroke in Marjory Chivvers. Furthermore, Lucille's caring and sensitivity also extend beyond her work duties, as seen when she prepares a warm water bottle for Nurse Crane and declares, "I thought you might need it, coming from a deathbed" (47:18–47:23). This neophyte nurse is "all things to all people" from the start.

It does not take long for Lucille to experience open racism on the job. She arrives for her first scheduled assignment at the hairdressing salon where her patient Marjory works and that is owned by Marjory's mother; before Lucille even enters, the mother, Mae, comments, "Get those curlers out, or she'll look like she is just fresh off the boat" (series 7, episode 2, 3:38–3:41). This is said within earshot of Lucille; this first encounter with Mae, in which the women stare each other in the face, shows Lucille obviously irritated but fully composed and professional. She initiates the conversation, firmly stating, "Midwife. To see a Mrs. Chivvers?" (3:46–3:48). This act of racial aggression from Mae is the first of many, including her snide, "Who died and made her the boss?" (4:48–4:40) when Lucille asks Marjory to get ready for her examination. It is not surprising, then, that when Marjory has a stroke, her mother blames Lucille in an attempt to quell the rumor that Mae is responsible because she overworked her daughter. A few days after Lucille delivers Marjory's baby, when Lucille touches the infant, Mae orders, "Hands off" (25:47–25:48). In the packed clinic, Mae adds, "There was nothing wrong with my Marjory until she got her filthy hands on her. What happened to my daughter has nothing to do with me working her in the salon but everything to do with her not having a proper English midwife" (26:15–26:21). Mae's mention of a "proper English midwife" illustrates that even at a time when the East End of London was becoming more diverse, even within the poverty-stricken urban area, there was spatial-social exclusion; this example highlights how, even at a time when West Indian immigrant nurses were not anomalies, the idea that professional spaces were white spaces continued to be part of the nativist mind-set of many people in this community.

Lucille's responses to these clearly racist insults offer insights into more than the extraordinarily hostile environment in which she must perform her profession; her reactions also tell their own story of her unspoken pain and even of her own perception of the grit she needs to show. In the scene just discussed, her facial expression conveys the shock and pain that one would expect from anyone who experiences that kind of hostility in any context. However, beyond the pain on Lucille's face, (nonverbal) communication is evident in the extended eye contact between Lucille and the only Black pregnant woman in the clinic. As the two women acknowledge the moment, it is the pregnant woman whose face shows more pain. Lucille's facial expression is harder to read, but there seems to be a combination of hurt and resolve, evident especially in her military-style walk away from the scene.

Illustrating the challenging landscape that Black professional women must constantly navigate, we also see Lucille inhabiting that ticklish question of how to use her voice. Here she is played as always outspoken, never allowing herself to be cowed or even defended in any situation. Her colleagues are obviously embarrassed and compassionate, but their efforts to rescue her are met with Lucille's stern refusal. She later asks Nurse Crane, "Why has Marjory Chivvers been put under Nurse Dyer's care? I have been the one most involved with her" (27:14–27:22). Nurse Crane's response, "Sister Julienne and I decided to spare you any more unpleasantness from that quarter," prompts more resolute action from Lucille (27:28–27:32). This young nurse, who has been on the job for only a short time, responds by confronting the head of the team. "I must be frank," she tells Sister Julienne. "It's not up to you or Nurse Crane to decide how much unpleasantness I can bear. But if you stop sending me to Marjory, it will look as though Mrs. Stanton's slurs are justified and as though you accept her attitude towards me." Sister's Julienne's response, "Nurse Anderson, I do not accept it," is met with, "Then, with respect, Sister Julienne, you know what you should do" (27:45). That any of the nurse-midwives would challenge a decision made by the kind but authoritative Sister Julienne is virtually unthinkable; this firm and unequivocal self-assertion from a young Black immigrant nurse is, therefore, especially remarkable, as is the overlooked toll on her body and psyche.

Lucille's return to her assignment with Marjory reveals more about her resolve, as it also tells a powerful story about what it meant to be a Black professional woman in the protean 1960s imperial city. The scene for a face-off is well set up: when Mae glimpses Lucille, about to enter the salon, Mae positions herself for battle; so does Lucille, who stops at the door, stands erect, and literally braces herself to take on what she knows will be hostility from Mae. In the presence of everyone in the room, Lucille strikes first: "Mrs. Stanton, I understand that you are looking for someone to blame, but what happened to Marjory was not my fault. And it wasn't your fault either." In response to Mae's "I never said it was," Lucille is unphased and continues, "I heard some gossip. People saying that Marjory became unwell because she was on her feet, working in here for her *whole* nine months. To think those silly gossiping women believe they know better than all the highly trained doctors at the hospital. Only the good Lord himself knows why she had that stroke" (Episode 2, 32:54-33:39, emphasis added). This is a powerful, dramatic moment, masterfully delivered by both actresses. The change in tone, particularly Lucille's lowering of her voice when she ends with "Only the good Lord himself knows why she had that stroke," captures her remarkable combination of strength and compassion even as she defends herself against open racism. As audiences watch Lucille's self-possession and humanity grow in this scene, we watch as Mae softens and concedes. And Lucille silences both Mae and the other women in the salon, some of whom are among "the silly gossiping women." When Lucille returns to the reason for her visit—"I brought a prescription for Marjory. May I take it upstairs?" (32:50–33:55)—Mae is evidently humbled; with tears in her eyes, she manages to say, "Yeah," as the women, some smiling, look on in awe.

As the series progresses, Lucille only grows in competence, increasingly demonstrating her academic brilliance and excellent hands-on nurse work: she is well read (and is able to recite Keats, much to the surprise of Sister Monica Joan); her English grammar is impeccable; and she is strong and assertive yet also a compassionate and gracious model Christian. But she has to endure and overcome, with utmost dignity, what no other nurse has had to suffer. Audiences never see her break down, cry, or react to the onslaught of racism in any way that shows the impact that this hostile environment has had on her. Apart from the headache that she mentions when Nurse Dyer chokingly says, "We missed you last night. We had the Scrabble board out and could've done with someone who can spell" (30:02-30:09), (once again indicating competence), there are no complaints. She is not just an excellent nurse; even in leisure, she has and can offer more. And her mention of a headache is cushioned between a quick smile and a serious, but not pained, facial expression.

Beyond the mammoth task of professionally standing firm and defending herself against racism, Lucille still has more to offer; she also demonstrates her capacity to rise above racism and to serve as the comforter, confidante, and even motivator for white people—representatives of the very group that renders her an outsider. For example, it is Lucille who insists that Marjory's husband, Dennis, assume responsibility for his wife's care, after Mae had bullied and sidelined him. Lucille spurs Dennis to action and ensures that Marjory receives rehabilitation, which Mae had refused. Lucille waits for Dennis outside his workplace, and her straightforward pep talk to Dennis challenges him: "You want to make things right for your family? This is your chance—your chance to build a proper future for your wife" (40:44–41:07). Watching the young Black immigrant nurse put "pep in the step" of a white male, whose gait immediately changes as he strides home and takes charge of his family, underscores the power and advantages of the audiovisual medium in advancing the analytical goals of this book. And when Nurse Dyer tells her own story about the class discrimination that she suffered in the military, it is Lucille who comforts her, despite the headache she confesses to having had after her earlier encounter with racism. Lucille consistently avoids any defense of her personhood that would be read as what Theodora in *NW* refers to as "aggressive hysteria" (Smith 285).[5] Lucille's compassionate and reassuring attitude toward Nurse Dyer is yet another example of her selflessness. At another level, these moments in *Midwife* illustrate the huge expectations that are often viewed as normal life for Black professional women. Thus, the absence of any exploration of the impact (intentional or not) on Lucille calls attention to how the wider culture elides fuller expressions of Black womanhood.

Midwife offers a representation of Black female experience in the early 1960s with verisimilitude. This is true not only for the series's representation of the racist landscape within which an immigrant professional had to work but also with regard to how that woman had to act to survive and to be taken seriously. Yet this is also a representation that allows us to ask, Where is the rest of Lucille? What happens to her when she no longer has to engage in the performance of competence, grace, and strength? And so the series leaves very open this question: What happened to women like Lucille and their daughters who could only bring part of themselves to the public? As *NW*'s Keisha-Natalie observes, women like Lucille had "to pass the entirety of [themselves] through a hole that would accept only part" (Smith 251). Only Lucille's most professional, composed, and competent self could be accommodated in this hostile space. And it is here that Smith's *NW* enters to open up the depiction; while it does not necessarily flesh out the totality of Black professional women, it does show more of them. Specifically, it makes visible what happens to the psyche of the woman when she is not allowed fuller self-expression; in other words, *NW* helps us to address the question, What happens when Black professional women have to always "put the best outside"?

Keisha-Natalie

In this section, I address how the fuller portrait of Keisha-Natalie that *NW* offers fills some gaps in the portrayal of Nurse Lucille Anderson, who functions in an earlier—and in many ways a similar—racist urban context; this, in turn, offers a more complex portrait of Black womanhood. Therefore, with a view to establishing the genealogy for which I am arguing here, I address Keisha-Natalie's self-making and self-representation—how the expectation of and investment in social mobility demand fashioning only a version of the self that is deemed strong, acceptable, or wholesome. An examination of her encounters, her relationships, and her psychological state and its concomitant onto-logical impact makes clear that self-fashioning and self-invention function both as necessities for social advancement and as the cause of Keisha-Natalie's undo-ing. Remaking of self will also be crucial in her path toward realization and recovery. Hui Wang's conclusion that in *NW* "the sense that we are all masters of our own destinies has been shattered" is beyond dispute, as is the suggestion that, for those who are born outside the middle and upper brackets of society, there is "very little hope for autonomy, self-making and self-definition" (386). Keisha-Natalie manages for much of her life to squeeze her way into that "very little" space that Wang leaves open. The novel shows that Keisha-Natalie does engage in some partial "self-making" and that she has reaped the material ben-efits. However, the novel further highlights not only the limits of such efforts but also, and perhaps more importantly, the enormous cost that Keisha-Natalie, who is so deeply invested in the promises of mobility within Western capitalist systems, must inevitably pay. *NW* demonstrates that the possibilities for self-invention exist on a continuum, with the possibilities, outcomes, and impacts being variously predetermined by society.

Smith's narrative strategy effectively offers a characterization of Natalie that, while not entirely predictive, makes the arrival at her ultimate place of psychic demise unsurprising and logical. *NW* scatters bits and pieces of infor-mation about Keisha-Natalie that offer a complex and expansive portrait of her as an insider-outsider in almost all settings and in all her relationships. Readers learn of Keisha-Natalie early in the novel, long before the extensive section dedicated to her past and present lives. The interaction between her and her best and longest-lasting friend, Leah Hanwell, whose story opens the novel, raises questions about the sincerity of the friendship between these two women and places Keisha-Natalie's insider-outsider position at the center of the novel.[6] A few pages into the novel, Leah answers the door to Shar, a drug addict and scammer who is asking for money. Shar recognizes Leah, and Shar's "Wait—you went [to] *Brayton?*" (10) leads to a conversation about the women's lives and Shar's question "Got kids?" (Smith 11). Leah's response, "No. A dog, Olive. She's at my mate Nat's house right now. Natalie Blake? Actually in school she was Keisha. Natalie De Angelis now" (11). This moment marks readers' introduction to Keisha-Natalie as a reinventor of self, and this introduction influences readers' perception and piques our interest in this character.

Even more significant is the way that Leah seizes this opportunity to (re)connect with Shar by filling Shar in about Keisha-Natalie's present life. "She's got kids. Lives just over there, in the posh bit, on the park. She's a lawyer now. Barrister. What's the difference? Maybe there isn't one" (11). While Leah does not say anything that explicitly indicates tension with or envy of her friend's position, her tone is not one of pride in and admiration of her friend's accomplishments. Instead, mentioning that Keisha-Natalie lives in "the posh bit" and frivolously showing that she does not know the difference between a lawyer and a barrister aligns Leah more with Shar, an obvious socioeconomic "failure," than with the woman with whom she has maintained a friendship since childhood. This moment, then, offers readers the first insight into the uneasy space that Keisha-Natalie occupies even within her intimate circles. This introduction to Keisha-Natalie's living "over there, in the posh bit" brings into sharp and early focus the significance of space in the construction of her character and, more specifically, her insider-outsider position. Though still close friends with Leah, Keisha-Natalie is spatially separated from the friend with whom she grew up in urban public housing, and Leah's introduction of Keisha-Natalie makes readers aware that the divide between them—aggravated by their spatial separation—is a point of tension that represents the overarching conflict of the story. And when readers finally see the friends together, Leah "looks up at her best friend . . . and hates her" (67). Leah's thoughts about her "friend" are revealed in a scene in which the women's families are together; they are, by all outward appearances, having a good time together. Yet only Keisha-Natalie; her husband, Frank; and Leah's husband, Michel—not Leah—laugh at a shared joke. It is even more noteworthy that it is her "best friend" that Leah hates, a revelation that makes the point about Keisha-Natalie's precarious position in different spaces even more disturbing. And soon after we gain access to Leah's thoughts, readers learn that the two friends "are annoying each other" (67). The hatred that the narrator eventually reveals goes unnoticed by the other three adults present, but the narrator's mention of it offers another early insight into the depth and extent of Keisha-Natalie's insider-outsider existence, even when she is oblivious to it. The shared recognition that they are "annoying each other" opens up hostility, but at this point, it is an understanding the women share with each other. So, while Keisha-Natalie might be oblivious to Leah's hatred, there is a shared tension in their mutual annoyance. The reality of their disconnection appears with even more clarity when Leah thinks, "It's humiliating being the cause of so much abject boredom in your oldest friend" (70). The obvious insecurity that Leah feels when she is in Keisha-Natalie's presence is mostly because "on the surface [Keisha-Natalie] appears to be an exemplar of self-making and self-improvement" (Wang 390).

Almost three hundred pages into the novel, the magnitude of Keisha-Natalie's insider-outsider status and the way this part of her life centers on place and space are dramatized during a visit to her childhood neighborhood and home, which includes a face-off with her sister, Cheryl. A moment in which the sisters share some child-care responsibilities turns into a huge quarrel between them. Right on the heels of bonding over and smiling together about their father's "innocence, . . . his optimism, and incompetence" (Smith 309), Keisha-Natalie seizes an opening to offer her sister (and extended family) financial assistance through more convenient housing. Keisha-Natalie's "I just can't stand to see you all living like this" (309) is met with Cheryl's "If you hate Caldie so much, why d'you even come here? Seriously, man. No one asked you to come. Go back to your new manor" (310). Keisha-Natalie's "There's nothing wrong with wanting to see you and the kids in a nice place somewhere" angers Cheryl even more; she defends her space with, "This is a nice place!" And Cheryl adds, "Keisha, if I wanted to get out of here I'd get another place off the council before I come to you" (310). Keisha-Natalie has to absorb this and defend herself, much as she has to in another space and context: when her husband, Frank, accuses her family of refusing to help her, she "launched into a passionate defense of her family, despite the fact she was not speaking to any of them" (271). The need for Keisha-Natalie to both defend herself from her family and defend her family from outside attacks underscores the zone of unbelonging that Keisha-Natalie always occupies. Cheryl's characterization of Keisha-Natalie's current abode as a "manor" highlights even further how place widens the distance between the sisters. Cheryl's expressed preference (true or not) for the British government—which has neglected this (ungentrified and ungentrifiable) community for decades—over her sister's obviously well-intentioned offer of help makes the extent of their distance from each other particularly remarkable; such an extreme response underscores the level of Cheryl's vociferous rejection of her sister's new upper-middle-class status and highlights the chasm between them.

The progress of the sisters' brawl makes clear the twin conundrum of physical and socioeconomic movement. Their confrontation comes to a head when Keisha-Natalie asks, "Why am I being punished for making something of my life? . . . I work hard. I came in with no reputation, nothing. I've built up a serious practice—do you have any idea how few—" (311). Keisha-Natalie's decision to name the problem, to make clear the "thing around [their] neck[s]"—to borrow a term from Chimamanda Adichie—moves the quarrel into the territory of what underlies the resentment about place (the projects versus the manor).[7] Cheryl's "Did you really come round here to tell me what a big woman you are these days" is, in part, what opens up the source of the tension. Cheryl's retort, "But no-one in here is looking for your help," made in response to Keisha-Natalie's "I came round here to try and help you" (311), represents a pivotal moment in this encounter, as it underlines the complexity of the city; it does so by opening possibilities for socioeconomic advancement within Western capitalist spaces, while at the same time laying bare the inequalities that, in turn, rip families apart. It also bears mentioning that here Keisha-Natalie is trying to fulfill one of the core values of her Jamaican, West Indian, Afro-based values: as one who has actualized and exceeded the hope of a better economic life that was the push-pull factor for her parents' move to London, it is her duty (within the context of cultural expectations) to provide financial support for family members who have not done as well materially. And even more, providing more comfortable living space is one of the most sought-after and expected kinds of support in this culture. There are more suggestions that this offer of help is well warranted, because the space that Cheryl defends as a "nice place" still has the markings of urban poverty. The room with "old twin beds"—which the sisters shared as children and which brings back fond memories for Keisha-Natalie—is where Cheryl still lives with her children. The "narrow hallway [is] made almost impassable by laundry strung from a wire along both walls" (308). This is the kind of living space that immigrants such as the sisters' parents imagine as temporary housing, a sacrifice they make in these harsh cities so their children will live in something resembling the "manor" where Keisha-Natalie lives. Yet Keisha-Natalie's accomplishments, made more visible by the contrast between the living conditions of her childhood and those made possible by her professional accomplishments, are the source of tension between her and her sister and are the basis of her exclusion from the social and physical space with which she is most familiar.

The insider-outsider position and unbelonging that defines Keisha-Natalie's adult life recurs in her encounter with an old schoolmate at a time when she confronts her alienation. After her husband, Frank, discovers the online identity Keisha-Natalie uses to contact young men in an underworld of debauchery, her departure from her suburban home takes her to the streets in ways she has not been brought back to the area for decades. Nathan Bogle, the childhood friend she runs into as she walks the streets of London at this moment in her breakdown, initially embraces her: "'Keisha Blake. Hold up. . . . You don't look too good, Keisha. Reach for me. . . . They jumped down to the other side together" (361). But even with this initial gesture of friendship, the tension between Keisha-Natalie's past and present, her physical and social distance from the community of her childhood, is already becoming apparent. Nathan's "You don't look like you got no real problems. Come join me. I'm flying" (362) is at once an invitation and a denial of her very real dislocation. Nathan's simultaneous embrace of an old "mate" and his denial of Keisha-Natalie's problems is further compounded by his desire to reduce and discredit her. Her initial refusal of a joint prompts Nathan's "Don't pretend you're a nice girl, Keisha. I known you from time. Know your family. Cheryl" (364). Even as Nathan repeatedly denies her the right to experience pain because she has "made it," his own sense of inferiority and insecurity drives him to remind Keisha-Natalie that she is, after all, just like him—a response that will probably aggravate Keisha-Natalie's fragile selfhood by reinforcing her already-wobbly existence in multiple in-between spaces.

Smith's crafting of Keisha-Natalie's character calls into question a key, taken-for-granted idea of Western capitalism: that economic progress translates into a full actualization of self and, even more preposterously, that such individuals are always more wholesome than those who have not made comparable economic "progress." Keisha-Natalie's tenuous bonding with Nathan is another stark example of the novel's confrontation with this warped understanding of socioeconomic success within the capitalist system. As readers follow Keisha-Natalie and Nathan on their walk, we witness a gradual breakdown of their initial long-time-no-see bond, due, in large part, to the distance that Keisha-Natalie's socioeconomic gains inevitably create. Their rekindled friendship also crumbles because of Nathan's insistence that, as a result of her new social status and move away from urban poverty, Keisha-Natalie has no "real" problems. Consistent with Smith's narrative strategy, mentioned earlier, the novel offers tidbits from their initial meeting that keep in sharp focus the fragility of their apparent reconnection. Ironically, the big breakdown of their reconnection happens when Keisha-Natalie tries to affirm Nathan's worth by telling him how much he was loved by Leah. In this meeting of two damaged urban subjects, even Keisha-Natalie's attempts to validate Nathan's personhood are met with hostility: "Everyone loves up a bredrin when he's ten. After that he's a problem. . . . Last time I was in your yard I was ten. . . . Your mum ain't let me past the gate after that" (376). By centering himself as the ultimate victim, Nathan does more than invalidate Keisha-Natalie's challenges; his suggestion that all is well with Keisha because she is no longer poor and is not "on the streets" as he is is indicative of his own investment in the very system that is responsible for his diminished existence.

Nathan's extended rant fully discounts the past of urban poverty, racism, and marginalization that he shares with Keisha, even if we do not take into account the persistent psychological damage made even more invisible because of the mask of prosperity:

They don't want you, your own people don't want you.... Ain't the same for girls, it's a man ting.... "We went to the same school." And what? What do you know about my life? When you been walking in my shoes? What do you know about living the way I live ...? And you go home to your green and your life and where's my green and my life? Sit on your bench. Talking out your neck about me. "How does it feel to be a problem?" What do you know about it? (376–377)

Nathan's tirade, his claiming of both race ("how does it feel to be a problem") and gender ("ain't the same for girls"), is notable because he articulates much of what makes life for the socially mobile Black female professional in an urban setting so virtually unbearable. Not only does Nathan's denial of any kind of suffering highlight the extent to which Keisha-Natalie's wounds are rendered invisible, but his dismissive attitude also illustrates why masking, "putting the best outside," is the default position for women such as Keisha-Natalie: What does a successful Black woman have to complain about? As Nathan adds, "Had some bust-up with your man.... You know you made it when you're crying over that shit" (377). Moreover, the reductive assumption that what Keisha-Natalie is experiencing is "some bust-up with [her] man" embeds the superficial understandings and characterizations that this representative Black woman undergoes. Therefore, at a time when Keisha-Natalie believes she does not need to "put the best outside" because she is with an old "mate," Nathan denies her that opportunity because he too has bought the more-money-more-happiness myth.

Where Is the Rest of Her?

My inclusion of performance as a structuring element of this chapter is drawn from Smith's foregrounding of the performative and develops more extensively an idea that some critics have raised. Lourdes López-Ropero has noted that Natalie, who significantly refers to her different roles as "drag" (Smith 245), comes to the realization that, "however ideal and strived for, her subject position is a construction, rather than something natural or authentic" (López-Ropero (131).[8] The novel invites attention to performance, not only in the crafting of characters, particularly Keisha-Natalie, who engage in overt acts of self-invention but also through its inclusion of performative elements and references. Smith's inclusion of "Daughter drag. Sister drag. Mother drag. Wife drag. Court drag. Rich drag. Poor drag. British drag. Jamaican drag. Each required a different wardrobe" (333) compels an engagement not only with Smith's recuperation of performativity but also, more importantly, with the necessity of performance for a socially mobile Black woman. How else does one survive in a world where only specific parts of the woman are acceptable?

The examples from Keisha-Natalie's encounter with her sister, Cheryl, and with her childhood neighbor and peer Nathan, as well as the conversation between her friend Leah and Shar illustrate both the inevitability of performance and the extent of Keisha-Natalie's alienation from even the ostensibly most intimate corners and relationships. The cramped city housing where she grew up and where she seeks connections with her family is as hostile and, in some ways, as foreign an environment as the new suburbs where she now lives and the public spaces where "putting the best outside" is an existential necessity. And as we see in all three examples, her relationships are at best tenuous. The examples in the preceding section also show that the part of Keisha-Natalie's self that her community considers to be consequential is her professional success and social mobility, the new place she now occupies within the greater city of London. This is why they no longer make room for her in her expected spaces of relief. Yet, in the novel's comprehensive portrayal of Keisha-Natalie, it also gives readers access to other parts of her character, including the persona she has had to cultivate, the semipermanent masks, and the necessary and deliberate constructions of self that make her "success" possible. This portrait also gives access to the scars she has carried since childhood, her insecurities, and the ongoing price of professional success and socioeconomic mobility. And as I suggested earlier, unlike Lucille, whose public persona is mostly what audiences see, readers of *NW* also witness the toll that these demands, as well as her investment in neocolonial-neoliberal definitions of success, take on Keisha-Natalie.

Beyond the tension between Keisha-Natalie and Leah that is part of readers' introduction to Keisha-Natalie's fuller self, the novel's setting is another aspect of Smith's narrative strategy that advances the comprehensive portrayal of this character. Readers are introduced to Keisha-Natalie as a "perfect wife" (Smith 68), an owner of "the grandeur of [a] Victorian house" (67), and the barrister in the "banker-barrister" duo (67), who is capable of balancing her toddler, Spike, while she holds a conversation with Leah (69). And in a backhanded way, Leah also paints a picture of perfection in Keisha-Natalie: "Leah watches Natalie stride over to her beautiful kitchen with her beautiful child. Everything behind those French doors is full and meaningful. . . . How do you get to be so full? And full of only meaningful things? Everything else Nat has somehow managed to cast off. She is an adult. How do you do that?" (73). Intentional or not, Leah's diction here raises questions. Her inclusion of absolutes, "everything" and "so full of only meaningful things," prompts a skeptical response from readers. Aside from the fact that readers know that Leah does not truly admire Keisha-Natalie, an earlier jab at Keisha-Natalie brings Leah's discomforts and insecurities to the surface and confirms her sarcasm. As Leah jogs Keisha-Natalie's memory of old schoolmates and the conversation turns to Nathan Bogle, she includes, "He sat next to Keisha. Back when she was Keisha. I was very jealous about that, when I was eight. Innit, Keisha" (70). This deliberate act to put Keisha-Natalie back into her inner-city working-class place (by calling her Keisha) elicits just the reaction Leah intended: "Natalie chewed at a nail, hating to be teased. She dislikes being reminded of her own inconsistencies. Leah dares to put it a little stronger: hypocrisies" (70). Here, then, is one instance in which, in the midst of Keisha-Natalie's performance of her new upper-middle-class persona, she appears uncharacteristically vulnerable, biting her nail in embarrassment. And in the same awkward moment, "Nat keeps her bright smile *pinned* to her face" (71; emphasis added), thus highlighting one of her necessary acts. As one who exists mostly as a performer, it is hard for Keisha-Natalie to just smile, an awkwardness that Smith captures well in the use of "pinned." And yet, not long after this uncomfortable moment, "Nat strides back out, looking serene, unreadable" (75), this time masking even more.

The parts of Keisha-Natalie to which readers have access in these moments call the narrative-authorial insights in the following quote into question. As Keisha-Natalie struggles to recall names and faces from her time at the Brayton school, the narrator intervenes: "Perhaps Brayton, too, no longer exists for her. It's gone, cast off. She is probably as surprised to have come out of Brayton as it is surprised to have spawned her. Nat is the girl done good from their thousand-kid madhouse; done too good, maybe, to recall where she came from. To live like this you would have to forget everything that came before. How else could you manage?" (70).

For onlookers such as Leah, Cheryl, and Nathan, Keisha-Natalie has forgotten (or must have forgotten) where she came from. In fact, her new station in life demands a performance of amnesia; while, ostensibly, she does forget, she does not and cannot really forget. Certainly, she may have forgotten some names of classmates and high-school details from almost two decades prior, but she may also have tried to forget some experiences. It is precisely the persistence of memory, however, that makes Keisha-Natalie the anxious, wounded person readers get to see because we have access to more of her. And the challenges are, in part, the result of the added burden of managing these memories, since the professional world of London "would accept only part" of her (251).

One part of the portrait that readers access in the making of Keisha-Natalie, the metamorphosis from Keisha to Natalie, is her movement between what many people would consider "normal" youthful behaviors and more unusual thoughts and actions that set her apart from her peers and prime her to be the anomaly she has turned out to be. So, from early on, Keisha-Natalie has to split herself in different parts, each of which must be held, performed, and managed, often outside public view. As a youth, Keisha-Natalie easily engaged in childhood mischief with Leah. They "sneaked a cigarette . . . wrote the word FUCK on the first page of a Bible, tried to get *The Exorcist* out of the video shop" (209). After Keisha-Natalie receives a vibrator as a sixteenth-birthday gift, "the following Saturday morning she began approximating the early signs of a cold, and on Sunday claimed a severe cough and stomach ache" (219) so she could make use of the gift. At the same time, she "watched her family walk to church, not without regret: she was sincerely interested in the topic of Abraham and Isaac" (219). While much of this kind of youthful, adult-pleasing hypocrisy is neither unusual nor surprising, when put in the context of Keisha-Natalie's "cerebral willfulness" (211), a more complicated picture emerges. These teenage actions are dress rehearsals for a set of performances that will make it possible for Keisha-Natalie to, at once, reap success and fall victim to the accompanying psychological burdens.

Once Keisha-Natalie receives this sex toy, readers witness her awareness of her sexuality and come to understand her orientation toward sexual liberation, experimentation, and even risk. But consistent with Smith's narrative strategy of leaving tidbits that create the mosaic of Keisha-Natalie's character, even in this early launch of her sexuality, there are signs of the character traits that will eventually get her to the barrister's office, the suburbs, and the mansion she occupies with her family: "She had the dildo for only a couple of weeks but in that time used it regularly, sometimes as much a several times a day, often without washing in between, and always in a business-like way, as if delegating a task to someone else" (219). Even here, in her private space, there is evidence of her capacity to separate. This is the skill that is so necessary for the kind of social movement she experiences in the city, which simultaneously makes her viable and credible but also precipitates her collapse.

What appears to be Keisha-Natalie's innate drive and aptitude for learning manifest themselves in multiple snippets throughout the novel: when she received a home computer for her fourteenth birthday, "Keisha Blake read through the accompanying booklet and was able to figure out how to program a basic series of commands so that in answer to particular prompts text would come up on the screen as if the computer itself were 'talking'" (215). And when we hear of Keisha-Natalie's visit to her "Head of Year's" office, it comes as no surprise that "Keisha Blake had not been called in for a reprimand, she had come to discuss her options for a set of exams still three years into the future" and that "she did not really want to discuss these exams, she simply wanted it to be noted that she is the kind of person who thought three years ahead about important things in life" (212). So, in addition to drive and sheer brilliance, we also see here an investment in image, in self-making, in shaping and making known to the world a persona that she knew would be validated and marketable. This is also why she worked out for herself how to handle the bullying that a youth such as Keisha-Natalie would inevitably attract:

> When being bullied Keisha Blake found it useful to remember that if you read the relevant literature or watched the pertinent movies you soon found that being bullied was practically a sign of superior personality, and the greater the

intensity of the bullying the more likely it was to be avenged at the other end of life, when qualities of the kind that Keisha Blake possessed—cleverness, will-to-power—became "their own reward," and that this remained true even if the people in the literature and movies looked nothing like you, came from a different socio-economic and historical universe, and—had they ever met you—would very likely enslaved you or at best, bullied you. (214)

Keisha-Natalie understands from early on that, as a survivor of urban poverty, there are costs for social mobility. Furthermore, her acceptance of these costs, evidenced in the no-pain-no-gain attitude that she has cultivated, portends the alienation and isolation she experiences as an accomplished adult. It is not surprising, then, that despite her investment in being the "sole author of [her] own fate," none of this is sufficient to stave off a mental break and the potential loss of the family she has built. The cognitive dissonance of the late realization that "life was [not] a problem that could be solved by means of professionalization" (238)—and, in Keisha-Natalie's case, through the management and performance of multiple selves—precipitates her unraveling.

The shattering of this erroneous "sole author" notion is most visible when Keisha-Natalie confronts the limitation of professional achievement. The sense of homelessness and unbelonging that Keisha-Natalie experiences in her personal life is more devastating because these spaces did not offer a shelter from the homelessness she inevitably experienced in her professional life. "Why had she stopped participating in the social life of the set? Did she feel isolated? Would it help to talk to someone who'd "been through it?"" (282). This unnamed "it"—the gendered and racialized exclusions that are part of the package of her professional life and accomplishment—not only challenges the foundation of resiliency that Keisha-Natalie had so carefully built but also calls into question the very point of her parents' (and other immigrants') move to the city. Education, and its capacity to move individuals into new spaces of prosperity, is not enough to change one's place in this imperial city. What Keisha-Natalie learns from her conversation with Theodora, a middle-aged, seasoned barrister of similar Jamaican heritage, is instructive: Theodora passes "a hand over her neat frame . . . [stating], 'This [the Black female body] is never neutral'" (285). In confirming her own sense of isolation early in her career as a lawyer, Theodora demonstrates the urgent necessity of belonging in familial and other familiar and friendly spaces.

For the formerly colonized and their children, a move to the city is the logical step toward achievement of the "progress" that the new enduring capitalist system—now masked as globalization—demands. This examination of the depiction of the experiences of professional Black women offers a unique set of insights into how the city functions simultaneously as a facilitator of socioeconomic mobility and as a catalyst for the unraveling of the self. The (represented) Black professional women in this city must construct and perform selves that are necessary for their presumed success. Yet in that space that is so open to reintervention and for people for whom only self-reconstruction will do, these acts of self-fashioning always include the cost of fragmented selves; the city has already been carved up into spaces of inclusion, partial inclusion, and exclusion, thus making wholeness or anything approaching a full expression of self impossible for the Black woman. Readers are not sure where exactly Keisha-Natalie ends up or if, and how, she is able to move forward once her secret life in the underground of the internet is discovered. But what is clear is that the forward movement, the promise that led her parents to the city and drove her youthful imagination, is unattainable. Her circle clearly does not close, as the novel ends with her showing some agency ("Goodbye Nathan"; 385), but readers can surmise that she will have to start all over again, this time most likely on a lifelong path of self-repair and sustenance; to survive, Keisha-Natalie must engage in another kind of reinvention. And in *Call the Midwife*, while Nurse Lucille Anderson becomes increasingly comfortable in her professional and social spaces, for much of the series, she remains guarded; the understanding that she must always present only the self that will protect her remains a core element of her persona.

Returning briefly to genealogy—the framing idea of the chapter—I note that, while the characters are not identical, the resemblances between Lucille and Keisha-Natalie are notable, and chief among these is the necessity of performance. The context of the imperial-colonial city, in which these characters move into and through professional spaces, is marked by racism and unreasonable expectations, and their places in the city are clearly demarcated along the lines of inclusion-exclusion. Both texts show that these women do not feel a full sense of belonging in the spaces they occupy; rather, their survival in this system—whether in their intimate or professional spaces—depends upon the ability of each to present a carefully and consistently crafted persona.

3

**The Transnational
Semicircle and the
"Mobile" Female Subject
in Amma Darko's *Beyond
the Horizon* and Chika
Unigwe's *On Black
Sisters Street***

■■■■■■■■■■■■■■■■■■■■■■

This chapter continues the exploration of female experiences in modern cities, expanding the view beyond the imperial city of London, discussed in chapter 2, to cities located in "third world" African countries and "first world" European cities of former colonizers. The goal here is to advance the conception of cities as sites of colonial capitalist hauntings as well as locations of freedom—though a kind of freedom that is both ephemeral and questionable. A central question guides this chapter: How do these creative renditions of women who have been victims of neocolonial capitalism, ethnic conflicts, and gender oppression help us make sense of the state of Black womanhood in the era of rapid globalization? Keeping in focus Carole Boyce Davies's still-relevant assertion that "renegotiating of identities is as fundamental to migration as it is to Black women's writing" (2), this chapter considers the constraints that come to bear on such negotiations when the migrating subject is a trafficked (in some cases "willingly" traded) sex worker.

The context of Ama Ata Aidoo's "In the Cutting of a Drink," which frames the introduction to this book, sets up the stakes of this chapter in very useful ways. This work demonstrates how an examination of depictions of female experiences in creative accounts of cities offers additional points of entry for theorizing Black diasporic cities. Aidoo's 1985 story presents a city in the Global South, in an "African" country, as a space of liberation, if only partial, and certainly as a site of new opportunities for women—opportunities to define the course of their lives in new ways and, in so doing, to redefine the terms of female experiences in modernizing and globalizing "African" societies. Perhaps more directly than other texts analyzed in this book, Amma Darko's *Beyond the Horizon* (1988) and Chika Unigwe's *On Black Sisters Street* (2012) insist on a contemplation of familiar questions related to the interface and overlap between "tradition" and "modernity" in fresh ways. These works also compel us to reexamine general conceptions of morality, decency, and "good womanhood" within the context of a global marketplace. Additionally, they stimulate a number of related questions that shape this chapter: What particular insights do we gain into Janus-faced global cities when a reincarnated transnational trading of bodies is centralized in fictive accounts? What does the entry point of sex trafficking allow? What does it mean to be mobile, and what are the limits of mobility? What is the role of the city in determining the parameters of mobility? What do the context and opportunities of the city demand that one must trade in order to have access to an agreed-on set of material gains? And ultimately, how does one reconcile the inevitable trade-offs?

These questions in turn lead us to examine, rethink, and redefine freedom and agency, two concepts that take on particular relevance in this configuration of cities as complicated, limber, semicircular sites of shifting possibilities.

Extant scholarship on these two novels has centered primarily on multiple aspects of sex trafficking; the impact of the characters' outsider status in foreign, specifically European spaces; female subjectivity; and the novels' portrayals of male characters.[1] While transnational sex trafficking is the primary subject of both novels and naturally the point of departure for this chapter, sex trafficking per se—in its role as a modern, bold example of global commodification of female bodies—is not the main focus of the discussion here. Instead, I attend more closely to the insights into Black women's experiences in global city spaces that these depictions of global trade allow us, and I extrapolate from these fictive accounts to theorize the experiences of Black diasporic subjects. Arguing that these women are situated at the edges of freedom and bondage, I engage each of the themes listed here as well as others to arrive at working theorizations of a "mobile" Black womanhood made possible by the opportunities and disappointments that global cites facilitate. Darko's *Horizon* and Unigwe's *Black Sisters* successfully align this theorization of constrained, commodified, participatory, and tenuously agential Black womanhood with the conception of city spaces as fertile, semicircular sites that are always open to expansive possibilities for negotiation.

Darko's *Horizon* tells the story of Mara, a young woman from the village of Naka, who is first traded into an arranged marriage—within the context of her ethnic tradition—by her father. Mara moves to the city to live with her abusive husband, who later, unbeknownst to Mara, places her in a sex-trafficking ring between African and European cities. Mara's eventual uncovering of her husband's scheme illustrates the potentially forward-moving possibilities that even these sorts of debilitating circumstances of the city can hold for women because of the resources that cities uniquely offer. The four women who are the subjects of Unigwe's *Black Sisters*—Ana, Efe, Joyce, and Sisi—each find themselves in a sex-trafficking ring similar to that detailed in *Horizon*. The turns that their collective lives take illustrate the contained and tentative possibilities of female mobility and, to borrow a term from Davies, configure the "migrating female subject" as an agent of self- and community transformation.

The inclusion of both the village and the city in the portrayal of gendered experiences in *Horizon* epitomizes the confluence of postcolonial-globalization discourses in critical conversation about cities. One of the most significant contributions that Darko has made to the growing "African" literary tradition is the shift from the rural, traditional village as a primary setting for portrayals of what are assumed to be singular African experiences. In this way, Darko centralizes modernity as an ongoing site of contemplation in literature from the continent. *Horizon* takes up what might be regarded as stock postcolonial themes, including attitudes toward Western-oriented modernity, materialism, and the outward gaze to the West as the solution to "African" problems. There is, for example, a clear intertextual relationship between Darko's *Horizon* and the closing letter in *Our Sister Killjoy*, a novel that is well recognized for its interrogation of Euro-derived conceptions of progress. But even as Darko's novel is a clear recourse to earlier postcolonial themes, the fact that much of the novel's plot unfolds in urban spaces and centers on transnational trade renders this work fertile ground for both contributing to and expanding globalization theories.

Mara's foregrounding of materialism, money, and trade in the introduction of her home village of Naka sets the tone for the eventual emergence of the themes I have just outlined:

> Naka was a farming village, and Akobi's father, like most men in the village, was a farmer too. But unlike most men in the village, he was also an undertaker. . . . A man who once shocked the entire village and beyond when he threatened to give the dying chief's linguist a "banana funeral" because the old man owed him eight shillings, . . . he earned even more respect for using the money to educate his son Akobi at the Joseph Father of Jesus Roman Catholic school, making his son the first child of Naka to earn a Form Four General

Certificate. . . . They stood out in the village and were held in high esteem.
(Darko 4–5)

The prestige that Akobi's family enjoys in the village results from their possession of financial means that are unavailable to the rest of the village; ironically, the family's attitude toward money clearly runs counter to the village's
traditional values. The threat of Akobi's father and his eventual fulfillment of
that threat to "give the dying chief's linguist a banana funeral because the old
man owed him eight shillings" demonstrates the undertaker's willingness to
eschew traditional values by inaugurating standard, globalized, capitalistic
values in this still-"traditional" village, naturally "shock[ing] the entire village and
beyond." It is also notable that such an extraordinary approach to finances
and business earns the undertaker respect, not ostracism or even scorn, from
the villagers. If we put the villagers' "shock" (which connotes recognition of
outside negative influences) and their accordance of prestige together, we are
left with what appears to be a surrender to the inevitable dominance of Western
capitalism, if not an actual show of respect for the system.

Even more remarkable is the way in which Darko sets the stage for Western-
centered commodification and consumerism by positioning Mara as part of
the web of global capitalism that had already been inching its way into the village life. The story of the approach to business, debts, and relationships of
Akobi's father becomes relevant to the novel because this is the family into
which Mara would be married or, one might even argue, into which she would
be traded. While Mara's father does not have the means and business acumen
that Akobi's father does, he is equal to the undertaker in his ruthless pursuit
of money and his willingness to use his daughter as a pawn. Mara's representation of the serendipitous timing that her father was able to exploit strikingly
highlights the fact that the way Akobi's father does business is less an anomaly
than it is part of an emerging pattern—evidence of the steady and certain shift
from community-oriented village life to a more globally aligned capitalist mode:

> I don't know why of all the eligible women in the village his [Akobi's] father chose
> me. I only know that the choice, for my father, could not have come at a better time.
> A man he owed money to had come and forcefully claimed his debt in the form of
> eight of father's eleven goats. So, my dowry came in handy. And then, too, he was
> flattered that the first Naka son with a school certificate should choose his daughter
> for a wife. So much so that . . . drunk from palmwine . . . he had proclaimed that he
> would gladly have given me away even for one goat. (Darko 6–7)

Part of what is notable about Darko's portrayal of both fathers in these
examples is that she does not present the village as a pure antithesis of the

market-driven city. Instead, as I show later in the chapter, while capitalism and global commodification are more pervasive in the city, the contextualizing of the village's vulnerability and surrender to a market economy illustrates the seamless continuities between coloniality and globalism in "African" experiences of modernity. Taken together, the capitalist and exploitative orientations of the two fathers and the villagers' recognition and ambivalence are, as Chielozona Eze has noted, "the ultimate result of a global capitalist system of which Africa and Africans have become a part" (94).

Theorizing Bridge Cities

I begin the textual analysis of this chapter by highlighting the place and significance of "the village" to illustrate how the values and ideals of global capitalism that are amplified in cities shape female experiences. These cities simultaneously provide spaces of transformation and continuity, agency and debilitation, and thus illustrate other ways that one might contemplate the variable city experiences in which this book is grounded. Furthermore, in both novels discussed here, the fictional "African city"—what Rashmi Varma refers to as "the colonial city," later emerging as the more explicitly described postcolonial-global space—functions as a bridge for the imperial cities in which the women's uneven, mixed experiences are most apparent.

While Darko and Unigwe circumvent the "progress" narrative of colonizers and of proponents of globalization, they both creatively configure and recuperate these postcolonial-global cities as bridge cities. By this, I mean that while Lagos and the unnamed city in *Horizon* function as spaces that offer a prelude to the ways in which the marginalization of women is perpetuated, these cities are also where women will find spaces of recovery and regeneration from the debilitating conditions that they seek to escape. Ifeyinwa Genevieve Okolo offers a useful analysis of this connection in her suggestion that, in *Black Sisters Street*, the boundaries between Lagos and Antwerp are blurred, as both are unsafe spaces for the characters in the novel. Additionally, Okolo points out that the novel does not represent Lagos "as a nostalgic ideal home" (119). In Darko's *Horizon*, Mara similarly illustrates this varied set of women's experiences. Her entry into the unnamed Ghanaian city highlights gender inequity and disempowerment, as Mara is literally bounced from one man to another— from her father to her abusive husband, Akobi—in her move from the village to the city. It is solely Akobi's ambition that makes Mara's move a proverbial "done deal": "[Akobi] had tasted town life and was now craving city life. And returning to Naka . . . was out of the question" (Darko 5). In Mara's reflection on her sudden thrust into city life, she recalls, "And while Akobi returned to the city to work, the customs and traditional rites were got over and done with on his behalf. Three weeks later he came straight from work on a Friday evening, arriving in Naka on the same Saturday, and left for the city with me as his wife . . . and property" (7). The ominous inclusion of "property" here is striking, as it marks Mara's entry into a world in which her value in the market will henceforth determine the course of her life.

With the exception of Sisi,[2] the one woman in Unigwe's *Black Sisters* who meets a tragic end, Lagos is an in-between space, a bridge city, a location of both deliverance and entrapment into years of sex work. Unigwe details the persistent vulnerability of women on the African continent while making clear the critical role of cities in women's current complicated experiences and outcomes. For Joyce, whose original given name is Alek, the prospect of a life in Lagos far outweighs the existential threat she escapes when she leaves her native Sudan. Alek manages to make her way to a refugee camp after she is gang-raped by the same soldiers who brutally murdered her brother, father, and mother. The admiration and love of Polycarp, one of the soldiers guarding the refugee camp, offers both hope and despair for Alek-Joyce, underscoring how variegated her experiences there, and later in Antwerp, will be: "The day they got into Lagos, Polycarp asked Alek what she thought of it. She thought this: Too many people. Too many houses. An excess of everything. . . . Houses juggled for space, standing on one another's toes. . . . Lagos streets were rutted, gutted, and near impassable, yet they were jam-packed with cars: huge air-conditioned Jeeps driving tail to tail with disintegrating jalopies. . . . Broken-down trucks dotted highways, their flanks huge banners of wisdom" (Unigwe 183–184). Yet, even in this disappointing reality of the urban decay and inequities that is so stark in Lagos, Alek-Joyce could see the beauty and the much-improved life that this city could offer her: "Lagos was not all pollution and dirt. It had a splendid beauty that was sometimes enough to make her cry. The first time Polycarp took her to the Bar Beach on Lake Victoria Island, the day was made to order: clear skies and a sun that shone straight onto the beach, a dazzling show of splendor. . . . She was sure she would be happy in Lagos. . . . She felt very lucky to have been given another shot. And with Polycarp by her side, there was little else she wanted" (186).

The differences in the physical spaces that Alek-Joyce describes also capture her eventual mixed fortunes in this bridge city. After the visit of Polycarp's mother and his final admission that he can neither marry nor remain in a relationship with Alek-Joyce, it is Polycarp—the person who had rescued Alek-Joyce and the one whose presence by her side would leave her wanting nothing—who also delivers her to Dele, the Lagos-based sex trafficker. It is in this space that Alek-Joyce recognizes the control that Polycarp and Dele exercise over her and where she also establishes her resolve. They treat her as they would handle any piece of property for sale; they give her a Fanta that she did not ask for, rename her, and most egregiously, in her presence, decide her future without even allowing her any input: "The soldiers who raped her that night in Daru had taken her strength, and Polycarp's betrayal had left her unwilling to seek it back. From now on, she resolved, she would never let her happiness depend on another's. She would never let anyone hurt her. She would play life's game, but she was determined to win. Her resolve gave her thirst, and she downed the Fanta without tasting it" (197).

The shared set of notable experiences of Darko's Mara and Unigwe's Alek-Joyce in "African" villages and cities captures this chapter's central point about the capricious characteristics of cities, as both women are coerced into the sex trade and experience their dehumanization prior to their entry into a European city. Mara's initial downward slide begins in the village in her native country; Alek-Joyce, who also barely survives a genocide in her birth country, is thrust into an African city, Lagos, that precipitates her exploitation even as it plants the seeds of resolve that will both sustain and deliver her. Perhaps not tasting the Fanta (in the scene just quoted) foreshadows the steely disassociation from her body and feelings that Alek-Joyce will need to harness to survive in Antwerp; there, sex work will require her to marshal extraordinary grit and detachment to get through each job, each day, and each year.

The persistence of sexual abuse of women as a push-pull factor for entry into the city is also detailed in Unigwe's representation of Ama's story. From age eight to the time she has her first period, Ama is sexually assaulted by her stepfather, the hyperreligious pastor Brother Cyril. It is Ama's mother, an otherwise docile woman who remains eternally grateful to her abusive husband, Cyril, who facilitates Ama's escape to the city. During the most unbearable instances of Ama's childhood abuse, she copes by imagining herself in cities: "She wanted to go to London.... Her other choices were Las Vegas. Or Monaco" (Unigwe 115). Underscoring the significance of the "African" city as a bridge city, the narrator explains, "When Ama did leave home, thirteen years later, it was neither to Las Vegas nor to Monaco. It was to Lagos. Bigger and wider than Enugu. It was a good place to start from" (116). But even as Ama notes and celebrates Lagos's promises and possibilities, her view of Lagos as a bridge city persists: "Ama looked forward to the customers, for sometimes they came with bits of her dream. Reminding her of what she might otherwise have forgotten, keeping her on her toes, so that she could never be complacent: young women slinging expensive handbags, ... bringing into the *buka* the sweet-smelling fragrances of perfume and freedom.... She saw the life she could live.... And Ama knew she had to leave" (136–37).

The connection between the city, modernity, and material prosperity shapes Ama's negotiation of her new space. She also makes clear her awareness of the constraints of the "African" city and a global marketplace. Ama's acknowledgment of the need to leave Lagos both illustrates her understanding of the limits of this Global South city space and represents a modern iteration of

Varma's conception of postcolonial cities as unhomely spaces for formerly colonized peoples, spaces that have become more tempting because of the dangling global capitalist fruits.

The notion of Lagos as a bridge city—better than the village but not enough to provide the kind of healing and prosperity that Ama desires—becomes central to her economic goals; she reconsiders her initial rejection of Dele's offer to travel to Europe to work in the sex trade:

> Brother Cyril had taken what he wanted, no questions asked. No "please" and "may I" or "could I." . . . And strange men taking and paying for her services. And it would not even be in Lagos. But overseas. Which earned you respect just for being there. It was not like she would be standing outside nightclubs in Lagos Island, hoping that she would not run into someone who might recognize her. So. Why not . . . ? She gave herself two days. *Two bloody days.* And then she went back to see Dele. "I am down with it," she said, relieved by the option of choice. (Unigwe 141)

Even the way the sex trade operates in Lagos renders this city inadequate for advancing the women's economic dreams. In this economically wounded Nigerian city, the people's enduring values place limits on the degree to which the new-age idea that "any kind of work is work" (Aidoo, *No Sweetness Here* 37) holds significant sway. Therefore, being recognized as a sex worker would place Ama outside the parameters of traditional expectations of respectability.

Yet the failure of the postcolonial city is centered primarily on the economic dwarfism of this representative "third world" city. Chisom-Sisi, the only university graduate among the four women, opts to enter the sex trade because of the inadequacy of Lagos; it is not a city in which her and her parents' dreams of upward mobility can be realized. Indeed, the failure of postcolonial cities is most clearly dramatized in Chisom-Sisi's gradual descent into despondency as her dreams of a job and all its benefits become increasingly elusive:

> The days after graduation were filled with easy laughter and application letters, plans, and a list of things to do (the last always preceded by "Once Chisom gets a job," "As soon as Chisom gets a job," "Once I get a job"). . . . Yet two years after leaving school, Chisom was still mainly unemployed . . . and had spent the better part of two years scripting meticulous application letters and mailing them to different banks in Lagos. . . . But she was never even invited to an interview. Diamond Bank. First Bank, . . . then the smaller ones. . . . No envelopes came addressed to her, offering her a job in a bank considerably humbler than the banks she had eyed while at school, and in which less intelligent classmates with better connections worked. (Unigwe 19–21)

The context of Chisom-Sisi's frustrations makes even more visible the importance of choice and agency in a city that, at first glance, diminishes agency through its failed promises, its corruption, and its relatively diminutive status in the modern global economy. At the same time, this city—with its sleazy, transnational sex trade and easy access to a global market—is paradoxically also the urban landscape on which Chisom-Sisi will be able to act as an agent of both her escape and her ultimate demise: "So, when she got the offer she did, she was determined to get her own back on life, to grab life by the ankles and scoff in its face. There was no way she was going to turn it down (22).

The way Unigwe leads readers to this woman's decision to accept Dele's offer of sex work abroad establishes in very clear terms the important role of Lagos in shaping these women's lives and ultimately how sex work, global capitalism, and travel impact them:

> When she ... had to eat *gari* and soup for the third day in a row, she thought nothing of the man's offer. The next day when her father came home to announce that there were rumors of job cuts in the civil service, . . . Chisom merely brought out the card and fingered it. Like she would something beautiful. . . . When she went to the toilet and found it broken and overrun with squirmy maggots and a day's load of waste—there was a citywide water shortage—she felt short of breath. She needed to get out of the house. Go for a walk. A breath of fresh air. And even then she had no destination in mind until she found herself at an office on Randle Avenue standing at the address on the gold edged card, which she had somehow, without meaning to, memorized. (31)

Unigwe's strategic use of incremental disappointments—looming job loss, food scarcity, a water shortage and its accompanying sanitary inconvenience—sets the context for the way Chisom-Sisi is almost inevitably lured into what can only feel like an opportunity amid the despair that seems to predominate in Lagos, a city whose glaring wealth disparities leave large segments of its population in poverty, and also lays bare the inequities that result from neoliberal economic policies.

At the same time, the contrast that Unigwe sets up between Chisom-Sisi's living conditions and Dele's office (31) underscores the duality—even the multiplicity—of the varied living conditions and socioeconomic possibilities within the city. In this way, Unigwe keeps the focus on the postcolonial wreckage that the city of Lagos so clearly exemplifies: "The office was large, with carpeting that yielded like quicksand under her feet and air-conditioning that kept out Lagos's oppressive heat, keeping her skin fresh as if she had just taken an evening bath" (31). The opulence of Dele's office, set against the squalor of Chisom-Sisi's dwellings, edges her further toward accepting Dele's clear proposal of sex work: "I get connections . . . . You work hard and five hundred euros every month no go hard for you to pay. . . . You fine gal now. Abi, see you back-side . . . come see you assets! As for those melons wey you carry for chest" (40). Chisom-Sisi's initial imagined questions—"What kind of girl he thought she was? . . . Do you know I have a university degree . . . ?"—are overridden by visual-izations of the mostly (economically) failed city of Lagos: "Instead, images flashed in front of her like pictures from a TV show: the living room with the pap-colored walls. A shared toilet cistern that never contained water, a kitchen that did not belong to her family alone. Her father folded, trying to be invisible. Her mother's vacant eyes interested in nothing. . . . She did not want to be sucked into that life. She imagined her life, one year from now, if she stayed in Lagos. But could she really resort to *that*? She turned to go, but her feet stuck in the quicksand. They would not move" (40). Chisom-Sisi may not yet have experienced the side of Lagos displayed with such vulgarity in Dele's office and manner, but she *has* witnessed her parents' hopelessness. In a city and world shaped by, and understood only in terms of, global capitalism, the despair of her parents' circumstances renders the choice Dele puts before her the antidote to a debilitating "third world" city.

Black Sisters presents Lagos both as an unhomely city for an aspiring young professional such as Chisom-Sisi and as a bridge city for sex work, which within the crevices of urban decay, also offers possibilities for access to the trappings of modernity that elude Chisom-Sisi. Yet, Lagos emerges as a broken bridge, thus complicating even further its place in the context of global capitalist exploi-tation. This is particularly evident in the experience of sixteen-year-old Efe, another of Unigwe's female characters, who ends up in Antwerp; the death of Efe's mother plunges her father into years of depression, interrupts her educa-tion, and places the running of the household into Efe's hands. In this role of premature motherhood, Efe is equipped with only the bare essentials—just enough for food. Significantly, this change makes Efe vulnerable to yearning for elusive consumer goods, which in turn contributes to her entry into sex work.

Although "work" as the forty-five-year-old Titus's kept woman makes eco-nomic gain possible for Efe, the nature of her gains is itself indicative of the limits of Lagos in making meaningful and sustained economic mobility possible: "Titus gave Efe the money she needed for the jeans and the blue T-shirt" (Unigwe 49). And over the course of her several months in this role, the money Efe earns gets her "Biscuits. Nail polish. Lipstick. A red handbag. Sweets for the little ones. Chewing gum in varying colors and flavors, . . . a suitcase, . . . a musical jewelry case, . . . a cassette player. New sandals" (50, 51). The extensive list of petty consumer items illustrates the meager offerings of Lagos for sex trade. But, more importantly, these inexpensive purchases that Efe amasses make clear the improbability of meaningful economic gains and socioeco-nomic mobility for most of the city's poor.

Given Efe's awareness of both the pervasiveness of global capitalism and the limited access that she and her then-infant son are likely to have to it, "she had agreed to Dele's terms before she asked what she was expected to do abroad." Dele does, however, imply "what sort of sales she was going to be involved in," as "he sized her up, his eyes going from her face to her breast to her calves under her knee-length skirt." Yet Efe agrees "to be Dele and Sons Limited's export" (71), and, as the use of "export" makes clear, it is this moment that marks her official assent to commodification. The small consumer items that sex work with Titus has brought her has given her a taste of what is possible, but she is aware that this small-scale sex work is in no way sufficient for her increased (adult) financial needs; her decision to be an "export" emanates from this awareness. It is significant to note that the local, Lagos-based sex work ends the moment Titus learns of her pregnancy. In a city where the death of a parent automatically turns the eldest girl into a woman who "missed her classmates whom she no longer saw because other responsibilities had taken over and made her a lot older than they were," Efe is an overnight grown-up who "missed the smell of new books . . . [and] missed the smells of ink" (49). And when she finds herself the sole provider for her son, it takes three cleaning jobs for her to be able to provide the minimum for her child. Here, too, readers are invited to understand what this clear offer of sex work outside the city of Lagos means: "L.I. [Efe's son] would get a better life. Go to good school, become a big shot and look after her when she was old and tired. L.I. was a worthy enough investment to encourage her to accept Dele's offer. And even though leaving him would be the hardest thing she would ever do, she would endure it for his sake" (71). Furthermore, Efe is well aware of the possibilities that work in a city abroad can open up for her. Not surprisingly, then, when Dele, her third and most generous employer, asks if she wants to go abroad, Efe's response is, "If I wan' go abroad, Oga Dele? anybody dey ask pikin if de pikin wan' sweet?" (70). The narrator's insertion of "Who did not want to go abroad? People were born with the ambition, and people died trying to fulfill that ambition" (70) underscores the limits of Lagos as a mere bridge to a city where economic prosperity is actually conceivable. The subtext of the postcolonial city's inadequacy in making social mobility possible embeds yet another subtext: that of the constraints that this same system inflicts on urban citizens of the Global South.

Of the four women who land in Antwerp, Alek-Joyce is not only the sole woman who is forcibly sent there but also the only one who believed that Lagos was a place of promise for her. Given the women's awareness of their choices, *Black Sisters* harks back to Aidoo's observation that "any kind of work is work." At the heart of this comment is the recognition of the wide-ranging possibilities of cities to reshape not only the accepted notions of what is acceptable as gainful employment but also "traditional" ideas about decency, good womanhood, and the relevance of established ways of being when economic survival is paramount. This new and seemingly unshackled sense of what counts as work obviously dispenses with boundaries of respectability and opens the door to a range of options that would make one economically viable in the new economic order. Such a shift naturally raises questions about "choice" and, moreover, the notion that urban residents, in this case mostly women, can now "choose" how they will make a living. My use of quotation marks in representing *choice* and *choose* indicates my problematization of choice—particularly whether choice is possible in constrained contexts where other opportunities are so limited and the need for survival is so urgent. Thus, even as urban locations such as Lagos serve as only bridge cities, they make visible what is possible in Western market-based cities.

The intertextual relationship and points of intersection between Unigwe's portrayal of Lagos and Darko's representation of the city where Mara lives after she leaves the village highlight the pattern of paradoxes that I argue these writers offer for the cities they represent. Mara says,

> To say I was shocked when Akobi brought me to his home in the city would be an understatement. I was stunned. Our home in the village were of mud and leaves but no one needed to tell a visitor they were homes. Akobi had to tell me this was his home before I believed it. [There was] a cluster of shabbily-constructed corrugated-iron sheet shelters that looked like chicken houses, . . . and between them shallow, open gutters wound their way. . . . All the water from dirty washing and bathing, and urine too, collected and stayed until it vaporated. . . . I was soon to discover that these would not be my only headache. (Darko 8)

The squalor detailed in this description, which is typical of inner-city poverty across the globe, serves as an especially powerful way to launch Mara's city experience; it compellingly and appropriately sets up her subsequent experiences, not only in this "third world" city but also in the German city where she will be sold into sex slavery.

The fact that Mara's initial response to the conditions in the city is tempered by her later exuberance about it is illustrative of the city's complexity and varying possibilities. Not surprisingly, the global capitalist system, one of the debilitating aspects of the city, offers the first glimpse of the constrained empowerment that Mara will develop not only in her home country but also in the European urban and suburban spaces where she will eventually find herself. The conversation with her neighbor Mama Kiosk, which precipitates Mara's first job, is particularly striking for the way it informs our understanding of the possibilities of cities, as are Mama Kiosk's questions. What is most significant and shaping about this encounter with Mama Kiosk is their exchange when Mara returns with the garbage can and then turns to leave: "Hey, do you work for free in the village? . . . You are in the city, and in the city nothing is for free" (Darko 10). This moment marks Mara's entry into the world of work and affirms, yet again, the framing quotation of this chapter that "any kind work is work." After this, Mara regularly dumps garbage in exchange for food, and paradoxically, it is Akobi's abusive and domineering attitude that offers Mara her first opportunities to participate in that system.

Illustrating the conception of cities as sites of in-betweenness, the Ghanaian city in which Mara is thrust once she leaves the village allows for a kind of abuse and vulnerability, even as it provides space for shades of agential action. The city makes the emotional and physical abuse that Mara suffers from Akobi more difficult because she is away from her family. Yet, by allowing Akobi to ignore traditional practices that created more built-in systems of accountability to families and communities, the city—and its attendant shift toward a more modern, globally oriented culture—also makes it possible for Mara to enact new terms of engagement for male-female relationships. Mara's sense of the city and her place within it is made most visible and facilitated by her access to work: "I never imagined it to be such a brisk trade as it turned out to be. Neither did I consider that trading this way would be so exciting. The lorry station was a place of colour. The people in their various coloured up-and-down clothes and headties. The kiosks . . . and then the lorries and trucks and their colours and inscriptions . . . I began to enjoy my trade very much. . . . My eggs, too, were going so fast that by the second week I had doubled the quantity I took for sale" (18). For Mara, the landscape of the city is a varied one, as is her own experience with the economic system that characterizes the city. And even as her partial freedom and time away from her home attract more abuse from Akobi—such as the "nasty kick in the knee" (19) that she receives from him—Mara's hope rests in the increased independence that making a living for herself makes possible. Her revelation, "I was always calculating my money to see when I could pay Akobi back his capital and still be left with something after I had" (19), signals the possibilities for liberation and perhaps a modicum of economic independence because of the opportunities that the city continues to present.

Notably, this moment of burgeoning economic self-empowerment, which triggers more physical abuse from Akobi, is a breaking point for Mara, even though the break from abuse manifests itself in unexpected ways. Because of what Mara learns about the expectations of men in the city, she musters the courage to expose Akobi as an abusive husband. Mara is shocked, confused, and unable to pay the interest that Akobi demands on the capital he lent Mara to start her egg-hawking business. Mara reports that he reverts to his default response to any conflict between them: "I saw his clenched knuckles ready to knock pain into my forehead" (21). But for the first time, she refuses to accept Akobi's abuse in silence, mostly because of the potential support from the residents of the dilapidated tenement yard that had been such a source of shock and disappointment when she first entered the city:

I don't know what made me do what I did, but suddenly I wasn't prepared to take any more of it. . . . I rushed out of the room screaming. . . . Mama Kiosk took me in, gave me cold water to drink and settled me down on her old sofa. . . . Outside, people were gathering and grouping in the compound. They were talking and gossiping their hearts out but I didn't care. Indeed I liked it because it was my screams that had brought them out and very soon they were all going to learn the one thing that I wanted them to know, that Akobi maltreated me. . . . I knew for sure that if he had known that I was going to take this action he wouldn't have done what he did, for he was a man who craved recognition as a civilized person and a gentleman . . . and, as the saying went in the city, only bushmen beat their wives. (22)

The overcrowding in the city's tenement yard, the lack of privacy, and the different ways that city residents engage with their neighbors give Mara the confidence to reject abuse and to deny Akobi the privacy that facilitates his ongoing assaults; this provides not just relief but also a shift in Mara, a recognition of the relative autonomy and opportunities for self-remaking that the city makes possible. Indeed, Akobi's only act of violence toward Mara after she returns home is his usual (though not to be minimized) impersonal sexual intercourse. And so the value that Akobi places on a more sophisticated, city persona undercuts some of the power he previously exercised over Mara, thus marking an important, predictive moment in the way the city will eventually provide quasi-liberation for Mara.

In this section, I have sketched the backgrounds of selected female characters, highlighting the catalyst for each of their departures to illustrate some important ways in which Global South cities such as Lagos typify the more general understanding of cities as spaces of opportunity: these women's ways out of debilitating socioeconomic situations were possible only in urban spaces where the lines of cultural expectations were being redrawn to align these societies more closely with global values and expectations. At the same time, each woman's experience—her push factors, so to speak—makes clear how such urban locales necessarily fall short of the promise of cities. Taking these factors into account, then, my theorization of these "third world" cities as bridge cities illustrates the way they serve as gateways to what Caroline Herbert refers to as "neo-imperial" cities—sites of simultaneous prosperity and destruction (204).

European cities, created for the sole purpose of advancing European societies, are arguably the centers of global capitalism, the spaces where the possibilities for economic advancement are most feasible. But for immigrants, the working class, and anyone outside the privileged groups, these cities fall short of that promise. This reality notwithstanding, the women in *Black Sisters* arrive in Antwerp steeped in their own interpretations of the iconic and widely proclaimed elevated view of such spaces: "Before Efe came to Belgium, she imagined castles and clean streets and snow as white as salt. But now, when she thinks of it, when she talks of where she lives in Antwerp, she describes it as a botched dream, . . . created for elegance but never quite accomplishing it. In her part of Antwerp, huge offices stand alongside grotty warehouses and desolate fruit stalls run by Turks and Moroccans" (Unigwe 23). Speaking very pointedly to the city's failure to deliver and the variances between image and reality, this passage also highlights the imperial cities as sites of decay and of "dreams deferred"—a fact that is especially striking given the alluring tales of economic prosperity that continue to beckon people in the Global South, who in reality often experience the failed margins of global capitalism.

Sisi's characterization of Antwerp as "*a city that is collapsing under the weight of its own congestion*" (242) underscores both her realization of the similarities between European and African cities and the way the inequities wrought by global capitalism render cities as repeating sites of decay. Her focus on the physical landscape in one part of Antwerp offers even more striking descriptions of a city that is at least partially in ruins; this observation highlights how closely locations in Antwerp resemble the features of Lagos that were her ultimate push factors: "Every time she took the bus outside Antwerp, she was aware how easy it was to tell that one had left the city. Or had reentered it. The landmarks could not be missed: houses with peeling paint and broken windows. Derelict buildings looking like life had been hard on them. They always reminded Sisi of drug users . . . scars of hard living. . . . Sometimes, Sisi thought, stepping over a mound of brown stool, Antwerp seemed like a huge incinerator" (242). The ironies of this description of a European city are self-evident, and the comparison of Antwerp (or at least parts of it) to an incinerator is indicative of Chisom-Sisi's realization that this European city potentially burns dreams more than it nurtures them. When placed within the context of these characters' and their compatriots' unquenchable desires to travel to Europe (recall, for example, Efe's rhetorical question, "Who didn't want to go aboard?"), Sisi's remark calls into question the neocolonial narrative of the superiority of Europeans cities. Depictions such as these hark back to some cornerstone postcolonial themes, even as they locate themselves within more recent globalization discourses. The colonially generated misrepresentations that inform thoughts such as Sisi's in the preceding quote constitute new iterations of travel writings that frequently market European locations, especially their cities, as superior antitheses of African countries or, in this case, African cities. Tales of success in Europe, and European cities in particular, where immigrants most frequently expect to realize their dreams of economic splendor, function as stock-in-trade in the marketplace of ideas where Western-oriented narratives prevail. The commodification of abroad, of European cities, with prosperity-laden narratives such as Dele's—"Every month I send gals to Europe. Antwerp. Milan. Madrid. My gals dey there" (39)—set the partial reality of a decaying Lagos against the images of "luxury cars" and other splendors that only the European city can make possible.

Yet, in Unigwe's depiction, the inherently complicated status of cities is underscored in the novel's simultaneous confirmation and undermining of the women's expectations. Even for Sisi, who is arguably the character who loses the most as a result of her move to the European city (Sisi is murdered in Antwerp), the capacity of the city to deliver on some of its promises is also centralized. Sisi describes another side of Antwerp, one that gives her a taste of the freedom that she craves, even though in her current job she has lost much of what would be considered her freedom and even as, more disturbingly, she walks toward her death. On this day, Sisi experiences—if only briefly—a taste of the paradise that a European city is supposed to be: she "walked in perfect weather. . . . [She] had a song in her heart and money in her purse" (242). This is exactly what she had envisioned when she contemplated Dele's offer only months before: material prosperity, freedom, and the prospect of a new life away from her squalid living conditions in Lagos: "In central Antwerp, people did not care whether you lived or died. When they said hello in shops, you could tell it was routine. . . . They said hello and looked past you. . . . There was a furious pace to the city that hindered people from stopping to smile. . . . Even her fellow Africans did not talk to her. . . . Central Antwerp was a city of strangers, of anonymity. It was the anonymity that she craved sometimes" (241). That Antwerp facilitates tenuous freedoms, agency, and some "choice" for women, whom the combined local and colonial traditions render as mere property and bodies to be exploited, is more the norm than it is the outlier in *Black Sisters*. As the preceding quote makes clear, because of the impersonal nature of the city, Sisi now has the freedom to enjoy the upscale environs because she has decided to leave the bondage of the brothel; she is therefore able to briefly experience exactly what she desires. Capturing the give-and-take of the city, the way people's disengagement facilitates the freedom and anonymity that Sisi craves, this quote encapsulates the multifaceted capacity of cities to simultaneously liberate and constrain. Patricia Bastida-Rodriguez compares Sisi's wanderings in the city of Antwerp to the *flâneur*, an "upper-middle-class" man who, out of boredom, walks the streets of Paris. Bastida-Rodriguez tweaks the term to account for Sisi's lower-class, outsider, immigrant status, arguing that "Sisi seems to be subverting power relations at work in contemporary cities while at the same time she gives way to her fantasies" (208). Even fleetingly, Sisi's success at "subverting" class structures and temporarily breaking away from the apartment where she is housed is illustrative of both the possibilities of cities to offer some liberation and the tenuous nature of such "freedoms."

Drawing on deep-rooted spiritual worldviews, Unigwe's narrative strategy supports the conception of the city as a space of the proverbial mixed blessings.

In a somewhat circuitous manner, the narrator gives readers access to the women's pasts, their present lives in Antwerp, and their futures. Sisi's freedom to move around the city is quickly contained by the anonymity that gave her that freedom; Segu, the man who lures her from Luc's home and kills her, is able to easily corner and murder her without even being suspected of anything untoward precisely because in this urban space, "people did not care whether you lived or died." But—even as we are on the verge of believing that Sisi's circle is closing, that she has paid the ultimate price for daring to end her bondage—Unigwe's inclusion of the spiritual dimension of Sisi's existence further complicates the outcome of her city experience. Rather than simply learning of Sisi's death, readers last encounter Sisi as an active spirit, thus leaving open the question of whether the end of Sisi's life is indeed her final demise. In the time between Sisi's being almost dead and stone-cold dead, the instant when the soul is still able to fly, she escapes her body and flies down to Lagos (251). She checks in on her father and her mother; she then visits Dele's home in time to hear him conversing about her with Madam back in Antwerp, and finally she goes upstairs to Dele's daughters. The narrator reports that "anyone who knew Sisi well might say that she cursed them" (254). The last we see of Sisi is an image of her soul "bounc[ing] down the stairs to begin its journey into another world" (153–154). By also situating the story in the realm of the spiritual, making it possible for Sisi to traverse transnational cities, and by ending her story with her metamorphosis into a spiritual being who possesses different kinds of powers, Unigwe affords readers the possibility to consider Sisi's sojourn into the city as, perhaps, more than simply a lost or wasted life, destroyed by the city; rather, Sisi may be seen as one who loses and gains in Lagos and Antwerp and, ultimately, in the great beyond.

Consistent with the novel's move beyond the temporal present, the narrator gives readers a futuristic snapshot of each of the other three women's outcomes. They all leave the trade (or, in Efe's case, her past iteration of it) financially better off, though they are excluded from the honorable lives that women in their culture are expected to lead: Joyce opens a school in Sisi's name; Efe, perhaps the most complicated, becomes a madam in the trade, exploiting women the way she has been exploited; and Ama opens a store.

However, as we observe in Darko's representation of Mara's city experience, particularly the economic independence the city makes possible for her, the money she earns becomes the catalyst for both her forced entry into the sex trade and her ultimately more decisive actions. Even as she resigns herself to a life devoid of the dignity that is so essential to her sense of self, to her understanding of womanhood, personhood, and her place in a centuries-old set of traditions, Mara takes from the city what it can offer her. Later, after years of sex work—and serial disappointments—she tells Kaye,

I am no longer green. . . . As for the morals of life my mother brought me up by, I have cemented them with coal tar in my conscience. If the gods of Naka intended me to live by them, they should have made sure I married a man who loved me and who appreciated the values I was brought up with. I lived by those values until I could no longer do so. The rot has gone too deep for me to return to the old me. And that is why Kaye, I am going to do the films and stage shows and all there is to it. But I want every pfennig of what I make to come to me! (Darko 131)

What Mara articulates here is not only a sense of resignation but more so an interrogation of the system that places huge demands on women yet offers them little protection. Hence, readers observe a shift that is more philosophical-moral—a critique of a lopsided set of expectations. Mara's comments exemplify the capacity of cities to simultaneously diminish and empower its mobile female subjects.

Further illustrating the mixed returns Mara receives from the city, her extensive list of what she has been able to provide for her family is telling: a video player and television set for one brother, a pickup truck for another, a cement-block house for her mother, and eventually a home for her children and herself: "Material things are all I can offer them. There's nothing dignified and decent left of me to give to them . . ." (140). Thus, the pattern of simultaneous opportunities and losses that begins for Mara in her "third world" city continues in a European city that clearly delivers on its promise of economic prosperity while also taking from Mara much of what defined her and shaped her as a rural "African" woman.

Critics have addressed this question of agency for Mara from multiple angles. While Barberán Reinares acknowledges what might be termed "agency" because of the actions that Mara takes at the end of the novel, she ultimately casts a bleak shadow on Mara's transformation, noting that while it is true that agency and victimhood are not mutually exclusive, "Mara has become a battered drug addict still dependent on exploiters because of her limited options" (*Sex Trafficking* 105). In her discussion of "consent" and "agency," Barberán Reinares eschews the binary characterizations of sex workers as either helpless victims or agents, instead arguing for a "third space . . . in order to redirect the discussion to the structural causes that enable sex trafficking" and to "examine sex trafficking fictional narratives within frameworks that interrogate how systemic gender inequality, xenophobia, racism, destruction of third world environments . . . directly correlate with sex trafficking" ("Pedagogies" 58). María Frías sees Darko's representation these female sex workers differently: "Darko's disturbing discourse on prostitution aims to designate African women as active subjects, recalcitrant rebels, and victim-survivors who . . . [offer] resistance to sexual/colonial domination." Even more pointedly, Frías concludes that Darko's female characters "ironically chose prostitution less as an act of subjugation, despair, and subservience than one of vengeance, defiance, self-assertion, and financial independence." In this regard, Frías reads the novel as demonstrating "subversive power" (12). Despite the somewhat different conclusions, the main point of convergence between these two critics is their agreement that there is evidence of partial agency. Okolo reads the women in Unigwe's renditions "as not just a vulnerable and stigmatized category of person but as resilient individuals with hopes and dreams" (121).

When these novels are read through the frame of the city, as I have attempted to do here, it is the space that the city provides in a globalized urban context that allows Mara and the other women to make the "choices" they do. The decision not to return to family in the village is indicative of the recognition of the cover, albeit torn and imperfect, that the city affords Mara and others like her. Thus, the circle remains open for Mara, as it does for the women in *Black Sisters*—Mara returns to neither the self she was forced to relinquish nor the Western-defined poverty of "crude thick-soled rubber-tyre slippers" and "mud and leaves" housing of her first home (Darko 25).

Gender in the Urban Space

One notable point of intersection between these Global South bridge cities and European cities is that they both provide fertile ground for the development of certain kinds of female relationships and solidarities, even though these do not fully eliminate intragender oppressions. In contemplating the women's experiences in the two novels through the lens of the cities to which they move and then inhabit, I find that the relationships that these women form with each other to be among the most pivotal aspects of their city experiences. For example, the fortitude that Mara is able to build in her home city and later in the European city where she is traded is the result of her friendship with the older woman Mama Kiosk. It is Mama Kiosk who introduces Mara to gainful employment. Mama Kiosk is the one who initiates conversation with Mara, laying the groundwork for a deep friendship that will become the source of any modicum of liberation that Mara experiences: Mama Kiosk is also the person from whom Mara comes to understand the city as a space not only of gender oppression and marginalization but also of opportunity. Mama Kiosk's preamble to economic agency is significant, as it surfaces in the first set of exchanges: "You are the new tenant here? You come from the village? Do you work? Are you going to the rubbish dump? Can you take mine with you? Hey, do you work for free in the village? You are in the city, and in the city nothing is for free, you get me? Come!" (Darko 10). As Mara reports, "She beckoned and I followed her into her house. Minutes later, I emerged with a paper bag filled with a piece of yam, two cassavas, some okros and a handful of garden eggs. 'For throwing my rubbish away for me' she added" (11). Mama Kiosk's deliberateness in engaging Mara in a barter system that she had not experienced in the village makes Mara aware of this new way of being; Mama Kiosk conveys to Mara that the city she now inhabits is a marketplace to which she must adjust and where she can participate in mutually beneficial exchanges. Later in the story, Mara reports, "it was Mama Kiosk who suggested that I take up hawking boiled eggs to travellers at the lorry station" (18), a move that precipitates lasting and consequential changes for Mara's city experiences.

The friendship that Mara forms with Mama Kiosk and the mentorship that she receives from the older woman also plant the seeds of female resistance to gender imbalance. This woman-inspired intervention provides the baseline tools that Mara later mobilizes in a European city, with its vaster possibilities and resources, making it possible for her to finally achieve justice. Referring to Akobi's ill treatment of Mara and her acceptance of her husband's dominance, Mama Kiosk's observation "that is not normal" (13) does not immediately move Mara to liberatory actions; instead, her words germinate years later, in part through a bond she forms with another woman, Kaye. The relationship that Mara forms with Kaye, the co-owner of the sex-trading establishment where Mara begins life as a sex worker in Hamburg, illustrates Mara's mixed experiences—the beginning of her agential acts as well as her acceptance of her new life and persona. Mara describes Kaye as "my trusted friend," even as Kaye "polish[ed Mara] up splendidly to the standard of Peepy [the pimp]" (116). Despite the fact that Kaye participates in the exploitation of Mara's body, she is the "first person [Mara] told [her] whole true story" (116). Forged out of a shared exploitation, the friendship that these two women form makes it possible for Mara to earn money that the male pimps are not able to claim. Kaye "passed customers" on to Mara (12) and covers for her when she leaves to earn more money through private clients. Significantly, too, it is Kaye who finds a private detective for Mara; the detective provides Mara with all the information she needs to bring Akobi and his criminal network to justice. But the most defining act of solidarity between Kaye and Mara is the way Kaye facilitates Mara's relative freedom. Kaye's carefully orchestrated plan gets Mara far away from Hamburg—where she is still constrained—to Munich, where, even as she continues work in the sex industry, she will have greater autonomy. While I remain cognizant of the danger of subscribing to a village-to-city progress narrative, it bears noting that as a "contact zone"—a term defined by Mary Louise Pratt as the space where Europeans and the range of peoples they colonized met and necessarily exchanged cultures—and as a site of competing ideas, the city offers more ideological, physical, and economic space for fostering the kind of communally driven, covert act of resistance that Mara's journey highlights.

Along similar lines, Unigwe configures life in the city of Antwerp—where the four sex workers are mostly powerless and vulnerable—as a circumstance that makes supportive female relationships possible, despite the uneven nature of these supportive bonds. As Okolo has noted, "The locale 'Black Sisters' Street' is not only a space of female bondage but of potential female bonding," and a "fragile 'sisterhood' begins to grow" (119). The narrative structure of *Black Sisters* also signals the novel's deliberate attention to the women's eventual positive relationships, as the story is structured around the women's gathering at an informal wake that they hold for Sisi after learning of her death. It is in this moment of their most significant bonding yet that each woman opens up and shares her story. Their telling, in turn, is the means through which readers gain insight into each of the characters' pasts and into how they ended up together in a European city where they have individually and collectively lost what appears to be everything—their families, their human rights, and most disturbingly, the rights to their bodies and to any say in how they are traded as a commodity in the city.

The novel's affirmation of female bonding is reinforced as readers are introduced to Sisi, as she walks the streets of Antwerp on the day on which she will eventually die. Even as Sisi basks in her newfound freedom, she is stopped by feelings of guilt for leaving the house she has shared with three other women: "She hadn't abandoned them. Had she? She had just . . . well, moved on. Surely, surely, she had that right. Still, she wondered: What were they doing now? When would they notice that she was gone?" (Unigwe 4). Sisi's internal monologue—her self-reassurance that "surely she had [the] right" to leave them for what seemed like her freedom—and the fact that she considers this self "pep talk" necessary speak eloquently to the connection, though previously unspoken, that Sisi feels to the other women. As the women point out, Dele, the sex trader in Lagos who has sold all of them, is their one link to each other; despite the conditions under which they meet, these women forge a bond that illustrates how, in modern cosmopolitan contexts—particularly in the ways that urban settings create new challenges for women—such circumstances also create opportunities for the new kinds of female relationships that both Darko and Unigwe detail in these works.

Yet, while the city facilitates the kind of female community that I have suggested here, consistent with this chapter's and this book's more general theorization of the city as a space of simultaneity and variance, I propose that both novels also complicate their representation of women, showing how some women exploit the possibilities of cities, particularly cities' commercial opportunities. The most egregious of these, by far, is Madam, Dele's transnational business partner; her cold, inhumane, strictly business approach to her relationship with and management of the women is among the worst examples of women's complicity in the exploitation of other women detailed in the novel. Among the most striking demonstrations of Madam's callousness and her treatment of the women as chattel—or, worse, inanimate commodities—is her "business as usual" response to Sisi's death, a response that serves her well in reminding the surviving women of their tenuous and dispensable position: "Nobody says it, but they are all aware that the fact that Madam is going about her normal business, no matter what they are, is upsetting them. There is bitterness in the realization that for her, Sisi's death is nothing more than a temporary discomfort. They watched her eat a hearty breakfast, toast and eggs chewed with gusto and washed down with a huge mug of tea, and thought her appetite, her calm, tactless" (37). Madam's cruelty and nonchalance also demonstrate how, within the context of a global marketplace, values such as female solidarity, as illustrated by Darko's Mama Kiosk and Kaye, cannot be assumed when women are placed in circumstances where competing values such as individualism and capitalism also exist; additionally, this representation illustrates *Black Sisters*' disavowal of a binary approach to gender relations in the city. Instead, what we see here is a continuum of possible ways in which women are likely to engage with each other within the context of global capitalist exigencies.

Of the numerous examples of Madam's treatment of the women as bodies to be traded, I have chosen to discuss her belief that Sisi's death is just collateral damage because it highlights in such a vulgar way the performance that Madam stages as the women openly mourn. That she eats with "gusto" is especially notable for the degree to which this act makes visible the disregard for life within this woman-run, capitalist setting. This example also illustrates one crucial way in which the city allows for the diminishment of traditional values: As the women contemplate how to mourn Sisi's passing and mark her life as their "African" tradition would demand, Madam's actions in a European city where, as Sisi observes, "people did not care whether you lived or died" show a disregard for life that deviates significantly from the way life is valued in Sisi's culture and the way death is marked. Viewed through the prism of Madam's exploitation of the women, Antwerp emerges as a space of loss— loss of values and loss of opportunities for women to challenge capitalist-patriarchal institutions and practices.

The Sex Trade, Women, and the City Space

The dangers, level of exploitation, and tragic outcomes of sex trafficking are beyond dispute. So, what insights does an examination of late twentieth- and early twenty-first-century transnational trade provide? It is important to recall here that, except for one of the story's female protagonists, all of the women in *On Black Sisters Street* enter the trade willingly, out of frustration with their economic prospects—more precisely because of the devastating effects of global capitalism on their "third world" countries and bridge cities. Yet even those who "willingly" enter the business find the conditions of their work much more restrictive and exploitative than they had anticipated or had been told they would be.

Because of the complicated pictures that emerge, we are compelled to consider questions of agency, marginality, loss, and so forth in layered, nuanced ways. With a group of women who mostly consent to engage in sex work abroad and with specific and stated intentions to access global capitalist networks and their gains (ill gotten or not), women are portrayed as partial agents, complicit (perhaps necessarily so) in presumed and actual exploitations. Given these choices, women also reckon with multiple belief systems and values that so obviously compete with the values of the marketplace. There is therefore the suggestion that in the age of rapid and unparalleled globalization, choices are few, and even the notion of choice itself is called into question. The novels demonstrate that, in the inevitable urgency of survival in urban locations into which all the women have been thrust by someone who sees them only as capital, characterizing sex work as a choice does not offer a comprehensive or accurate enough picture of the conditions that drive the women's decision or of their experiences in these cities. Ostensibly, most of these women "choose," but—given the limited options available to them in cities created by colonialism and, later, excluded and exploited in the global capitalist milieu—"choice," "freedoms," and "options" should at least be interrogated, even as we acknowledge the new possibilities for survival that these spaces open up. Experiences such as Mara's allow us to consider the sex trade against the backdrop of classical postcolonial themes because of the ways in which the novel centers the city as a foil for the village; the novel further enables our consideration of these postcolonial themes through its depiction of how characters view colonizers' lands as what Aidoo refers to as a "dress rehearsals for paradise" (*Our Sister Killjoy* 9) and of how some traditional values are undermined, challenged, and in the end necessarily disavowed. But overall, both novels and each woman's experience insist on readings that are grounded in a longer and more present globalization, while they remain cognizant of how past colonial hegemonic economic actions inform their stories.

Ultimately, then, along with the opportunities cities offer for anonymity, reinvention, and nuanced ways of thinking about agency and work, even sex work—which allows women some shift in status, tempered but not necessarily negated by significant exploitation—they also allow women diverse kinds of movement. Cities emancipate women from economic stagnation, even as they demand a relinquishing of old ways of being and foreclose any kind of return to the women's pasts or reconnection with the communities they left behind. Women do indeed move within the socioeconomic and cultural contours of the cities they inhabit with some degree of freedom, but always on a metaphorical leash and always with others taking from them. Their quest for social mobility always includes surrendering much of themselves, because cities almost always demand some self-reinvention as trade for any modicum of economic success.

Reflections on the conditions of the women's entry into the sex trade, their experiences as sex workers, and their outcomes facilitate greater understanding of their individual experiences and also help readers to make sense of the interplay between the historical postcolonial period and the contemporary globalizing times. Critical inquiry into these depictions of sex work provides a window into globalization as a phenomenon. It is hard to read these novels and not notice the explicit ways in which they recover some patterns of the transatlantic slave trade. The presence of these traded female bodies in these cities— all of which are colonial creations—renders the cities as sites of colonial hauntings; in these modern capitalist-oriented urban locations, these women are ghostly presences of their slave-traded foremothers. The women's fictional journeys therefore contribute to a broader understanding of what it means to exist in a Black itinerant body in modern cities, where the allure of economic prosperity and even actual gains are always undermined by the historically based and enduring exclusions.

4

"Writing the Sprawling City"

■■■■■■■■■■■■■■■■■■■■■■

The Transatlantic Drug
Trade in *A Brief History of
Seven Killings*

> You might as well call the whole place
> Kingston 21.
> —Marlon James, *A Brief History of
> Seven Killings*

A few related observations and utterances in recent history capture the key concerns of this chapter. The first is Tom Barry's and Dylan Vernon's remark, "The common opinion in the Caribbean was that the free trade train was coming, like it or not, and it behooved them to join the negotiations rather than get left behind" (Barry and Dylan Vernon 31). In other words, Caribbean countries such as Jamaica—where the novel under consideration here is set— are mostly powerless in free-trade markets. This is a hallmark of globalization: these countries' only two choices are to sign on or be left behind. In dialogue with Barry's point, in the film *Life and Debt*, Michael Witter shares with a group of students, "The economy today is much more under the control of foreigners, not necessarily through direct ownership but through the mechanism of debt." What Witter articulates here reads like an explanation of what results from the choices Barry has laid out; based on the new conditions in which Jamaica finds itself within the global marketplace, there seems to be little room for negotiations because the country is being controlled by foreigners and, we can safely assume, Euro-American foreigners.

The second example relates to the 2016 US presidential elections: one of the key points of debate and a position that played a role in handing the White House to Donald Trump was the impact of job losses that many working-class US citizens had experienced over the prior decade. As part of the global free-market economy, many of these jobs went to "third world" countries, the kind that the global "trade train" was believed to have left behind. This is not how globalization was supposed to work. The citizens of "first world" countries were not meant to compete with those in marginalized, mostly Global South regions of the world for jobs and other economic gains. The election of Trump, with his "America First" mantra, was seen by some "Americans" as a way to rectify this wayward turn of globalization.

I have often pondered the irony inherent in both examples: as the preceding comment about being left off the train indicates, globalization was meant to continue, renew, or consolidate economic and other forms of subjugation of smaller, economically weaker countries that were brought into being by colonization and exploitation in the first place. Yet, in the latter example, here was a presidential candidate making his case, and a credible one too, to those whose lived experiences were evidence of this globalization gone awry—those in "first world" countries who had been failed by globalization. The basis of Trump's claim was understood as the marginalization of people in the most powerful, wealthiest country in the world, a kind of globalization "in reverse" (to borrow from Louise Bennett)—at least in part.[1]

The preceding examples provide a useful backdrop for Marlon James's fictional—and historically grounded—account of the simultaneous marginalization and warped display of agency among poor urban men as they confront both historical and current global capitalist injustices in Jamaica.

Representing the dominant scholarly view of the impacts of globalization on economically weaker countries and former European colonies, Patrick Chamoiseau characterizes globalization and its impact in the following way: "Never before has humanity found itself in so global, total, totalitarian, and totalizing a system. . . . Economic globalization is a loose, baggy system that no longer affords the slightest prospect of elevation. It threatens the fundamental equilibrium of the planet, indeed the survival of the species, while telling stories about 'sustainable development' in an effort to persist with and conceal its folly" (4–5). Justin Edwards's characterization of the 1999 antiglobalization protestors in Seattle raises similar concerns:

The new technologies, new media and new political landscape (following the fall of the Soviet Union), protestors said, enabled multi- and transnational companies to enter global markets outside of the established markets of the West. This expansion has led to outsourced manufacturing, call centres and other business deals in any country that is poor. . . . For many of the protestors, then, globalization encouraged dependency, disenfranchisement and dis-empowerment deriving from Coca Cola-ization and McDonaldization that eroded cultural differences. . . . In this, wealthier western powers can call the shots in poorer countries, thus undermining the independence of the poor nation. (160–161)

Consistent with widespread views of globalization, Chamoiseau and Edwards see smaller nations—such as the fictional Jamaica of Marlon James's 2014 novel *A Brief History of Seven Killings*—as victims, with their people being constantly squeezed by the heavy weight of large global hegemonic players who, according to Edwards, "call the shots." There is much evidence to support the foregoing characterizations; yet, while *A Brief History* exposes some of the dev-astating impacts of globalization and its attendant neocolonial capitalism, James's account leans toward a shift in the power relationship between oppressed "third world" urban residents who, by design, should bear the brunt of a neo-subalternization wrought by globalization and the dominant neocolonial, global powers.

A Brief History offers a fictional account of a crucial period in Jamaica's his-tory between the 1970s and 1990s. The novel focuses on the political upheav-als of the period: the increased visibility of political garrisons—described by Damion Blake as "don-ruled shadow versions of the official state" (58)—and related gang violence; the effects of US/CIA intervention; the well-known 1976 attempt on the life of an international reggae artist, whom the novel refers to as "the Singer";[2] and the expansion of drug and gang warfare beyond Jamaica's (inner-city) borders. Given the novel's setting in recent history, when post-colonial, global power imbalances were becoming increasingly tangible, *A Brief History* is central to the larger arguments of this book because, like the other texts under consideration in this book, it takes up and insists on reflection about a broad set of questions that must be considered in any discussion of the repre-sentation of postcolonial, postindependence Global South cities and their relationships to cities in the Western world. Most significant among these structuring considerations is the recurring question of what unique features cit-ies possess that warrant an examination of creative accounts that are set in cities in the first place. Because of the novel's scope, style, and historical and overt global reach, and most importantly because of the genesis of the specific cities on which it is based, *A Brief History* functions as a kind of touchstone for the broader analyses in this book. James's novel addresses in specific and unique ways the relationship between colonialism and the formation of cities—in particular, cities in which substates such as the fictional Copenhagen City exist. *A Brief History* gets to the heart of one of this book's structuring questions: How might cities and the conditions they engender potentially challenge power relationships between "first world" and "third world" countries and, relatedly, reshape frequently addressed themes such as agency and marginality, center and periphery?

As a work of art that locates itself so deeply and explicitly within discourses of globalization, *A Brief History* also insists on a consideration of the importance and stakes of creative writing and the role of writers in a globalizing world, which makes it conceivable to read James as the kind of writer that Chamoiseau addresses here: "Today, the author-wayfarer's context is globalization. . . . The writer now finds themself confronted with the world as if standing on the threshold of an immense landscape: an indecipherable landscape with its own impossibilities, its avalanching burdens and vertigo of possibilities and inspirations awaiting definition. The first effect of today's globalization is to thrust the writer or artist into a totalitarian regime of a new kind. . . . I can imagine no true wayfaring towards art that ignores the urgency, dominations, or impossibilities of its time" (3). In the novel's treatment of a number of themes pertinent to globalization and its intersection with cities, it is exactly the kind of creative writing that Chamoiseau argues is essential in today's global context. Additionally, because of its sheer size, broad sweep, and representational ambitions, readings of *A Brief History* are enriched by attention to the novel's engagement with the challenges and opportunities of artistic representation in a globalizing context. In its performative quest to capture an extensive historical arc and associated present-day challenges in one book, *A Brief History* wrestles with and necessarily engages readers in broader questions about literary representation—its challenges, limits, and possibilities—as a place for documenting, exposing, and in some instances charting new ideological terrain. As a discursive companion to scholarly writings, including Chamoiseau's reflections on the impact of current globalization trends, *A Brief History* makes visible the cross-genre and cross-disciplinary conversations that this shifting and demanding global context necessitates.

Because James recovers recent history, and a past well known to many people still living, a number of scholars have written about the parallels between this fictional work and the lived, remembered, and much-talked-about period in postcolonial Jamaica. While I ground my analysis of this work in its context, I read this work strictly as a fictional account but, at the same, as an example of a version of the kind of dangerous artistic creation on which Edwidge Danticat elaborates in her book *Create Dangerously: The Immigrant Artist at Work*. Near the novel's end, James addresses the risks and limitations of writing, an aspect of this work that is deeply intertwined with its global reach.

My central argument is that *A Brief History* presents readers with other ways of understanding the impacts of globalization on urban residents. This novel proposes a more complicated set of negotiations, if not an actual disruption of power, rather than the one-way street of "first world" domination or the paradoxical marginalization of white, working-class people in the United States. Informed by these shifts, I theorize the "third world" urban city space as a sprawling and semicircular space that offers some of the would-be marginalized a space within which to claim their personhood and experience partial social mobility. At the very least, the urban citizens who temporarily take the reins of transnational power allow for a reading of the city as a contested space and of globalization as less unidirectional in the way that it impacts less powerful nations and urban communities and their occupants.

Saskia Sassen's characterization, quoted in the introduction to this book, is helpful in its synthesis of the particular role of cities in the current globalized context: "The city has indeed emerged as a site of new claims: by global capital, which uses the city as an 'organizational commodity,' but also by disadvantaged sectors of the urban population, frequently as much an internationalized presence in large cities as capital. The denationalizing of urban space and the transformation of new claims by transnational actors raise the question, 'whose city is it?'" ("Whose City" 309).

A Brief History is an especially notable representation of the "denationalizing of urban space" because of its explicit treatment of "city-to-city" interactions through the constant global flows of people and of commodities, specifically drugs. In its portrayal of these interactions, the novel dramatizes the undermining and, in some cases, the actual collapse of apparent boundaries and power relationships between wealthier and poorer nations. From the perspective of urban studies, I am mobilizing the term *sprawl* as a way of capturing this novel's treatment of boundaries to characterize how one Global South city space—inner-city Kingston—is represented in *A Brief History*. The term *sprawl* helps me to characterize the literal spreading out of the clandestine economic activities and culture of the fictional Copenhagen City into cities in North America. This sprawl, then, is one way of illuminating the notion of denationalization of cities that Sassen suggests in the preceding quote. Urban sprawl, in the simplest terms, is the literal spreading out or expansion of the city space and its characteristic features beyond previously defined borders. Urban sprawl, as Gregory D. Squires points out, most often includes an expansion of characteristics of particular cities, including the problems inherent to most urban spaces beyond the city's geographic boundaries.[3] Nadia Ellis uses the term *sprawl* to describe both the size and the stylistic and narrative scope of *A Brief History*. The specific sprawl I am suggesting here is the novel's representation of not only the extension of the particular areas of inner-city Kingston—reaching far beyond the borders into the greater Kingston area or even the whole of Jamaica—but also a sprawl of international scope. More specifically, the drug trade, its attendant violence, and its particular dominance of some citizens over others take on global proportions. Notably, it is not the well-known or expected poverty and inequities of cities, which scholars like Squires address, that spill over into other national borders; in James's rendition, it is mostly the assertion of a violent and resilient brand of masculinity and dominance. The men who wield this localized and transnational power are the area "dons," men from among the urban poor who are handpicked by politicians to violently control their urban compatriots. This control is exerted to ensure votes for specific political leaders, whose consolidation of power in a perverted, clientelistic democracy is dependent on the votes of the inner-city residents.[4]

It is this kind of distorted manifestation of urban sprawl that Michael K. Walonen addresses in his 2018 essay "Violence, Diasporic Transnationalism and Neo-imperialism in *A Brief History of Seven Killings*." Describing James's novel in contrast to what he terms "salubrious forms of transnational flow," Walonen argues that "violence in all its different social registers" is a significant element of the "global flow" that James's novel details (2). Walonen also notes that the novel sheds light on one of the ways that Jamaica experiences globalization, suggesting that "Jamaica has been bound up in the transnationalisms of globalization in its exportations of violence" (8). Walonen's observation that James details "a wave of political violence that travels through the Jamaican diaspora and transmutes itself slightly into violence in the service of the informal economy of black-market capitalism" (10) speaks to the nature of the expansion I address through this theorization of sprawl to highlight the role of cities, specifically inner-city areas, in making such transnational flows possible. My use of sprawl here moves the conversation beyond Walonen's valid point about the "exportation of violence" to engage a broader significance of the portrayal of violence: What might James's representation of this "third world" inner-city community tell us about the disruptive potential of the ostensibly economically insignificant national players in the workings of globalization?

The urban sprawl that emerges from the way area dons marshal their power through the drug trade and its ensuing violence highlights both the proverbial "Frankensteinian" outcome of politicians' exploitations of the urban poor and the more complicated picture that James paints in this novel. This portrayal of dons, therefore, disrupts the usual perceptions of the subaltern urban characters as disempowered pawns in the hands of opportunistic politicians or global power brokers, thus complicating the dominant view of globalization as yet another opportunity for the powerful Western countries to further marginalize countries of the Global South. For example, Chamoiseau's framing of the new globalized economic space as "the totalitarian regime" illustrates this prevailing view of globalization as a neocolonial threat to formerly colonized societies, whose people are being constantly squeezed by the heavy weight of large global hegemonic players. However, James crafts characters as both victims *and* perpetrators of the kinds of marginalization that are routinely enacted on poor citizens in urban spaces and in multiple cities, which by their very nature provide space for reinvention. The city—in its enclosed and sprawling iterations—is therefore a paradoxical space because, among other questions, readers must also interrogate their standard understanding of what it means to be marginal: Can we consider urban poor men from "third world" cities marginal when their impact on the economic, social, and political dynamics of these cities is as consequential as James represents them to be in *A Brief History*? A fictional account such as James's, which compels us to problematize our sense of the impact of globalization, makes the anxieties of some of the 2016 voters in the United States plausible, if only partially so, even if their responses were debatable.

One result of these characters' newfound access to power on a transnational scale leads me to the other key concept of this chapter's representation of the city as a semicircular space: while the movement that this sprawl makes possible also, and necessarily, involves the main characters' breaks from poverty and exploitation, because of the unsavory, clandestine, and illegal nature of the transnational relationships they form, the movement—both physical and socioeconomic—is semicircular in a few important ways. Although the main characters often return to their communities, such returns are generally only physical and temporary because the changes in their economic circumstances and the power relationship between them and their fellow city dwellers sets them apart from their communities. Hence, they can no longer truly integrate into these communities. Thus, the main point of semicircularity that I want to explicate here is how the term captures the extent to which residents may escape how they were meant to exist in the urban space only to then confront the limits to such advancements. For these men who have ostensibly escaped the worst of ghetto marginalization, movement does occur, but almost always in the form of a loop or a "virtual return" to a place that is very close to but not quite where they began. Because their movements are a result of the drug trade, with its accompanying violence, movement across cities ("third world" to "first world") tends to aggravate more than ameliorate this despair, mostly flattening the transnational experience of urban dons and their subordinates.

Multiple critics have read *A Brief History* as part of a larger corpus of Caribbean literature that explores specific postcolonial themes; these scholars also read colonial resonances in the events the novel details and the issues it explores.[5] Among these resonances are the colonial-postcolonial connections in James's depiction of urban spaces in inner-city Kingston and the transnational sprawl they create. These simultaneously sprawling and restrictive sites are, in a sense, reincarnations of the plantations of the seventeenth to nineteenth centuries where Africans transported to the "New World" were enslaved. I do not simply mean that there is the presence of the oppressors and the oppressed or that the city space bears the markings of colonization and slavery in unique ways. While these claims are reasonable and relevant, my goal here is to extrapolate two other important parallels that make the point about the sprawling, semicircular city even more remarkable. Like the plantation, these urban locations are spaces of enclosure and limitation. Even as they are part of a larger nation-state, inner-city communities such as those imagined or creatively recuperated as the setting for *A Brief History* restrict their inhabitants in unique ways. Although residents can ostensibly move about the city and beyond in a democratic country, for inner-city residents, movement within and beyond these locales is more complicated than it is in other parts of the city and country. Second, the relationships that elected leaders of these communities encourage among the urban residents ultimately lock the overwhelming majority of these urban citizens in a cycle of violence and dependency. Plantation life was much the same for enslaved peoples: the exploitation of their labor depended on close monitoring and restriction, and violence was the mechanism of both control and survival.

These uniquely inner-city restrictions have emerged as part of multiple conversations about the experiences of the urban citizen, particularly of minority communities in the United States and other industrialized nations. For example, in *The New Jim Crow*, Michelle Alexander argues that urban communities in the United States also function as prisons, as spaces of enclosure. Alexander describes US ghettos as spaces of "hyper-segregation" (64) "constructed to contain and control" (165) the bodies and movements of poor residents of color. Tweaked to address the specifics of different historical and contemporary conditions, the point is applicable to postcolonial, postindependent cities throughout the Global South and, in this case, to Kingston's inner-city communities. In the specific context of *A Brief History*'s fictional Copenhagen City and Eight Lanes communities, poor urban citizens are confined to their communities, not only because of limited access to education, jobs, and other means of social mobility; these citizens are also restricted by the (imposed) political affiliations that render their communities political garrisons, and their neighbors in some nearby communities, enemies. This is because the engineered political culture of these communities bars residents from entering neighboring communities aligned with the rival political party. This particular kind of confinement and exclusion fosters an even more sinister exclusion: it prevents citizens who share the socioeconomic ravages of neocolonialism and globalization from creating potentially empowering alliances.

Extending the genealogy of the constant surveillance that is so endemic to the experiences of enslaved peoples, police patrols, states of emergency, and other restrictions are often put in place to control the movements of the urban citizens in this fictional account. One remarkable point of convergence between urban communities and the plantations where enslaved people were contained is how power is used and its connection to labor exploitation. The overseers' strategic use of enslaved people to control the bodies, movements, and actions of other enslaved people is recovered in *A Brief History* through the representation of politicians' manipulation of specific spaces and their deployment of dons—strong men from among the neighborhoods' people—to destructively manage their neighbors in communities such as Copenhagen City and Eight Lanes.

With that said, *A Brief History* illustrates a clear shift in power and agency among poor urban men. At the same time, because of said structures of power—particularly the nefarious ways in which power and agency are attained by these "leaders," or dons, chosen from among the urban poor—such power is constrained, partial, transient. What amounts to a partial, reprehensible kind of power substantiates Harrison's characterization of *A Brief History* as a novel of despair and hopelessness in which urban dwellers are virtually locked in a cycle of violence, one that is made even more troublesome by its transnational, even global reach. Harrison takes into account how *A Brief History* illustrates "global capitalism at work" and addresses the novel's portrayal of "the impact of the global on the local" ("Global Sisyphus" 89) to demonstrate how urban spaces in newly independent nations are still very much haunted by the ghost of colonization.[6] Fraser reads *A Brief History* along similar lines of hopelessness and futility.[7] Fraser's point that James's depiction underscores the hopelessness of changing the system by working within it is well taken. But beyond the undeniable futility that Fraser addresses in his analysis, the novel also highlights the fact that those who are designated to be at the bottom of this global capitalist system can exercise agency only if they create a parallel system. I mean parallel in two ways: existing alongside the official economic modes of trade, travel, and organizational structure but also parallel in its own form of brutality, cruelty, and destructiveness.[8]

If we stop at the debilitating circumstances of postcolonial and postindependence urban life that the novel details, Fraser's and Harrison's readings of the novel as a work depicting futility and despair are undeniably accurate; in this case, the novel undoubtedly inscribes a circle back to where enslaved and indentured people began in this "New World" Caribbean space. However, even if we read the depictions in the novel as modern iterations of enslaved people's experiences, as these and other critics have suggested, part of what must be taken into account is how enslaved people responded to the conditions in which they were made to exist. With that fuller picture in mind, I find the term *semicircularity* to be useful in capturing the novel's representation of a postcolonial urban subject. Despair and futility are valid characterizations, but these terms do not go far enough to convey the range of experiences the characters undergo and, even more importantly, their response to such experiences. Reading the novel in this way highlights the author's depiction of the capacity of the urban poor—one segment of a present-day population that faces the (re)newed onslaught of colonially induced capitalism—to not only survive but also find spaces of resistance. In this way, the novel draws on a long tradition—going back to the plantation of enslavement—of undermining systems set up to keep those who are rendered lower-class (enslaved, peasant, or urban poor) locked in cycles of dependency and marginalization. That is to say that, in addition to highlighting a sustained presence of colonialism that Fraser, Harrison, and others address, I am also interested in the possibilities for empowerment among the former political underdogs. In this way, then, my reading of *A Brief History* moves beyond the sheer enclosure, the shocking representation, the "excess amount" of brutality that this work fictionalizes to address a wider spectrum of marginalized people's responses to exclusions.

Semicircularity serves as a useful conceptual anchor for my reading of this work, because although there is a trajectory of change, there is no celebratory triumph or redemptive "I made it out of the ghetto as a wholesome, upstanding citizen" story here in James's depiction. His novel affirms the agency of the oppressed and some possibilities that exist in today's globalized world economy to disrupt (oppressive) established systems. Thus, James configures resistance and agency in the fissures of global capitalist and transnational criminal organizations, showing how subaltern urban citizens, ostensibly used to further the will of Western powers and local politicians, undermine these debilitating systems, even as they turn on each other as the enslaved people did in James's *The Book of Night Women*. Through this representation, then, *A Brief History* forces us to open ourselves to the possibilities of a wider range of understanding and definitions of agency, power, and what it means to be marginal. Because while the standard view of "first world–third world" relations holds that there is an imbalance of power tipped in favor of dominant countries, the cities' dynamic underbelly allows for a constant renegotiation of power and even diverse ways of conceiving of empowerment. In this global landscape, powerful countries must constantly defend their turf through surveillance via their standard criminal-justice systems and, as the novel illustrates, through their covert operations. Although only a few leaders undermine this system in these ways, the scope of their impact on another global, powerful city is illustrative of the disruptive capacity for which I am arguing here.

Power, Agency, and Control Revisited

The inherently Janus-faced nature of cities as sites that foster self-fashioning, invention, reinvention, and renewal but also ruin and ongoing marginalization is especially meaningful to a reading of *A Brief History* and for the ways

I theorize cities in this book. The semicircularity of the city, its constant (virtual) loop back to decay and marginalization, is most usefully addressed through an examination of the sociopolitical and physical space from which the stories that James tells proceed. This is part of the backdrop that Harrison offers in her analysis of the novel. Among the three hauntings that Harrison isolates in *A Brief History* is the "fall of Balaclava City" ("Global Sisyphus" 87), a recurrent plotline of the novel, which appears as frequently as it does in the novel to keep in focus how some characters eventually come to understand the roots of their current sociopolitical conditions. Mentioned over a dozen times in the novel, the literal flattening of the old Balaclava City is significant to this argument because this recurring aspect of the novel's plot calls into question the notion of renewal, showing how the literal cityscape functions as the ground on which old modes of colonial subjugation are reinforced.[9]

It is this connection between old and new modes of disempowerment that shapes the interaction between the American writer who in the 1990s is gathering material to write about the events of the 1970s and Tristan Phillips, the incarcerated former gang member from Kingston. Phillips paints a picture for the journalist, who is intent on learning more about Copenhagen City, insisting that the two places, the old Balaclava City and Copenhagen City, are inseparable as sites of postcolonial debasement:

> But how you going know about peace if you don't know what start the war in the first place.? . . . Picture it, white boy. Two standpipe. Two bathroom. Five thousand people. No toilet. No running water. House that hurricane rip apart only for it to come back together like magnet was the thing holding it in place. And then look at what surrounding it. The largest dump at Bumper Hall, the Garbagelands where they now have a high school. The slaughterhouse draining blood down the streets right to the gully. The largest sewage treatment plant so uptown people can flush they shit straight down to we. (James, *A Brief History* 452)

As a city space that embodies the socioeconomic debris of colonialism, the former Balaclava was ground zero for postcolonial squalor; paradoxically, like many other homes for the urban poor in Kingston, the current Copenhagen City is a destination for rural migrants seeking jobs and the fulfillment of other dreams that the city promises to help them realize. Yet, as James's character Don Papa-Lo makes clear, in spite of the socioeconomic deficit apparent in the lack of access to clean water, privacy, basic sanitation, and other conditions characteristic of urban squalor, this is also a space of opportunity for politicians. Outlining the way this otherwise-sterile social space emerges as fertile ground for political exploitation, Papa-Lo, as don of the former Balaclava City and the first major don of the new Copenhagen City, offers what reads like a sociological perspective:

Nineteen sixty-six. No man who enter 1966 leave the way he come in. The fall
of Balaclava take plenty, even those who support it. I did support, not quiet but
loud. Balaclava was a piece of shit that make you beg for the richness of a
tenement yard. Balaclava was where woman would dodge murder, robbery and
rape only to get killed by a cup of water. Balaclava get bulldozed down so that
Copenhagen City could rise and when the politicians come in after the
bulldozers with their promises they also demand that we drive all PNP man
out. Before 1966, man from Denham Town and man from Jungle didn't really
like each other, but they fight each other on the football field and on the cricket
pitch and even when two boy get rowdy and a mouth get punch bloody, there
was no war or rumour of war. But then politician come. Me welcome them
because surely better must come for we too. (89)

This extended commentary from Papa-Lo lays out very clearly the stakes, culpa-
bility, and more subtly, the power negotiations that the change in economic circumstances made possible for the ones like Papa-Lo and Josey Wales, one of the
main gang leaders and political activists who controlled this inner-city community. These men, whom the politician chooses from among the residents to consolidate and sustain power, are allowed to exist on an empowerment-marginalization
continuum. The exchange of peace and free will for economic survival is apparent, but the tone of the passage and inclusions such as "there was no war or
rumour of war" suggest that there is nostalgia for the past, a recognition of the
cost of "urban renewal" as well as an acknowledgment of the privileges that
the community "leaders" now enjoy. And the closing line, "Me welcome them
because surely better must come for we too," is notable. While the sarcastic reference to the opposing political party's slogan would appear to be the main critique
here, with this statement, Papa-Lo makes a more far-reaching comment about
the residents' necessary reliance on politicians to improve the quality of their
lives; the tone also suggests an inevitable surrender to a system that offers equally
debilitating options for the poor inhabitants of this city space. When he admits
to making what at face value feels like a choice, Papa-Lo articulates the paradoxical helplessness and empowerment that urban men with constrained power experience. As this passage embeds the agency of the formerly downtrodden such as
Papa-Lo and those whom he would eventually bring into the fold, the subtext of
being cornered with these two almost equally abhorrent choices—remain in
squalor or become a pawn for exploitative politicians—makes clear the conundrum of the urban poor in the new capitalist milieu.

 Much of *A Brief History* is devoted to examining the consequences of this
no-choice choice that urban citizens have been offered, because even as readers
witness the brutality of characters such as enforcers Josey Wales and Weeper and
are reminded of the past sins of the mostly repentant and reformed Papa-Lo, the
context that passages such as those just quoted provide and the persistent ghostly

presence of the late politician Sir Arthur Jennings consistently complicates the narrative.[10] Keeping the past in the foreground provides a constant reminder that also casts these hardened criminals as victims not only of a longer history of colonization but, more pointedly and immediately, of contemporary local and global constraints. Wales, who succeeds Papa-Lo as the politician's point man and is arguably the novel's least sympathetic character, lays out the situation in the following way:

> People think that I have animosity towards Papa-Lo. Me have nothing but love for the man. . . . But this is ghetto. In ghetto there is no such thing as peace. . . . You have people living in the ghetto who can only see within it. From me was a young boy all I could see was outside it. I wake up looking out, I go to school and spend the whole day looking out the window, I go up to Maresceaux Road and stand right at the fence that separate . . . Kingston from St. Andrew, uptown from downtown, those who have it and those who don't. People with no plan wait and see. People with a plan see and wait for the right time. The world is not a ghetto and a ghetto is not the world. People in the ghetto suffer because there be people who live for making them suffer. Good time is bad time for somebody too. (416)

With a portrait such as this one, painted by the most notorious gang leader in the novel, readers are compelled to consider the making of a drug lord and how, as Papa-Lo, Wales, and the imprisoned Tristan Phillips reflect on the ghetto, the urban space is presented as an engineered space—a construction put in place to advance the political ambitions of people who have not, and will not, live there. By reflecting on his childhood, with his ever-outward-looking orientation and the suggested thirst for better, Wales forces readers to consider his context, to see him as a victim, even as we watch him consolidate his own power through equally brutal acts of violence.

The "disenfranchisement" and "dependency" that Edwards addresses is illustrative of the "first world–third world" model that the unscrupulous politicians use to exploit the urban poor, whose experiences bear the combined negative consequences of the impacts of postcolonialism and globalization. As Bam Bam, one of Papa-Lo's protegees, explains, "Two men bring guns to the ghetto. . . . I grow up in Copenhagen City and watch the guns change and know they don't come from Papa-Lo. They come from two men who bring guns to the ghetto and the one who show me how to use it. We the Syrian, the American and Doctor Love out by the shack near the sea" (9, 15). The presence of "the Syrian," a local politician; the American, a "first world" representative; and Doctor Love, another foreigner who also happens to be a CIA agent, makes clear the convergence of local and global interests that share a stake in the control and manipulation of poor urban youth. With Papa-Lo first and then Wales as more influential puppets, the stage seems set for a tight control of marginalized urban residents. However, my central point here is that while all of this was unfolding—and as the observations of Chamoiseau, Edwards, and others reflect—of equal importance in this work is the space that such uneven power relationships open for parallel power structures and even a destabilization of the official postcolonial Western country–Global South country relationship.

Papa-Lo articulates a similar connection between foreign and local marginalization:

> The Singer tell me a story. How back when reggae was something only a few people know, how white rock and roll star was him friend. . . . But as soon as the Natty Dread sing hit songs and break the Babylon top 100, everybody start treat him a way. They like him better when he was a poor cousin that they can feel good for taking notice. I tell him that politician do the same thing to me when they realize me can read. In 1966 they carve up Kingston and never ask we what slice we want. . . . Me fight hard until me get tired. I raise the men who now run with Josey Wales. . . . I swell Copenhagen City two times it size. (90)

What Papa-Lo explains here makes clear what all subalterns experience or are vulnerable to experiencing in their different spheres, whether such exploitation emanates from white foreigners or local politicians who exert class and sometimes color privilege. Additionally, part of what this passage highlights is the absence of a reward or any kind of recognition of equality. In such cases, not only are material rewards thwarted, but the people's personhood is also always undermined.

With this standard approach to relationships with working-class urban citizens, the way James configures characters—Wales, in particular—instantiates the unforeseen limits of the assumed powerful to exert full control over the urban citizens. In this regard, Wales's strategic use of the power he earned as a politician's strongman complicates the narrative about the place of small countries in a globalized world. More specifically, James's representation sheds a somewhat different kind of light on the role of "third world," inner-city residents—among the most oppressed—in the new global capitalist apparatus. The possibility that a politician's exploitation of these citizens can create access to a globalized world produces an unintended and unexpected consequence of a somewhat twisted kind of empowerment. The access to foreign modes of economic engagement, trade routes, and understanding of transnational negotiations that Wales gains from his relationship (facilitated by the politician Peter Nasser) with Doctor Love and other foreigners provide him with the tools to launch his multinational drug cartel.

Shifting Power Balances

Josey Wales's remark that "people with no plan wait and see. People with a plan see and wait for the right time" (James, *A Brief History* 416) sets up his ultimate break from Peter Nasser to become his own different, but in some ways similar, kind of leader—a choice that illustrates both the semicircularity of this representation of the city and a (partial) shift in power relationships. The clientelistic system of politics that political scientists such as Carl Stone and Carlene Edie theorize is at the heart of the portrayal of the relationships among Nasser, Papa-Lo, and Wales. Nasser is the politician who represents the former Back-O-Wall and the person also responsible for the "renewal" of this particularly debased urban space. Nasser installs Wales as his informal representative—the "strongman" who controls the area. Part of what James's depiction demonstrates here is that such relationships are much more complicated than they sometimes appear to be, that the power dynamics are fraught with distrust and simmering grievances, and that they shift over time. Thus, the control that politicians exercise over these urban gang leaders has a proverbial shelf life. For example, Demus, one of the members of Wales's gang, reports that Wales tells him that he has "bigger plans": "is high time we done be ghetto stooge for white man who live uptown and don't care about we until election time" (57). Beyond the obvious—that there is agency in what appears to be a strategic use of urban citizens to control and terrorize each other—there is the return of "plans," which intimates that this agency will transcend any politician's use of Wales and others acting as proxies for politicians. More pointedly, in reference to Nasser, the politician to whom Wales answers, Wales asserts, "truth be told, both he and I know that I long past the days when politician say jump and I say how high. Now when politician say jump, my woman say he can't come to the phone right now but I will take a message" (400). And just in case readers miss the import of this moment in the way this novel asks us to think about the postcolonial, urban-grounded system of power, Wales adds, "Talk about fool, what do you think was going to happen once you give a man with a head a gun, that he was going to return it? Even Papa-Lo wasn't so fool" (400). Even as this passage unmasks James's authorial insertion, Wales's point is fundamental to the discourse on power relationships in this novel and the unique role of cities in complicating narratives about power relationships. The passage underscores the historical basis of the novel and validates some critics' reading of *A Brief History* through the lens of postcolonial and postindependence experiences and discourse. The drug lord's forceful self-assertion here—choosing not to answer the phone and do the politicians' bidding and claiming a sharper intellect by calling Nasser a fool and himself "man with a head"—reinforces the link between politicians and violence and illustrates how politicians' intended subordinates carve agency out of the politicians' initial violence and disregard for citizens in urban communities.

A major plotline in this work is the much-talked-about attempt on the Singer's life. On closer examination of this subplot, readers can come to appreciate that it is through Wales's involvement in this complicated multi- and transnational assassination plot that he develops his acumen to successfully launch his own transnational and international drug trade and his own reign of terror. Strikingly, too, Nasser later loses control of Wales, whom the novel presents as the chief architect of the plan to assassinate the Singer. This is the job (killing the Singer) that first connects Wales to Doctor Love, who is also one of Wales's links to a world of crime beyond inner-city Kingston. What appears to be Wales's deliberate choice to shoot but not kill the Singer and his people is one of his major early acts of agency and one that convinces him that he has an intellect greater than that of Nasser, who is formally well educated; this realization in turn gives Wales further impetus to wrest himself from Nasser's control:

> It's a bitch of a thing . . . that though you're the only one who didn't go to top-class school and foreign college, you is the only man in the room with any sense. I really wanted to educate this ignorant, bad-chatting, Syrian shithouse. That it's bad enough that plenty man and woman have the Singer off as a prophet, but kill him and the man graduate to martyr. . . . I shoot that man off the pedestal and he fall back down to man size. I didn't tell Peter Nasser any of that. You have to look past a man, below the skin to the real skin to know that for all the whiteness . . . Peter Nasser is just another ignorant Naigger. But at least he was calling me busha these days. I must ask my woman when exactly I change into white man who drink at Mayfair hotel. (399–400)

Part of the power dynamics that *A Brief History* explores here and over the course of the novel is the huge advantage that wit and intellect potentially bestow. This moment is pivotal, even transformative, because it marks a point when Wales claims intellectual superiority to assert his personhood. While he returns to the remnants of colonialism that got him to the place he is now—an assumed puppet of the recast colonizer Nasser—in his inclusion of race and the uneven class system that persist, Wales excavates dignity, which seems to be at the heart of his quest. Getting Nasser to call him "Busha," a title that harks back to slavery, marks a dramatic turn of fortunes. The fact that the white man, for whom Wales ostensibly serves as Johnny Jumper, or foreman, is the one who ascribes the title that was historically reserved for the plantation owner to Wales is an obvious "crowning moment" for him.[11] Yet there are multiple layers of irony here: the entitlement only exists within the context of a seedy, parallel political system in which the work of one such as Wales cannot be publicly acknowledged because of its vicious, illegal, and covert nature. The question of whether one can even call this a genuine change of fortunes therefore arises. But if this change is read as a point of man-to-man respect, then Wales makes some meaningful gains out of the service he has given—the respect and acknowledgment of personhood that is as important to men in the urban context represented in this novel as is their economic mobility.

A Twisted Global Machinery

At the time of the novel's setting, the late twentieth-century iteration of globalization was in full motion; the global squeeze on poorer countries was becoming increasingly tight, making residents in places such as Copenhagen City all the more vulnerable to politicians such as Peter Nasser. Consequently, the disenfranchisement that Chamoiseau and Edwards feared had, in many ways, become the lived experiences of Global South citizens, with a particularly debilitating impact on urban citizens. Additionally, because of the strategic interests that the United States had in the local affairs of Jamaica, part of the transnational-global crossing that *A Brief History* fictionalizes is the US CIA's interference in local (Jamaican) politics. This local-global alliance unmasks the close links between local politicians' interest in controlling urban citizens and the interest of a global power in ensuring the victory of a political party that is more closely aligned to its ideologies.

In James's rendition, it is at this historical moment that Josey Wales finds the space, experience, and agency to extend the system for the illicit drug trade that he had developed on the ground in Kingston's inner city into an international franchise; here he expands and consolidates power that he had been plotting to acquire since he was a boy thinking about a "plan." The hint of power negotiation that Papa-Lo outlines in his reflections quoted earlier, the pushback from Wales on the dismantling of Balaclava, the making of Copenhagen City, and the intellectual superiority that Wales proclaims are yet other instances of a recourse to his talk of "having a plan." This plan unfolds when Wales converts what was a political machine with the purpose of ensuring one politician's control over a particular urban space and the co-opting of a foreign agency such as the CIA into his own transnational drug trade, with all its accompanying guns and violence.

Furthermore, once Wales becomes integrated into this transnational trade, his relationship with his business partners presents him with the opportunity to be more than simply a disgruntled second fiddle to Nasser. His attitude toward his work with the Columbian cartel makes clear that at the heart of this move away from political activism is a larger quest for personhood and agency. Once he gets into the drug trade, where he is expected to be an adjunct to the Columbians, a similar resistance to being managed and an insistence on having command over his turf and the trade surface: "I say to Doctor Love, who also call me that night, that I done deal with proving things to people from 1966 and if they really think this is prep school where they feel they must test and test, then Medellin can go right back to using those batty boys in Bahamas" (James, *A Brief History* 400). Here Wales reveals a deeper understanding of the power landscape that he must navigate; this is a context in which being a "stooge" for politicians such as Nasser and an underdog in the drug trade are decidedly out of the question. What ensues from Wales's decision to act on the plans he had been orchestrating since he was a boy observing the postcolonial inequities is a multicity, multinational drug cartel in which he is a central player. His insistence on taking the skills he developed as Nasser's enforcer and the founder of a locally run drug transshipment agency to what he believes to be a level befitting his intellectual capacities is, in large part, a carefully orchestrated move to recover his personhood.

For a long time after Wales opens his own transnational business, he lives in Kingston and does not travel, even as the other characters who manage different branches of his business are dispersed across the United States. By locating the characters under Wales's command in multiple cities, James offers us a nuanced representation of Kingston as well as the "first world's" cities. Paradoxically then, particularly because of Wales reengineering of this locale as his own underground marketplace, these sites provide a space within which said system of economic imperialism is disrupted; thus, some of the main actors in the movement of bodies, goods, and drugs within these city spaces emerge as those who were intended to remain the marginalized descendants of enslaved peoples and as pawns in a clientelistic relationship with local politicians. These would-be marginalized residents of urban areas stage a covert takeover of the economic machinery in which drugs and therefore the "illegal" drug industry emerge from within their own global marketplace. In this new scenario, some of the urban citizens who were supposed to be left behind, to not be on the globalization train, are the conductors, drivers, and engineers on those trains. The creation of markets—trade routes, so to speak, in the designated official global marketplace—ironically facilitates this parallel system, along with an unexpected and unwelcome set of leaders.

Relatedly, one of the ideas used to support the "postcolonial perspective" that globalization "is one of the most powerful forces fueling imperialism" (J. Edwards 161) is the way globalization, through its empowerment of wealthy countries, reinscribes colonial notions of center and margin. Exemplifying James's complication of these accurate but incomplete characterizations of globalization, once Wales wrests himself from being Nasser's political strongman and from being a deputy for the Columbian drug cartel, his location in Kingston shows how such taken-for-granted ideas about margin and center are disrupted. As Phillips tells the writer interviewing him in prison, "Him [Wales] and this man name Eubie who be here since 1979 selling weed and coke, almost turn they dealing into a legit business. Almost. I told, you the one thing about Storm Posse why they will always be bigger than Ranking Dons, is that them boys have ambition. They got plans. Man in here tell me that Storm Posse running things in New York, D.C., Philly and Baltimore. . . . Since I in prison them push all the Cubans back down to Miami" (565). The passage conveys more than the long reach of Wales's transnational operation. Phillips's adoption of the language of business is notable. His rhetorical positioning and understanding of the stakes involved are salient here. His choice of words such as "ambition" and "having plans" ostensibly fits the narrative and expectations of progress as articulated in the mainstream business parlance in the global capitalist structure. The comparison to another drug cartel and the "pushing out of the Cubans" to Miami resonate with mainstream business practices and expectations around competition. Strikingly, it is after six years of commanding this business that Wales arrives in New York, which is one of his cartel's key operations sites—a detail that illustrates the centering of Kingston as the hub of the illegal drug operation. And while Wales commands from Kingston, his man on the ground in New York easily passes as a mainstream businessman—in wearing a business suit and silk handkerchief and in the way he comports himself—or, at worst, a pimp (but never a drug dealer). Eubie's ability to seamlessly move through New York City and elude association with the illicit drug trade is another illustration of the permeability of the official global capitalist structure that has been established to curtail the movement—physical as well as socioeconomic—of poor urban people.

Listening in on Wales's phone call from his base in Kingston, readers are brought back yet again to his reflection on his childhood and his suggestion that he is one of those with a plan who waited for the right time to break free from a politician's control. The result of his waiting is a masterful transfer of the skills he gained as the politician's strongman, albeit in a subordinate position. While he is on the phone in Kingston, Wales outlines the tight organization that he has successfully managed:

When a man have to skip borough just to get two or three packet that sound like a problem. Make me tell you, in the Bronx me run a tight ship, even from the days me just 'lowing little weed. Back in 1979 me set things up like any business, better than any shop because I know from the devil was boy that you can never expand if you core base didn't set right. I don't take kindly to no kind of slackness. . . . You know what me tell the last man who fuck up? Me give him a choice, me say to him, my youth, this is what I going do for you. You get to choice [sic] which eye you want to lose, the right or the left . . . and what go for Bronx also go for Queens. (494–495)

Without the context of the drug trade that the novel provides and the hint in the last few lines, this passage could convey the sentiments of a legitimate, even admirable approach to business. Wales runs a "tight ship" with no "slackness," talks about his need to "expand," and uses standard business terms such as "core." Wales manages a space from which he is physically absent, yet he is able to apply the same rules set in place by the global capitalist system in which he was only supposed to be a pawn.

Through Wales's articulation of his business "ethics," the transnational drug trade is presented as a business like those sanctioned by the big global players, and therefore it requires a similar kind of management: "Brethren, New York look like a monopoly to you? Ranking Dons, Blood Crew and Hot Steppers all want a piece of each street and that's just the Jamaicans. You don't supply they find another supplier, simple as that. And then thanks to people who think like you, I have to come to New York and put everything back in its natural order" (468). In his choice of terms and phrases such as "I let him take over Miami," "I have to come to New York and put everything back in its natural order," and "they know they can't set foot in the Bronx or in Queens" (550), Wales not only suggests but explicitly asserts a control and domination of the physical and economic spaces. These articulations illustrate how, in this parallel economic system where these men operate almost in the clear light of day—and in the case of Wales, mostly from a kind of satellite location—leaders with the wherewithal, the plan, as Wales frames it, can exert control and reterritorialize North American city spaces. It is this parallel system of trade and governance that establishes the collapse of spatial boundaries, the sprawl of inner-city Kingston over into mostly North American cities, resulting in the flattening or leveling of the sociocultural city space. In the scenario where Wales's control is so significant, the differences between Copenhagen City and the Bronx, Queens, Miami, and other cities where the drug lords and former area dons exert their power diminish; official control over city spaces is drastically reduced, and the level of control of assumed global players is equally compromised.

That sense of control and the capacity to coordinate a business that Wales projects, along with his transcendence of the system designed to marginalize him, is perhaps most apparent in his reflections on Eubie:

Eubie in the Bronx. People can't understand why I check for that brethren. . . . Hard to like a man who cut him hair every two week, talk like he stay in a posh high school for the full seven years and always wear silk suit. . . . But here is the reasoning nobody catch: If people busy thinking that you is a pimp no body going think you is a drug dealer. Eubie is a school boy and that make him think he have class. And him do, a little. Boy all set for Columbia law school but leave because he wise up about law. Eubie perfectly fine in Queens and the Bronx and I let him take over Miami from Weeper. (466–467)

Wales—whose class position rendered him useful to a politician because of the perception that his lack of education and other requisites made him incapable of navigating the official system of global, or even local, commerce—emerges as the one who manages someone educated in the very system Wales would never be able to enter: Eubie was set to attend law school at an Ivy League university, which implies that he has matriculating credentials, with a background that we can safely assume was strong enough to get him to Columbia Law School. And here he is the point man for the (formally) uneducated man, who is a product of the inner city.

Michael K. Walonen pits some aspects of globalization in James's novel against the intended goals and in many instances the realities of official global movements:

> The diasporas of our contemporary era are a key part of the intricate system of interconnections, transfers, and exchanges that have been steadily reconfiguring the societies of our world on a more global scale since the 1970s to a greater degree than ever before possible. This system of globalizing "flows" is commonly conceived of in terms of the cross-border movement of people; expressive and material culture; money, in the form of foreign investment and remittances in particular; and ideas that move through the digital mass media and through diasporic intellectual networks, or what social scientists sometimes call, in contrast to the popular concept of brain drain, "brain circulation." (1–2)

However, James draws attention to a less salubrious form of transnational flow that may also circulate through the diasporic networks of the world of neoliberal globalization: that of violence in all its different social registers, from means of social control to response to the traumas of past violence.

Walonen's claim about the exportation of violence is illustrated in Wales's statement about the consequences of falling out of line. Undoubtedly, as Walonen argues in his essay, globalization has engendered movement of a plethora of ideas, goods, and services that have disrupted the official global marketplace, and the drug trade is central to this disruption. The parallel system that I introduced earlier is part of this "global flow" (in the form of violence) that Walonen reads as a key element of James's treatment of globalization in *A Brief History*; this is the dramatic shift that illustrates that the outflow of goods and services and culture and its resulting power are only part of the story of globalization. Furthermore, the Kingston–New York drug network illustrates how the contributions that smaller countries make in this entangled network exponentially change the landscape of the countries that are supposed to make the rules, resulting in a reverse globalization in which power is interrupted or constrained, if only at an informal level.

The significance of Walonen's contention about the reverberation of violence across international lines is an important marker of the city sprawl under consideration here. This observation is further illustrated in the experience of Nina Burgess/Dorcas Palmer/Millicent Segree, the woman who has spent years hiding from Wales because she was a witness to his shooting of the Singer and members of his team.[12] The difficulty this woman experiences as she attempts to escape being killed by Wales illustrates not only his power but also the extent to which Copenhagen City has extended itself globally. When she operates under the identity of the nurse Millicent Segree, Nina Burgess notices a steady flow of Jamaicans coming into the New York City hospital where she works and soon learns that the shootings that took place in New York were reprisals for the killing of Benjy Wales, the son of Josey Wales, the man she had been trying to elude for well over a decade. Noting that what happens in Jamaica—Kingston, in particular—is "spilling into Bronx" (615), Millicent ask a series of questions that underscore not only the power of an incarcerated gang leader in Kingston to negatively impact lives in New York City, one of the "first world's" premier cities, but also, and more importantly, the interconnectedness of these cities. She wonders, "If all this is true why . . . am I in Jamaican Bronx? Corsa, Fenton, Boston, Girvan, you might as well call the whole place Kingston 21" (615).[13] Kezia Page has theorized the diasporic reach of Kingston in similar ways, as "almost Kingston but not quite." Page further explains, "The term [Kingston 21] was coined by Jamaicans in Jamaica to explain the 'scattering' and 'planting' of Jamaica abroad. Kingston 21 signifies Kingston expanded" (6). This is the urban sprawl that the careful unfolding of Josey Wales's expanded drug cartel illustrates to ultimately make visible the way this novel exposes the global reach of urban Kingston.

This sprawl of Kingston beyond its physical and official geopolitical boundaries marks a significant disruption of demarcations and exclusions. The "spatial exclusion" of urban citizens is one of the primary ways in which the poor continue to experience the impact of colonization in its revamped form, as globalization. As the work of Alexander, quoted earlier, demonstrates, keeping the bodies of urban citizens in their designated spaces is essential to sustaining socioeconomic disparities. *A Brief History* painstakingly illustrates how such exclusions have been impeded: not only are boundaries, or lines of exclusion, crossed, but also whole spaces are taken over, in the way that Josey Wales explains his control of parts of New York City. The result from such subversive takeovers is an undermining of the level of control that leaders of powerful countries have historically sought to exercise over colonized spaces and the people living in these locations. And paradoxically, it is the global network, with its efforts to simultaneously open the marketplace and keep small countries—and, even more so, poor urban citizens—in their designated places, that has opened the door for the upending of the neocolonial project.

Writing the Sprawling City

I now turn attention to the specific and larger questions about representation that James tackles in his rendition of this period in Jamaican and transnational history. The central point that Chamoiseau makes in his essay about the state of globalization and its corollaries is that the role and significance of creative writers is even more important in the current globalization moment. That point is worth restating here: "I can imagine no true wayfaring toward art that ignores the urgency, dominations, and impossibilities of its time" (5). As one of the most well-known novelistic voices of the moment, James engages in this necessary wayfaring in, among other features, the way he fictionalizes a different kind of urban sprawl through the expansion of the drug trade, violence, and the iron rule of inner-city Kingston's local area dons turned transnational drug cartel managers but also through specific engagement with the act and process of writing.

It is hard, if not impossible, to read *A Brief History of Seven Killings* and not be impacted by its style and the novel's narrative performativity. Nadia Ellis's review essay, titled "Marlon James's Savage Business," and Sherie-Marie Harrison's rejoinder in "Excess in *A Brief History of Seven Killings*" are two of the foremost early reflections on this novel to take up the questions of style. Ellis refers to the novel as "an idiosyncratic, highly formalistic piece of historical fiction" and argues that "the virtuosic polyphony of the book does create an occasionally bewildering sense of sprawl—there isn't really a center to the novel" (3). Furthermore, Ellis contends, "James's use of multiple voices in *A Brief History* can feel dizzying in its frequent shifts, baroque and self-conscious in its experimentation, and sometimes opaque even to a speaker of Jamaican Patois" ("Excess" 4). Harrison argues in her piece that *A Brief History*'s formal complexity is inseparable from its "poetics of excess." She sees more purpose to James's excess and overall style than does Ellis and passes the following verdict on the novel: "James' 'poetics of excess' intervenes in this decoupling tendency by displacing the centrality of discrete nationalism in Caribbean narratives and creating wild and risky new possibilities for thinking about the region's place in our contemporary reality" (6). While these two early critical responses evaluate the novel in different ways, they both observe that *A Brief History* is a different kind of Caribbean novel that has the potential to chart new formal pathways; it *does*, as Ellis notes, "create an occasional bewildering sense of sprawl" (2). This novel performatively—and necessarily, I would argue—engages in excess.

Taking these early reflections as points of departure, I contend that *A Brief History* is as much about writing as it is about the events of the period from 1970 to 1979, the place of Jamaica and other small nations in the new global space, transnational violence, and so forth. The novel tackles with comparable force the problem of representation and, more specifically, the challenge of writing about the sprawling, semicircular city in the era of a complicated globalization. *A Brief History* grapples very explicitly with the conundrum of the writer in the global context. Thus, the violence, the "excess amount" of many things, is a performance staged to engage readers in a conversation, to invite them to wrestle with a variety of questions: How does one write about all of this? Is fiction adequate? How far will writers get if they work within their established (though still growing) local literary traditions? And, even more thought-provoking, Can one even tell the stories of these sprawling cities?

A closer look at the range of characters developed in the novel highlights the reflexive engagement with writing and the related performativity of this work. Although Bill Bilson is listed among the cast of characters, it is Alex Pierce, the *Rolling Stone* journalist, whose character and point of view are extensively explored in the last few chapters of the novel. In this final section of the novel, Pierce is writing a multiple-part story titled "A Brief History of Seven Killings" for the *New Yorker*. At one point near the end of the novel, Pierce comes home to find Eubie, Ren Dog, and other Storm Posse members waiting for him in his kitchen. Through their interrogation of Pierce, readers learn that the main purpose of their visit is to challenge his authorial rights by telling him to change the story he is writing: "Part four: T-Ray Benitez and the Jamdown Connection. You send this in yet?" And to Pierce's affirmative response comes the Storm Posse member's retort and command, "Too bad. Because you going to call them right now and make a whole heap o' changes" (James, *A Brief History* 661). In another exchange, one Storm Posse member tells Pierce, "All this shit you write about Storm Posse, most of this shit not even true. For one Funnyboy is from the Eight Lanes and him still there, so there's no way he could be Storm Posse" (672). They even tell Pierce, "You writing a brief history of seven killings, right? Then you have four more killings to write about" (675). They instruct Pierce, "You go back to writing your *Brief History of Seven Killings*" (678).

The self-reflexivity of four chapters in the last eighty pages of the novel at least complicates, or even casts doubt on, the stories that James has been telling. The fact that the gang members ambush, confront, torture, and threaten Pierce in order to force him to revise his story is striking; thus, James's meta-narrative engagement makes visible the challenges of telling this story of the expansive, semicircular city. More importantly, these closing scenes link readers back to all the novel's formal choices and its narrative excesses. The fact that even after much research, many interviews, and cultural emersion, Pierce is not allowed to write the stories he thinks he has collected is noteworthy. Moreover, he has to write the version that these gangsters, who have a vested interest in the representation of history, want represented in written form. In setting up these scenes, then, James implies that the task of writing is a difficult one, that having full control over what gets written and eventually published is unlikely, and that interference of some kind is inevitable. All this is to say, then, that James's narrative extends beyond what Harrison suggests is his homage to the Chilean novelist Robert Bolaño's *The Savage Detectives* and even beyond his possible charting of fresh, formal possibilities ("Excess," 1).

A Brief History of Seven Killings demonstrates that the quest to tell stories about the place of one particular "third world," inner-city community within the context of a global economic framework is vast, that the task might be as unwieldy as the tales that need to be told, and that ultimately the telling is necessarily an act of inventiveness. Authors often "create dangerously," as Edwidge Danticat outlines, and sometimes they write to save their lives. Pierce manages to get some of his story out but must halt, adjust, revise, and even fabricate a new version of his story as a way to live to tell more stories or at least some parts and versions of more stories. Thus, the semicircularity for which I argue here extends beyond the city-globalization experience to also include a characterization of writing: though the fictional writer Pierce makes some gains in telling these stories, in complicating these representations of cities, he does not make it all the way; he manages to write and publish three sections of his representation, but the rest of the seven killings, the other four, though not eliminated can only be told in an adulterated fashion. Therefore, even with a "multiple-part story" in the *New Yorker*, in this big sprawling book, with all its excesses, the book and the telling have their limits. Thus, one of the main points that James makes about writing in general in the last section of his book is that to tell stories does not necessarily require truth or complete accuracy—that this novel is, after all, a work of art, fiction—and that more important than accuracy is the engagement with the pressing exigencies. In another sense, with the inclusion of these closing chapters in which the writer literally fights for his life and his right to tell stories, *A Brief History* also makes a case for the necessity of fiction as a way for writers to carry out their creative wayfaring—because fiction keeps important issues at the fore and also frees them from the shackles of accuracy and potentially keeps them alive to tell more stories.

5

A Door Ajar

■■■■■■■■■■■■■■■■■■■■■

Reading and Writing Toronto
in Cecil Foster's *Sleep On,
Beloved*

Two contrasting entries into the city of Toronto—one experiential, the other fictional—capture my theorization of creative accounts of the city in this chapter. In the summer of 2015, I, along with members of my immediate family, embarked on a journey to Toronto. This trip was driven in part by the research for this chapter and the larger project, but it was also driven by the quest to fulfill a long-harbored desire to experience the world's largest Caribbean festival outside the region and to reconnect with other West Indians in this city that is well known for its cultural and ethnic diversity. We pulled up to the window of the immigration officer at the US-Canadian border, ready for the often testy, if not downright hostile, exchange. But with a smile, the officer asked, "Are you folks here for Caribana?" I, of course, read this as the first sign that my hypothesis had some traction: Caribbean culture does permeate these North American cities (even if only temporarily). This inkling was further supported by the extensive media coverage we had access to on local Toronto television. This included weather reports centered around the forecast for Caribana events; a live telecast of the opening event, which included city officials such as the police chief officially opening the Caribana; and media announcements that the police will open high-occupancy vehicle lanes to all traffic to accommodate the heavy Caribana flow. And when we actually attended and saw the way traffic was diverted and how the city was literally reconfigured to accommodate the festival, we had no doubt that this decades-old celebration of Caribbean culture had become an integral part of the city of Toronto. This is, by most measures, a promising entry into the city. On this occasion, we experienced Toronto as a friendly and open cultural landscape.

By contrast, Dionne Brand's compelling story "No Rinsed Blue Sky, No Red Flower Fences," one of my fictional entries into Toronto, offers a bleak picture of one immigrant's experience in the city. The story opens, "The apartment had tried to kill her again" (85). Located in what the narrator later describes as "the white Toronto Street," the menacing living space is introduced as an existential threat. And in reference specifically to Toronto itself, we also hear that "the city could be so nasty when she had no money. Money was so important" (86) and that "the city was [also] claustrophobic [and] she felt landlocked" (87). These examples, and multiple others, configure Toronto as a cold, hostile, and inhospitable city. The implications of racism, or at least racial difference as a point of tension, are effectively woven into the story: The main character is "black, silent and unsmiling; the child, white, tugging, and laughing or whining" (87). There is also "a little white hand in hers, her other hand kneading a headache from her brow" (93). But most explicitly troubling is "the smell of whiteness around her, a dull choking smell" (92). Within this city space, then, the unnamed character exists on the threatening fringes of Toronto, and central to her sense of unbelonging is her intersecting subjectivities: female, (undocumented) immigrant, Black, and poor.

Brand's short story and my experience with Caribana are useful points of departure for this discussion because they open space for an understanding of Toronto as a site of multiple paradoxes. Like other cities under consideration here, Toronto functions as a space of openness, of inclusion and exclusions, of material prosperity as well as of destitution, where one's personhood is measured in dollars and cents. Yet as a space open for and accommodating of multiple cultures, Toronto is also fertile ground for the seeds of temporary relief, providing an opiate for the pain it also inflicts. In light of the divergent but equally accurate representations and experiences of the city, this chapter reads Toronto as a city with a door ajar because there is no denying its gestures of accommodation. Yet, as the the novel under consideration here and the experiences of immigrants and people of color make clear, Toronto's is a carefully managed accommodation; the door is never left unattended, surveillance is always active, and any inkling that the house is being overtaken is summarily and forcefully eradicated.

Cecil Foster's *Sleep On, Beloved* tells what is in many respects a familiar story about immigration from a Caribbean country to one of the most popular destinations in the Global North: A young woman first moves from rural Jamaica to the city of Kingston to seek opportunities that are unavailable in her rural community. This move is especially necessary as the young woman, Ona, will pursue a career in dance, a vocation well outside the standard professions such as teaching, law, medicine, and so forth. Ona's religious and spiritually gifted mother opposes this move, but after being coaxed by the dance instructor, she relents and signs the permission form. Ona's career is cut short by an early pregnancy, and while being employed at a bank in Kingston, she takes advantage of an opportunity to move to Toronto, Canada, for a job as a nanny with a family there.[1] Ona leaves her daughter, Suzanne, in the care of Ona's mother, Mira Nedd, with the hope that in a few years, Suzanne will join her in Toronto, where together they will take full advantage of the opportunities for economic advancement. (But Ona must wait twelve years before she and Suzanne are reunited in Toronto.) As is often the case, Ona is exploited by the family that employs her; she is sexually abused by the man of the house, and after a painful abortion and in the face of continued abuse, she flees her place of employment one night. She is rescued by another West Indian, Fanny, who connects Ona to a wider Caribbean community that offers spaces of cultural regeneration and a strong support system.

The novel is about the lives of both Ona and Suzanne; it focuses on the challenges they encounter integrating themselves into the fabric of a city whose institutions and practices are designed to keep them on the margins of the society even as, paradoxically, their culture becomes increasingly visible and integral to Toronto. Suzanne's delinquency, the mother-daughter estrangement, Mira Nedd's illness and death, and Ona's mental breakdown mark a turning point in Suzanne's life. And while the linear socioeconomic movement that brought this family to Toronto is still out of reach by the end of the novel, the story ends with some sense of possibility. The city, which has been such a source of agony for this family, is still the place where Suzanne believes she has a chance to claim her agency and forge a different future for her much-younger brother, Telson. *Sleep On* moves between Jamaica (mostly St. Ann) and Toronto, with a narrative strategy shaped by associational loops but with chronology intrinsic to the different subplots that constitute the novel.

John Doyle writes in his review of the novel that *Sleep On* is "firmly rooted in a specific environment." He also credits Foster for eschewing the tendency among Canadian writers to refuse to deal with "the city in its harshness or to relay the ugly cacophony of noises and voices that make up any major city" and notes that "the book asks us to see Toronto with new eyes and dares us not to look away from the despair of the immigrant who doesn't fit smoothly into the city" (2). Yet Doyle also contends that the novel is "choked by the accumulation of parallels to real events," adding that the "the attempt to document reality is the undoing of *Sleep On, Beloved*" and that the novel "tells us what we already know" (2). The apparent discrepancy in Doyle's reading of the novel—that it "tells what we already know" but also asks us to see "Toronto with new eyes"—is precisely the reason I find this work so relevant to the intervention that this study seeks to make into discourses about current Black experiences in cities. This is because to write the experiences of Black immigrants with any kind of sensitivity to current global exigencies, artistic considerations notwithstanding, necessarily involves engaging in verisimilitude.

While this familiar tale of immigrant aspiration, disappointment, and possibility for regeneration takes us along a frequently trod literary path, *Sleep On* is an important inclusion in this project as it allows for what Alison Donnell refers to as "new," and I would suggest renewed, "peepholes." This is true not only because of the way the novel simultaneously allows a window into the complexity of a city that—at face value and to some degree in practice—welcomes an ongoing flow of immigrants but also because the novel specifically affords an opportunity to engage with immigrant African derived and infused culture. This novel, along with Caribana—the yearly festival that uses Eastern Caribbean carnival and other forms of Caribbean performances as the base on which it builds multiple layers of a regenerated diasporic festival—allows us to consider the significance of the dynamic Caribbean cultural practices in Toronto and other cities.[2] The opportunity that these texts—Caribana and *Sleep On*— make possible for the engagement with culture enriches and complicates our understanding of Black experiences, particularly those of immigrant women in the kinds of urban spaces represented in this study. Additionally, with the novel's explicit and extensive engagement with African spirituality, related performance, and culturally inspired anticapitalist discourse, *Sleep On* opens additional avenues for addressing the structuring concepts of the study. This work is especially useful for the theorization of the complexity of cities—their openness, in this instance, to new cultures and their simultaneous position as locations of exclusions and enclosures. This novel also engages with the value of cultural memory, a well-known survival mechanism for immigrants. Yet here, even within the context of cultural regeneration, the novel exposes fissures that exist, due in part to structural, mostly racially motivated territorialism, the desire to control Black bodies, or the tensions among Black immigrants that are aggravated by pressures to retain and preserve personhood in the face of dehumanization and marginalization.[3] Finally, this novel, like no other text in this project, draws a through line between colonization, ongoing imperialism, and the current state of fragmentation that West Indian immigrants experience in a North American city.

The cue that African-derived creole cultures are central to the story comes early, in the first lines: "Grandma Nedd loved to dance." Yet the author adds, "but only on the right occasions and in the right places" (Foster 3). From this mixed introduction, readers are made aware of a tension in which dance will be implicated, if not central. The novel also centers the city early on as more than just a backdrop where these important events happen to take place.

And significantly, the first major conflict, and what in retrospect may well be regarded as the pivot point of the story, brings culture and the city to the fore because it is Ona's move to Kingston—Jamaica's capital and the larger of the island's two official cities—to pursue dance that precipitates the cascade of events and therefore drives the plot. Thus, the interplay between culture and the city that *Sleep On* addresses is central to one of the recurring questions that this study addresses: How does the city in each of these representations emerge as a site of simultaneity where opportunities are gained and personhood often lost, where agency and self-fashioning are at once facilitated and undermined?

The way that Foster lays the groundwork for the conflict between the spiritual roots of dance and the threatening or corrupting influence of the city is notable: while Ona dances alongside other Pocomania congregants in the way that Grandma Nedd and Pastor Grant approve of, her more personal relationship with dance develops in the secular space of the school. Remarkably it is someone from outside the village and not affiliated with the church who gets Ona excited about dance in a new way: "Ona became addicted to dancing at the village school, under the direction of Mrs. Small, or Miss English Lady as everyone disdainfully called her. Mrs. Small had returned home to teach after living and studying in England" (57). A native of the community and a "returning resident," Mrs. Small is never fully accepted back into the community.[4] She remains, in the community's mind, an outsider. Mrs. Small's place as an insider-outsider highlights and preempts the conflict between the sacred and profane understanding of Caribbean performance culture, as well as the related conflicts between mother and daughter and between rural and urban values. Mrs. Small's lessons on the history and origins of Caribbean dance forms introduce Ona and her classmates to an understanding of the spiritual and the secular as integrated, having the same African origins. The "music from Africa" that Mrs. Small brought to the classroom "sounded familiar to Ona. . . . It made sense when Mrs. Small said that the Pocomania dancers, whose freestyle dances Ona and her mother danced at Pastor Grant's church, were from Africa." The connection appears seamless to Ona because "now [she] had another reason for going to church" (58). This first connection between sacred and secular dance is important because it marks and sets up the high cultural stakes in the novel: it signals not only the ensuing conflicts between mothers and daughters but also how urban spaces, which treat dance as a commodity to be traded, create the circumstances for women's exploitation and fragmentation.

When Ona hears that she has been recruited to audition for a dance troupe in Kingston, she runs "home with the permission letter and shove[s] it in her mother's hand, thinking Mira Nedd could not but revel in the good fortune. She had to feel proud that some big shot in Kingston, the capital of the entire country, wanted to see her daughter dance. . . . After all, Ona thought, her mother found it so difficult to contain herself at the sound of drums. Without trying, she had passed on the love of dancing to her sole offspring; she had to be happy her daughter had learned it so well" (59). Pride, happiness, and good fortune in Ona's articulation here link dance, the cultural resource with which the Nedd women are gifted, with the allure and importance of the city of Kingston. But the conflict between what Mira Nedd holds as a sacred gift and the marketplace for every resource that this and other cities require neutralizes Ona's enthusiasm: "But Mira Nedd didn't see it that way. She said dancing in Kingston wasn't for the honor and glory of Christ. It was the work of the Devil to increase lust and wickedness in this sinful world. . . . This was not for a baptized child of God who has dedicated her soul to Christ" (59–60). Foster fittingly describes the "opportunity" for Ona to audition for the dance troupe as "the first crisis with [Ona's] mother and Pastor Grant." Mira's refusal to sign the permission slip is also based on her understanding and perception of the city as a dangerous, threatening space: "More than that, Mira Nedd said Ona was simply a country girl and wasn't ready for life in a bustling city like Kingston" (60); with her refusal, she introduces the conflict between the city and her understanding of the place and uses of African-derived cultures.

Kingston: Another Bridge City

In chapter 3, I argue that the cities in African countries function as bridge cities for the women who become sex workers in European cities. I return to this idea here to establish some connections between Kingston and Toronto because, in similar ways, Kingston functions as miniature version of the North American Euro-dominated city, as a space of both opportunity and ruination. Mrs. Small's perception of Kingston as the ultimate place of promise for anyone with the talent to excel as a dancer provides the dance teacher with the impetus to strategize to ensure that Ona does not lose this unique opportunity. Drawing on her insider skills and knowledge, Mrs. Small meets Mira in her yard and implores, "Tell me, nuh, you going to sign the piece o' paper for the pickney to go dancing or not?" (60). Mira surrenders, but even as she consents, the city reemerges as a source of angst: "But she'd be alone in the city." Small's reassurance, "Think of it this way: this is one of God's talents we are taking from under the bush. We letting it shine for all the world to see" (61), conveys the disjuncture but also the competing truths embedded in the women's views of the city and what it makes possible.

As it turns out, the truth about Kingston as a place of both promise and destruction lies somewhere between Mira Nedd's, Mrs. Small's, and Ona's conceptions of this Global South city. Mrs. Small's recognition of Ona's talent is validated "because all the teachers" in Kingston deem Ona "the most gifted of the students" (61). Ona reaps the benefits of the opportunities for advancement, recognition, and anonymity that cities naturally make possible: in the prestigious National Dance Troupe that Ona could join only by being in Kingston, her exceptional dancing skills are immediately recognized, and she finds a boyfriend, Lawson Heron, a senior dancer from the community who "had never spoken to Ona in the village [but] was glad to be friends with her in Kingston" (61). And she "enjoyed the double thrill of dancing and living dangerously.... For the first time in her life she enjoyed freedom and a liberation from her mother's watchful eye. For the first time, she felt in control" (62). Mira Nedd, who is firm in her understanding that the allure and dangers of Kingston would bring nothing but trouble, is not surprised when Ona returns home pregnant and abandoned by the (unbeknownst to her) married Lawson: "I could see this thing happening, how it had to happen once a young girl like you start living in Kingston" is Mira's predictable response (63). Although she attributes the circumstances around Ona's pregnancy to the unavoidable "curse" on the Nedd women, Mira always returns to her belief that Ona's presence in the city would foreclose any possibility of staving off that curse. And although it is in Kingston that Ona finds a clerical job in Barclays International Bank, she now understands Kingston not as a haven of freedom and opportunity but only as place that offers more than St. Ann. Yet what it offers is perhaps not enough for her to be fully actualized, because she realizes, "She would have to seek redemption away from St. Ann's, or even Jamaica itself" (66). Kingston is, at best, somewhat better than rural Jamaica, but it is still better. And as the novel shows, this "third world" city might not be enough to extricate Ona from the depth of economic despair that she will face with a child to support and her prospects as a dancer now blighted. Kingston is at best a bridge city.

As a bridge to the "first world" city, one of the most significant ways in which Kingston portends how Toronto will unfold for Ona and Suzanne is the way Ona suffers specifically as a female subject. It is a pregnancy that ends her career and precipitates her undoing. While the character of Lawson (Suzanne's father) is not well developed, this suppressed narrative tells its own tale of male and class privilege. Lawson completely ignores Ona when she has to leave the troupe; there is no mention of him when support of Suzanne is addressed; the two women—Ona and Mira—are Suzanne's sole guardians. It is fair to assume, then, that in Toronto, Ona's suffering will be gender-based. Against this backdrop, I now turn to Foster's treatment of the intersection of female experience and African-derived cultures in the paradoxical, partially open city of Toronto.

A Door Ajar: Toronto

The portrayal of both Ona's and Suzanne's experiences in Toronto brings to light the city's façade of openness and inclusion.[5] The efficiency of the Canadian High Commission in advancing the work permit and immigration process for Ona gives a promising first impression that what it has promised is credible and that there will be adequate follow-through. The familiar promise that "the domestic servants scheme was a chance for young women to make a better life for themselves" is an easy sell for someone in Ona's position, and the process of interviewing and processing Ona's application for legal work in Canada is smooth, showing all the markings of "first world" efficiency: "Three months [after Ona completed the forms,] Kevin and Mary Jenkins offer[ed her] employment as a live-in nanny for their two sons" and requested that she also perform "light housework" (Foster 70). That this program, as Ona learns from older women waiting to be interviewed for placements in Toronto, "is only for women without any children" (71) is notable, if not ominous. The officer "speedily processed the papers, gave Ona several forms and a letter to present at the Toronto airport. She had a month to report for employment" (72). In less than six months, everything is in place for Ona to embark on life in yet another city—this time, the imposing city of Toronto, which should surpass Kingston in all the ways in which cities are supposed to provide economic opportunities and freedoms. Despite Ona's trepidations, she fully buys into the North American city's promise of more and better: "It was all in the hope that she and her daughter could live together without anyone intervening, the chance to build a new life for both of them" (72), that she readily took this leap to another city. This is not just a typical expectation; given European economic domination in the postindependence years for Caribbean countries, the success that Ona imagines is both reasonable and feasible.

The clearly laid out parameters of the contract rightly offer Ona some reassurance that Toronto is a place of laws and standard; but the Jenkinses' flagrant and immediate disregard for these laws demonstrates quite early in Ona's Toronto sojourn that in this well-regarded Euro-dominated city, there is often disjuncture between the proclaimed and the enacted, the imagined and the actualized: "Soon after Ona arrived, Mary stopped doing everything for the children, handing them over totally to the nanny, while she did her fitness exercises, looked after her career and entertained.... Late into the night, Ona cleaned up after them. There were some disagreements between the two women, particularly differences over interpretation of the employment contract and what constituted reasonable expectation" (75). While much can be attributed to the Jenkinses' willingness to abuse their power, the presence of "reasonable" in the contract raises questions about the complicity of the larger system that shapes and enforces these contracts. The openness of and nebulousness in word choice here logically, (perhaps) knowingly, empowers Canadian employers to be the one to interpret what constitutes "reasonable"; it is hard to imagine that that there would not be an awareness of who would be more vulnerable in this employer-employee dynamic. And as H. Nigel Thomas has pointed out, "That the Canadian government never thought it necessary to put in place provisions to protect the indentured workers from abuse shows that it was not concerned about workers' welfare" (491). Thomas also points to the racial overtones of the terms of domestic workers' contracts, highlighting how race and racism shape immigrant experiences in the city.[6]

The details of disagreements offer even more insights into the state- and city-sponsored exploitation that would become part of "normal" life for Ona during her time with the Jenkinses:

> Their first disagreement was over the hours of work, whether Ona should be on call night and day, every day. Then, whether making breakfast and supper, cleaning the kitchen, dusting, doing the shopping and laundry and tending the children amounted to light housework. Ona contended it didn't. Kevin Jenkins did step in once to explain his wife's demands were not unreasonable or outside the intent of the contract. He gave assurance that he was not the type to exploit Ona. He was a lawyer, he said. "I can't have people thinking I am capable of exploiting the very person looking after my kids. What would that do to my reputation . . . ?" At the same time, he said, he wanted to make as clear as possible that breach of contract was a very serious matter with painful consequences. It could result in Ona being sent back home. (75–76)

Because the Jenkinses have the power to interpret the contract, "breach" is logically defined as any action that runs contrary to their requests. Aside from the explicit statement that it is Kevin's reputation—not whether or not the Jenkinses are fair to Ona or whether she is entitled to basic rights as an employee—that matters, there is the threat of Ona's being sent home. Despite Ona's agency—she "contended" that all she was being asked to do did not amount to "light housework"—she quickly recoils, dropping her protest once she is threatened by Kevin Jenkins, who is not only a powerful white Canadian male but also a lawyer. And because Ona "knew no one in Toronto," she also had to accept without any further complaint "sixty-five dollars in her hand at the end of the month after Mary Jenkins subtracted rent, board, taxes and such things as health insurance, workers compensation and payments for plane fare to Toronto" (76).

The mixed and multilayered nature of cities becomes apparent even when immigrants face their daunting challenges. The repeated rape of Ona by Keven Jenkins and a painful abortion eventually spur Ona's departure and her confrontations with the even more extensive vicissitudes of the city. Her encounter with Fanny at the coffee shop where she seeks shelter on the rainy night when she flees more of Kevin's sexual assaults connects her to her most trusted friends—Fanny and Mrs. King (an older Barbadian woman who becomes Ona's close friend)—as well as to a larger community of West Indians. Through this experience and the relationships that she is able to build, Ona gains access to the most hospitable aspects of the city. But despite Mrs. King's assurance that Ona should "stay right there" until she catches herself, Ona also comes to the realization that "overnight she had been transformed into an illegal alien, without a secure identity. She was unable to work legally or to see a doctor without being exposed." And she learns that "in this city . . . no kindness should be expected, because none was usually given" (86).

In *Sleep On*, Toronto is portrayed as a city of labor paradoxes: On the one hand, work is almost always available, and immigrants often do better economically. On the other hand, labor exploitation of both "legal" and undocumented immigrants is an unspoken understanding between employers and workers in some work settings, such as factories. When Ona comes to Tiltman's Garments factory, the company is happy to receive

> 185 pieces of work weekly. The quota had risen steadily every week. There appeared to be no limit to the supervisor's demands. The previous maximum automatically became the following week's minimum, although the lump sum payment remained unchanged. The growing demand forced her to work late almost every night. . . . At the back of her mind was the hope that if she worked hard enough and made no waves, Harold Tiltman, the rarely seen owner of the company, might make Ona a supervisor and help legitimize her immigrant status. . . . But apart from the supervisor's promise, nothing much had changed in more than a year. (87–88)

An arbitrariness similar to the open-to-interpretation contract that Ona had with the Jenkinses reappears. Maximums and minimums change at the will of supervisors, while workers are silenced into hopeful acceptance. In this iteration of labor exploitation, the supervisor also tells Ona that he would "approach Mr. Tiltman for" her and that is why she "shouldn't be too strict demanding any pay for overtime that you work" (88). Undeniably, the city offers possibilities, but immigrants take these opportunities always with the understanding that they are virtually powerless. As a place where immigrant labor is available in abundance, the city is also an ideal context for unscrupulous employers, who, in this representation, are not held accountable for breaking labor laws and engaging in exploitative practices.

It is particularly revelatory that, through Mrs. King's agency and care for Ona, Kevin Jenkins, Ona's former employer and assailant, is the one who rescues Ona moments before the plane taking her back to Jamaica as a deportee takes off. Kevin's presence illustrates the location of power in Toronto and also represents the city's paradoxes. Kevin's understanding of the law and his awareness of Ona's immigrant vulnerabilities make clear not just his but the city's manipulative culture. Even more telling is Kevin's revelation about Ona's immigration status: "'Would somebody get those damn handcuffs off my client. . . .

Here are the letters stating that she was granted landed immigrant status eighteen months ago. Boy, is somebody ever going to pay for this mistake before I'm through.' He held up copies of Ona's immigration papers and the brand new social security card. . . . 'I mean . . . didn't anyone actually stop to check the immigration records before acting on this so-called tip? And who is this supervisor that called anyway? Is this how things are done around here these days?'" (95–96). Just minutes before what ensues in this quote, Ona was deemed a lawbreaker and "illegal alien," thus placing her at the mercy of powerful immigration officers. Yet once she becomes the "client" of a more powerful white attorney, her status (immigration and otherwise) changes immediately, underscoring how the city's laws, and not every resident's humanity, determines personhood in the city. At the same time, Kevin's authoritative presence instantiates the variability of those laws, because those who understand both the law and Ona's vulnerabilities—her employers—could use the law to dispose of her once she has outlived her usefulness. Her deportation would have happened without anyone checking a database to confirm her status because the immigration system—ostensibly governed by law—determines whose word is assumed to be true. Kevin's "Boy, is somebody ever going to pay for this" brings into clear view the colossal failure of a system that is presumed and often performed as efficient and fair in a country and city open to immigrants and also one having agencies and services to ensure that immigrants are settled and protected. This incident and Mrs. King's "I don't know who tell them that they got any right to keep exploiting all them women from poor countries" (96) make clear that, laws notwithstanding, power in this city rests in the hands of powerful white men. Even as Kevin shows up and undercuts the immigration officers' power, his performance unmasks his duplicity and manipulation of the law. This is the same man who threatened Ona with deportation when it was his turn to exploit her labor and her body. The clash of white male power here reveals, among other things, the treatment of Black immigrant women as pawns, as human beings whose place in this city of inconsistencies is always dependent on where the wind of white male power blows.

Sleep On also makes clear that even when the laws work as they are intended to, they do not protect women like Ona; they are set up to undermine rather than support the full actualization (or anything close to it) of personhood for immigrants. For example, the onerousness of the laws governing family reunification harks back to the kind of "social death" that was inflicted on enslaved people in the Caribbean.[7] As Ona left Jamaica in a state of uncertainty and with much consternation, "the only thing that made sense was the aim of whatever she was doing. It was all in the hope that she and her daughter could live together without anyone intervening, the chance to build a new life for both of them" (72). Yet the legal system puts that goal virtually out of Ona's reach, as it requires that she clear additional financial and interpersonal hurdles before she is able to reunite with her daughter. To illustrate, consider the law that requires that Ona's daughter live in a two-parent, Euro-determined nuclear family: to meet this demand, Ona must first assume responsibility for Joe, an undocumented Barbadian man, whose presence in the two women's lives aggravates the challenges they already face in Toronto. When Joe is caught and deported, Ona must defray all the expenses to make his return and their subsequent marriage possible; only then can her daughter join her in Toronto. This is because the thing "that Joe Morgan could give her" (112) is the daughter she so desperately wants to join her, a wish that can only be granted within the stringent legal boundaries.

Ona learns that the legal system that demands a family based solely on Western patriarchal standards paradoxically turns family life or the quest for it into a business, an arrangement of convenience with the shared goal of stability in Toronto: "Ona had known Joseph for ten months and, from what else was available, thought he was worth the effort. . . . He held some potential and there was some value in him" (116). The language used to describe a soon-to-be spouse is notable: "potential" and "worth" connote a calculated business approach that is very much in line with how Ona experiences life in Toronto, where "no kindness should be expected, because none was usually given" (86). Survival, if not success, does not depend on feelings, which in "normal" Western contexts are an indicator of being socially alive; instead, the foundation of a family for Ona and Joe has to be built on calculated business decisions.[8] Therefore, the only emotion that drives the union between Joe and Ona is Ona's love for her daughter. What motivates Joe and Ona is "the realization that they had to stick together to re-create their lives, and the fact Joe could give her the validating name Morgan to put on Suzanne's immigration forms" (116). Joe, in a similar vein, confronts his choices: he "could marry [Ona] and stay in Toronto," or "he could fall on his own sword" (119). And it is only after Ona pays the $787 that Joe requires to avoid deportation and begin immigration proceedings that they embrace and talk about a life together. This last-, or late-, step-in-the-process embrace is an embodiment of the necessary prioritization of the material, economically driven demands of Toronto.

The significant space and detail that Foster devotes to each character's immigration story foregrounds the real-life human impacts of immigration laws, practices, and failings. Despite explicit statements that "Canada was committed by law and international human rights codes to the reunification of families" (124–125) and although Ona complies with all the regulations, the process moves slowly, the immigration officials are nonchalant, and Ona receives very little support from the official legal system. The novel's painstaking attention to the effects of these laws is outlined, for example, in Ona's reflections: "In Ona's eyes, the results of the setback were near catastrophic. It took the bloom off everything, stripped the budding relationship of its newness. By the time Joe rejoined her, everything was so tainted, so jaded and without any spontaneity" (125). It is not enough for the system to force Joe and Ona into a marriage driven by their mutual desperation to remain in Toronto; any possibility of their building a stable Black immigrant family consistent with the two-parent family ideal is erased by the lethargy and indifference of the same system that insists on this family structure as a prerequisite for reunification. What is even "worse" in Ona's view is that "the unexpected delay laid the groundwork for the greatest damage of all—the later troubles she has with her daughter." As Ona articulates, "If anybody had to ask me to point out what I think caused me all these problems, as God is my witness, I would have to say it's them immigration people." Ona misses . . . [Suzanne's] magic age of ten, which "every West Indian mother knew was a crucial age, when a young girl was still in a shape for a mother to influence her. Ona still could have reconnected spiritually with Suzanne; make it up to her for being away from her for so long. To help her ease into the new environment of big city life" (125). The sociological feel of this passage is due in large part to the way Foster fictionalizes one of the central points of discussion and theorization of diasporic experience: the impact of immigration policies on Black West Indian families, women in particular, in a proclaimed open, diverse city such as Toronto. Foster's fictional account calls to mind the docudrama *Borderless*, directed by Min Sook Lee, which tells the stories of two undocumented workers in Canada, one of whom is a domestic worker who literally raises her daughter remotely, mostly through long and painful phone calls. While by the time Ona makes the decision to marry Joe, she is a landed "legal" immigrant, her experience, as depicted in *Sleep On*, is not much different from Angela's, the undocumented woman in *Borderless*, because "the Canadian authorities were never going to allow [a] single woman to bring a child into the country" (Foster 12).

Ona's desperation to reunite with her daughter drives her back to Jenkins, the man responsible for so much of the exploitation she has encountered in the city, because he is "the man with contacts in the immigration department, but also the only lawyer she knew" (112). This time, too, Jenkins is apparently sympathetic, even protective. His cautionary questions are revelatory and predictive: "Is that something you really want to do? I understand how much you want your daughter, but isn't what you're thinking a bit drastic?" (113). Perhaps based on his experience seeing how much Black immigrant women have been exploited in these situations, Jenkins could (rightly) predict that Ona was creating more trouble for herself in Toronto. Yet he has to concede, "It would help you satisfy the immigration requirements for your daughter. No doubt about it" (113). At a time when Ona needs support to reunite with her daughter, this lawyer with contacts in the immigration department chooses to surrender to the law. It is hard to believe that this is the best that Jenkins could do to facilitate Suzanne's reunification with her mother, but it is not surprising that Ona soon "felt Kevin Jenkins turning cold on Joe's case" (127).

Rather than the city protecting and supporting the immigrant women to whom it has supposedly opened its door, the city and its laws leave the women at the mercy of Black and white men.

While, as we see from Ona's experience with Jenkins and with the men in charge of the factory where she worked, the novel highlights how white Canadian men, protected by the law, and the official immigration system collude to exploit immigrant women, it is notable that *Sleep On* also engages with Black immigrant women's victimhood at the hands of Black West Indian immigrant men. The system creates the situation that forces Ona to marry Joe so that she may reunite with her daughter, and these same laws leave Ona, and later Suzanne, vulnerable to exploitation from Joe. His entry into Ona's life—as a husband chosen only because of his presumed ability to create a "stable" nuclear family—foretells the added weight he will bring to bear on Ona, especially as she balances working outside the home, attempting to reconnect with her daughter, running a home, and just being in a city that remains an unwelcoming space. Mrs. King warns, "As for you saying you sending money to this fellow every month . . . I don't like it. . . . Y]ou better train him right from the start otherwise, he'll walk all over yuh" (128). It is not surprising, then, that "the first really big problem was finding a job for Joe" (132); his marriage to Ona amounts to a kind of purchase—an arrangement in which, from the start, Joe understands that he is on the (financial) receiving end of this bargain.

All the positive parts of Ona's marriage to Joe and their time together as a family of three—visits to the West Indian dancehall, Joe's good cooking, TV time, and listening to Joe's music—are short-lived. Joe's financial contribution to the family is minimal or nonexistent most of the time. Even the better relationship that Suzanne establishes with Joe lays the groundwork for something more sinister. As Suzanne's new father, Joe cunningly sets himself up as a friend, unlike Ona, who was always "inundating" Suzanne "with information, challenging her to learn fast, to plan a strategy to quickly go out and conquer the city. Life was easier with Joe just floating around, smiling occasionally and once in a while offering her a Jamaican beef patty or a Ting soft drink from the West Indian stores" (143). Especially within the context of the challenges that the city poses for newly arrived immigrant children, Joe's casual, friendly treatment of Suzanne is unsettling, and it clearly undermines Ona's efforts, later making her necessary (even if too drastic) efforts to properly situate Suzanne in a challenging new city environment all the more ineffective. Quite contrary to Ona's expectation that Joe will be a coparent, his nonchalance and his passivity when dealing with school officials contribute to Suzanne's ultimate delinquency. For one of the many school visits expected of a parent, "Suzanne had hoped her stepfather would attend the meeting this time. . . . Joe simply sat nodding his head in agreement . . . just letting the principal or teacher unload whatever was on their chest" (158). Education is traditionally the most highly regarded vehicle for social mobility among West Indians, yet Joe actively and passively undermines the potential that education holds to help Suzanne to navigate this complicated city with greater ease. And most egregiously, his (mostly unspecified) sexual abuse of Suzanne traumatizes her and precipitates her entry into sex work.

Sleep On also details how, as an arm of the legal system, the education system in the city that superficially opens its doors to immigrants simultaneously fosters an environment that undermines learning and tacitly endorses the marginalization that students experience in the schools. Foster presents the school system to which Suzanne must quickly adjust as a version of the "school-to-prison pipeline," which is now a stock term used to describe schools and school systems in urban areas in the United States.[9] One of many meetings between Ona and the principal of Suzanne's school illustrates the role of the education system in ensuring the partial exclusions that define Black immigrants' experiences in Toronto. Initially, the principal insists that the purpose of the "psychological testing" of Suzanne to which he tries to convince Ona to agree is "to have [Suzanne] assessed: to find out what may be wrong and how [the school] can help" (160). Soon after, the usual reason for offering testing to immigrant and minoritized students is revealed: "Maybe Suzanne is a late starter. . . . That's why we want to have the testing done" (166). Later, he returns to what he hopes is a more palatable presentation of what the school wants to accomplish, by adding, "Maybe something in the home, . . . maybe something in her background is distracting her from her schoolwork" (166). But when Ona presses—"What would it prove, this testing?"—the ultimate goal, typical of many urban school systems, emerges: "We'll be testing to see whether we have her in the right academic stream. Maybe, and I am only tossing this out as an example, she might be more suited for basic education, such as learning life skills, . . . teaching her things like how to apply for a job, some typing and shorthand, remedial English, arithmetic, and possibly ESL, English as a Second Language" (167). Ona's intelligence and her experiences in Toronto, where she trusts no one, lead her to persist and unmask the school system's goal: to do its part to ensure that Black immigrants do not receive the kind of education that would empower them in the city and make them fully actualized citizens equipped with the skills to fulfill their potential in the way that white Canadian citizens are allowed to do.

Although one could (rightly) say that Suzanne contributes to the school system's perception of her and other "delinquents," Foster neutralizes this suggestion by also providing insight into the internal pipeline of the school that Suzanne attends, giving readers a sense of the frustrations that schools often create; these multiple acts of exclusion then legitimize their actions. Mrs. Trudel sends Suzanne and another recent immigrant, Bobby Ali, to the principal because "they persisted in carrying on a running conversation, disrupting the class with their bouts of giggles" (161). While these are undeniably disruptive actions, Foster provides the context that the principal and teacher, agents of the system, elide:

> Bobby Ali arrived with a thick accent. . . . Suzanne also had problems with her accent. . . . She and Bobby Ali had arrived at the school about the same time. It didn't take long for the two of them to realize that they were different. In the very first math class Bobby kept his hand in the air while the teacher overlooked him and moved on to others who she felt knew the answers. This was not the last time Bobby was overlooked. After a while, he and Suzanne developed their own system. They did not raise their hands but wrote the answers on pieces of paper they passed to each other. Sometimes they drew funny caricatures. Other times they scribbled a joke. (161)

As both a microcosm and an agent of the city, the school system has already carved out a space for Black immigrant students, forcing them to develop their "own system[s]," which in turn lay the groundwork for later and more stringent marginalization. In the way the school scaffolds the measures that eventually place minoritized students on the destructive side of the law and on the margins of Toronto, it, as Foster presents it, is an integral, subtle, and highly effective branch in the city's complex, unwritten system of ostracism and xenophobia. The novel's depiction of how school systems in immigrant-dense cities aid and abet the exclusions that West Indian children experience is widely supported in many other representations such as Caryl Phillips's *Color Me English*.[10]

As the novel makes clear, with the school's door only ajar and with a system set up to deliberately marginalize students, immigrant parents are virtually powerlessness. Ona knows the system well enough to understand that the "psychological testing" and subsequent demotion to "basic education" will undermine all she has done to offer her daughter an economically prosperous life in a "first world" city, so she pushes back hard on the principal: "How can she express sheself any better when every damn time the poor chile put up her hand to answer a question in class nobody bother calling on she? Or when they get 'round to asking, as soon as she opens her mouth, the first thing the blasted teacher say is 'Pardon me, will you repeat that.' When the poor child give it another try, the same damn thing all over again" (167). Ona further challenges, "How come Suzanne isn't the only West Indian child to have problems in this school? How come it's almost always Black people? . . . You ever heard this child here read the bible?" (169). Despite Ona's demonstrated understanding of the systemic problems that her daughter faces, despite her fierce defense of her daughter and her refusal to sign the permission to allow "psychological testing," because of the laws of the city, Ona "was beaten": "After an embarrassing court appearance, Suzanne was tested and dropped to the basic stream. . . . Ona promptly stopped going to meetings at school. She also stopped applying for promotions" (172). Foster's inclusion of the promotion here draws readers into the systemic nature of the marginalization of both mother and daughter in Toronto. The school's and workplace's actions are part of a web and constitute a repeating, even if differently enacted, mechanism of exclusion. Describing "Suzanne's deterioration in the basic stream [as] thorough and quick" (173), Foster charts a downward slide: discrimination in the classroom, unfair punishment, delinquency, further marginalization in the school system, increasing run-ins with the law, and eventual entry into an adult life marked by constant legal problems and gendered exploitation.

Culture as Opiate: The Hole and Caribana

Many studies of immigrant-diasporic experiences, including my analysis of James's *A Brief History of Seven Killings* in chapter 4, address how Caribbean immigrants transform foreign, usually urban spaces to make them more like the homes they left behind.[11] Despite the focus of the foregoing discussion on how *Sleep On* exposes the paradoxes of immigrant experiences in Toronto, as my opening paragraphs in this chapter suggest, this novel also illustrates how West Indian immigrants have changed the landscape of this city. In addition to Caribana—which the novel includes as part of its representation of Suzanne's journey—and the transformations that Joe's music creates in the intimate home space, there is also the "Hole," which serves as a constant cultural interlude and a meeting place for West Indians. This site, too, offers insights into the always-tenuous space that immigrants occupy. Culture, then, functions as what I term a *counterspace*, in which immigrants can be returned temporarily to parts of themselves that must be contained within the wider society in order for them to attain levels of acceptance that will allow them to achieve the economic advancement they seek.

The Hole functions as a permanent meeting place for West Indians. The Hole is a dancehall but also functions as a social-cultural place, a site for camaraderie and strategizing, a space literally away from the city. The name is itself evocative in how it not only connotes distance from the main space of Toronto but also suggests a kind of dungeon, a space of relegation. At the same time, the range of activities that take place in the Hole speaks to this cultural meeting place as an enigmatic location. Ona is introduced to, and induced into, the culture of the Hole shortly after fleeing Kevin Jenkins's sexual assaults and being subsequently rescued by Fanny; these moves mark a moment of multiple possibilities for sustenance as well as further complication. For a gifted dancer such as Ona, the Hole is in some ways the kind of space she needs at a time when she is already feeling beaten by the city. As Fanny reminds her, "You know nobody in that damn Hole can put down a dance step like you, so. I don't see why you have to keep moping around that damn apartment" (98).

Foster makes clear not only the way the Hole evinces cultural retention and regeneration but also the important therapeutic role that this space plays in giving West Indian immigrants some respite from a city in which their status as outsiders is consistently prominent: "Almost every weekend, something went on in the basement. This was particularly true in the winter, when for a fee of two or three dollars—a mere fraction of the cost of more formal balls and galas across the city—the immigrants for a few brief moments could escape back to the warm tropics of rhythmic language and strong fragrances, even if the odors were those of perspiring bodies bathed in cheap perfume. They wrapped themselves up in one another for one night and got on as badly as they wanted" (101). It is hard to overstate the role and place of culture as succor for Black immigrants in a Euro-dominated city and the importance of a specific place where, as the narrator puts it, "they wrapped themselves up in one another." Described also as "a refuge full of imported nostalgia, as well as the source of news that really mattered, . . . more meaningful and useful than what they read in Canadian newspapers, where there was hardly any mention of back home" (105), the Hole is also a place where attendees' personhood—as West Indians and as human being—is validated and affirmed.[12]

While serving as the obvious social space where Caribbean mating rituals are enacted, the Hole is also a place where men can stake out women who are, in their estimation, worth their while because of the possibilities for economic advancement that they offer:

> [When Fanny and Ona] entered, they felt the eyes of men, married and single, running up and down their bodies, assessing and undressing as they weighed possibilities. . . . And the fact that Ona was a woman with a good job, working as a teller in the credit union, put her head and shoulders above many men in the Hole. That she also had her own apartment and maybe a few pennies in an account somewhere added to her status. She definitely was the kind of woman any man wanted to take home or hoped was desperate enough to dip into her savings for a small loan, a shirt or even a few months of rent. (98–99)

Coming from a West Indian culture where, although women are often employed (formally or informally) and are sometimes the breadwinners of their families, the targeting of women for financial support is a different take on male-female relationships; that this is a practice, even a goal for going to the Hole, speaks to the overwhelming power of the capitalist system on which the city functions, a system that also shapes interactions in the parallel West Indian cultural space. The shifting gender dynamics illustrated here also call attention to how migration and the constraints of "first world" economics shape and change gender relationships.

As a space where "most of the faces were Black" (102), the Hole functions as a location of both racial relief and tension, where the gender dynamics described in the preceding paragraph are also aggravated by racial tension: "Some men brought white women [and] everyone seeing these mixed couples recognized a Black man using the woman as a trophy to prove he had attained a high level of acceptance, an accomplishment that remained a dream for so many" (102). This acceptance and recognition obviously function as a double-edged sword, perhaps on the one hand gaining the recognition that the man seeks while on the other marking him as a kind of outsider. But it is the impact that these mixed relationships have on Black women that most clearly demonstrates the only partial safety of this space:

> Ona knew that just like her, all the black women recognized this posturing as symptomatic of the weakness and feelings of inferiority that still dogged their men. . . . With time, Ona began to feel the same pain that she saw on the faces of so many black women in the Hole. As they got older and more settled, ironically growing more financially secure and estranged from their black brothers. . . . Gradually, Ona understood . . . how the expectations of these women were transforming and dying, . . . so they stopped going to the Hole as often. (102–103)

Clearly not immune to the racial tensions and exclusions of the city, the Hole gradually loses its place as a location of safety and belonging for Black West Indians. The Hole, then, like the city in whose literal and metaphorical basement it is located, undermines the very Blackness it sets out to validate and perpetuates the same outsider status it seeks to combat. Part of what this demonstrates, then, is the limits of racial solidarity when the pressures of acceptance are so urgent and when the promise of the economic prosperity in this "first world" city is the ultimate goal. This example further illustrates the instability of states of being and identities, particularly when survival in the city is the existential imperative.

The sense of emotional insecurity that women begin to feel in the Hole is intensified in the threat that the legal system poses: "Every so often a pair of policemen, usually white, and the occasional immigration officer walked through the hall. Ostensibly, the police were there to enforce liquor licensing rules and to discourage rowdy behavior and desecration of church property. . . . Once or twice, squadrons of police cruisers descended on the Hole and dragged people away" (104). So, while the Hole undoubtedly serves as a space of relative freedom for Black immigrants, the emphasis is on "relative," because the existence of a place that is well known in the city as an immigrant meeting place opens up new threats of surveillance. While an undocumented immigrant— who otherwise has to behave like what Mrs. King characterizes as a rat "scurrying secretively from one hole to the another" (87)—can at some level experience temporary freedoms by mingling with people from home, such freedoms are also contained because the laws and prejudices of the city enter every crevice of immigrant life. Even more disturbing with regard to the level of constant scrutiny is Ona's discovery that "these raids usually came when complaints from neighbors and real estate agents concerned with value of their homes and properties were most acute and the local politicians had to do something about the pressure" (104). The existence of the Hole, within the context of Toronto laws and the constant threat of police and immigration presence, make clear the police's and the State's almost total control over Black bodies through multiple mechanisms of the city; even the space within the city that they carve out for themselves is not shielded from the invasive laws of the city.

Mashing Down the Half-Open City: Caribana

Through the lens of Caribana, one might theorize Toronto as an alluring, seductive, even welcoming, open city, and this would not be an entirely inaccurate characterization. Unlike the Hole, Caribana is a recognized, public, city-approved celebration, where ostensibly Caribbean people and anyone who wishes to participate can freely do so. The longevity, expansion, and intrusiveness of Caribana as well as the scholarly attention given to it in the work of Frank Manning, Lyndon Phillip, and others demonstrate that Caribana is much more than a once-a-year event that gives Caribbean immigrants a little visibility. The festival is a point of intersection for culture, ideology, economics, and perhaps most significantly, the politics of belonging (Green and Scher). The festival has also been in existence for well over five decades.[13] According to Phillip, "Caribana began as a joint venture between black Caribbean communities in Toronto and the federal government's new stand on multiculturalism" (104). With the groundwork laid by the Canadian Negro Women's Association, which hosted carnival festivals from 1951 to 1976, and by Emancipation Day parades, a carnival parade was the logical and perhaps most fitting way to offer a "West Indian contribution towards Canada's Centennial celebrations" (106) as a way of showcasing multiculturalism, ethnic diversity, and inclusion in Canada. The government of the city of Toronto and wider Ontario has always had a political and economic stake in the festival, which at once gives credence to the city's multicultural-inclusive rhetoric and raises question about its intent and level of commitment.[14]

Sleep On, Beloved is explicit in its recognition of Caribana as part of the cultural balm for the achy immigrant journey through Toronto. When Suzanne decides that "until she receive[s] some definite sign of how to regain control, she must remain sequestered within the walls of her apartment" (Foster 266), her friends Bobby Ali and Henderson, understanding her withdrawal as depression, lure her out with the enticement of Caribana: "A weekend like this, and you say you staying home. With all this sweet music all 'round town. Millions of people from all over the world dancing on the streets, mashing down Toronto. And you say you're staying at home. . . . You coming with me. . . . I know a Caribana fete that is just the thing for you. The medicine the doctor ordered" (268). The therapeutic implications of this statement are self-evident; they speak to an awareness and self-reflectiveness about the value of culture beyond the "jump up and wind" or "get something and wave" fervor of the moment: culture provides healing, so much so that just the act of getting dressed for the Caribana party is enough to start Suzanne's recovery. It allows her to escape, if only temporarily: "This was the way she felt after a really vigorous dance on stage" (271). And the fact that this Caribana party was being held at a "house in the suburbs" (271) underscores the extent of the apparent "takeover" of the city for the Caribana season; again, unlike the sessions in the Hole, Caribana is not a private, enclosed party for West Indian immigrants.

While the size and scope of Caribana might convey the impression that West Indians and their ways of life are part of Canadian society, as Foster's use of "temporarily" (270) in the quote about Suzanne's renewed energy conveys, the West Indian community also understands the takeover as a brief season, an interlude—even if it is a recurring one. As one woman caught up in the excitement comments, "Music sweet so . . . This is Caribana man. This is we culture. Too bad it's only once a year. This is when we can really be West Indian in cold-arse Canada. . . . Just wait 'til tomorrow when the parade begins downtown. . . . We'll start mashing down Toronto with we dance" (275). The reemergence of "mashing down Toronto" in this woman's comment is notable, and though in West Indian parlance, this is a term used to express the intensity of a party, at its core, this "mashing down" conveys an overwhelming presence of the culture, specifically carnival. In this instance, given the context of Euro-dominated culture for the rest of the year, it is hard not to hear the suggestion of seizing the moment to make the Caribana cultural presence felt at a time when it is legitimized by the city, when the activities are not as clandestine as they tend to be in the Hole. The fact that it is a carnival celebration "mashing down" the city is also significant because of the anticolonial, inherently iconoclastic origins and orientations of Caribbean carnival celebrations.

Over the decades and through different iterations of the festival's existence, it has always been a site of tension that unmasks the inconsistencies and the protectionist, even racist, aspects of dominant Canadian society, in which historical controversies persist. For example, despite the Canadian government's public endorsement of the festival, early on, it was not a reliable source of funding, and when funds were allocated, other problems around fairness arose.[15] Relatedly, the kind and extent of commercial interest in Caribana further highlight the challenges organizers face, because commercial interest is generally self-serving and selective. For example, Scotiabank's virtual takeover of Caribana is indicative of the strength and potential of the festival to be lucrative and attractive to many Canadian businesses, but it also illustrates the fraught nature of commercial and governmental support. Despite the legitimizing implication of sponsorship from one of Canada's premier financial institutions, when a group of high school and college students sought sponsorship for a band to dress in graduation regalia to promote school completion among Black youth, over thirty businesses turned them down, and it was a record company in the United States that sponsored the group (Phillip 124).

Even within the context of the temporary freedom to affirm, display, and celebrate Caribbean culture, any notion that these celebrations happen with full freedom from police surveillance is unfounded. Beyond the challenges with sponsorship and the commercialization of the festival, if we take policing and its intersection with race and racism into account, Caribana is also an occasion for heightened scrutiny, which then exposes racially and xenophobically oriented fissures in the city. That the Canadian federal and provincial governments' interest might more be exploiting culture to support their performance of inclusion is further illustrated in the way the state has historically policed the event, because Caribana is also renowned for how it demonstrates the targeting and management of Black bodies. In the article "Policing Caribana like it's a threat to national security," Ajamu Nangwaya frames his reflections with Buju Banton's "Yardie" and asserts, "This street festival has been wrongly associated with criminality. It has much to do with the fact that African bodies are linked to this event." Nangwaya adds that police violence was an issue in the early years of the 1970s.

Further, Nangwaya documents multiple incidents that have taken place in different years during the festival, in which the police besieged the festival with aggressive and clearly racist police tactics. Nangwaya quotes a 1990 *Toronto Star* article that characterizes security at Caribana as consisting of an "army of Metro officers." Most significantly, though, to make the point that the aggressive approach to policing Caribana is rooted in racism, Nangwaya contrasts the approach to security for Caribana with that of Toronto Blue Jays baseball games.[16] Nangwaya includes Peter Jackson's observation that "there were fewer problems (at Caribana) than at most Blue Jays baseball games where 60 officers police crowds of 40,000–50,000 spectators." This comparison accords much credibility to Nangwaya's assertion of racial targeting (and perhaps xenophobia) as the driving factor in policing.[17]

Foster's creative account of immigrant experiences, which focus specifically on women's lives and which places culture at the center, lays bare the vicissitudes of diasporic Caribbean communities' precarious position in the city of Toronto. The synergies between this account and multiple others are illustrative of the continuities across cities. The ancestral cultures that women bring to the city serve as an anchor, a haunting, and a liability. On the one hand, the city provides a space where dance, a remembered cultural-spiritual performance, distinguishes and pursues the Nedd women. But within the context of Western capitalist demands, in an urban setting, the gift always leads them down the path of exploitation. For Ona, it is the move to her home country's capital city, Kingston, that precipitates the fulfillment of the warning that dancing for anyone but God leads to destruction. Suzanne's choice of exotic dancing as a vocation propels the line of Nedd women deeper into a place where the "sacred" performance of culture turns into an illegal activity, thus giving more credence to Mira Nedd's warnings against secular expressions of the spiritual culture. Yet Caribbean cultural practices, such as dance that takes place in the Hole or during Caribana, even within the secular space that Mira Nedd disavows, are life sustaining and arguably open up different kinds of spiritual-cultural regenerative possibilities. The examination of Foster's representation of Caribana and readings of the festival itself mark the city as an enigmatic space, where the Black immigrant body is simultaneously welcomed and surveilled, marked but allowed to move with some freedoms. These reflections bring me to a reiteration of the chapter's central point: the city of Toronto is by no means closed; it is a door ajar, allowing West Indian immigrants and their culture to enter, stay, and enjoy a modicum of inclusion. But the half-open door that is Toronto is never left unattended, and its entrants are never allowed to roam freely.

Conclusion

■ ■

In the final section of the introduction to *Color Me English*, Caryl Phillips writes, "I believe passionately in the moral capacity of fiction to wrench us out of our ideological burrows and force us to engage with a world that is clumsily transforming itself, a world that is peopled with individuals we might otherwise never meet in our daily lives, . . . for literature *is* plurality in action. . . . It relishes ambiguity. . . . It judges neither party and it implores us to act with compassion towards fellow human beings. . . . I believe the writer has a crucial part to play in this" (16). Phillips writes these closing affirmations of the power and relevance of literature, and I would add the creative arts, in an essay that reflects on the changing demographics of Europe; he launches the essay with a true story about his and a classmate's encounters with racism in the city of Leeds, in England, where Phillips grew up. The quoted excerpt is preceded and followed by Phillips's assertion that Europe is not and will no longer be a homogeneous continent and that the only sensible way to ensure proper functioning societies on the continent (and in all other places) is to adopt the kind of simple, but oh-so-challenging acceptance and embrace of each other that James Baldwin urges in *The Fire Next Time*. Phillips draws his example of the costs of intolerance from his and other immigrant youths' experiences. Like so many other cities in the 1960s, Leeds was seeing its first wave of rapid racial, ethnic, and overall cultural diversity.

The important role that Phillips ascribes to the arts in general and writing is particular circles us back to the "landscape of globalization" that Patrick Chamoiseau addresses in the essay "Globalization, Globality, Globe-Stone," discussed in the introduction to this book. Chamoiseau's contention that he "can imagine no true wayfaring toward art that ignores the urgency, dominations, and impossibilities of its time" (5) locates itself in the same ideological and discursive space as the introduction to *Color Me English*. At this juncture, just over two decades into the twentieth century, the increasingly complicated impact of globalization is even more visible than it was when Phillips wrote, in these post-9/11 essays in *Color Me English*; the concerns and debates regarding the relevance of the humanities have become even more vibrant, and any discussion about how humanity might successfully navigate this new world order will undoubtedly be helped by engagement with the creative arts.

As some of the first cities to experience huge waves of immigration, urban locations in England in particular and in the United Kingdom more generally have served as touchstones for the steady and significant globalization of cities. Urban centers in Birmingham, Leeds, London, and Manchester—to name just a few—saw what Louise Bennett has creatively characterized as "colonization in reverse" (106), whereby, as addressed mostly in my analysis of *NW* and *Call the Midwife* in chapter 2, droves of colonized and formerly colonized people flocked to British cities to escape economic deluge and to satisfy Britain's need for cheap labor. As Caroline Herbert has noted, "Perhaps the most well-established strand of urban postcolonial literary studies explores how writers invite us to 'historicize the imperial (and neo-imperial) history of the production of space' in 'postcolonial London' and to engage with the ways that formally imperial centers are represented and rewritten by migrant and diasporic communities" (203). Herbert includes Salman Rushdie's *The Satanic Verses* (1988), Samuel Selvon's *The Lonely Londoners* (1956), Grace Nichols's *The Fat Black Woman's Poems* (1984), Zadie Smith's *White Teeth* (2000), Hanif Kureisha's *The Buddha of Suburbia* (1990), and Gautum Malkani's *Londonstani* (2006) among the most notable works that have addressed European and specifically British cities from the perspective of residents who make up that significant immigrant population. I have mentioned these representative works here, in large part, to note the spread of time during which writers visit and revisit the city space in a way that centers the presumed marginalized population and simultaneously decenters the neoimperial European culture and experiences. Works such as Smith's *NW* (2012) also demonstrate the still urgent need to reflect on and portray neocolonial-global cities from increasingly diverse standpoints. These writers depict what Kevin R. McNamara refers to as "a more complete, but still subjective and non-totalizing, account of their cities by presenting the city from multiple, spatially dispersed perspectives" (3). Because *NW* relates the experiences of former and, mostly, current residents of northwest London public housing, the novel allows readers access to Keisha-Natalie's new, more privileged, but psychologically agonizing suburban life, while also granting readers access to her childhood home, where members of her family still live in relative poverty. *NW* also takes readers to the streets and on public transportation, where we meet and journey with Felix and

Nathan, who are, in different ways, still living on the margin of this imperial city. In this way, then, the intended homogeneous story of London is fractured, reframed, and problematized in a way that prevents any kind of Euro-constructed center from holding. *NW* and other texts therefore epitomize how creative accounts that open up the city to a diversity of angles, locations, and voices also necessarily disrupt hegemonic histories and intents.

Among the central questions I have sought to address in this book is the extent to which minoritized people, specifically those of African descent, have been able to create homes in cities that were not intended to be homes for them. Herbert argues that Frantz Fanon positions the Manichean city, "a town cut in two," "as emblematic of the spatial, social, and economic ordering of the colonial world" (201). Decades after Fanon offered these descriptions, the representations of cities in the works under consideration here are eerily familiar. The cities creatively recuperated in the foregoing analyses are certainly "cut in two," and the colonial and early postcolonial inequities outlined by Fanon remain mostly intact. For example, the parts of Kingston in which much of *A Brief History* is set almost mirror Fanon's "cut in two" characterization. But James also sprinkles the novel with contrasting images of two sides of Kingston. For example, as one character escapes after members of his family were killed, he ran until he reached "Garbagelands, nothing but waste and junk and shit stretching for miles. Nothing but what uptown people throw out, rubbish rising high like hill and valley and dunes like desert and everywhere burning" (14). The same character reports a typical scenario, in which a police beating ends with the officer saying, "Never take you dutty, stinking, ghetto self uptown again" (10). These examples illustrate the more pronounced and clearly defined spatial exclusions that almost always circumscribe life in cities. While Kingston is a city in a small "third world" island, it was built as a colonial city space, and the vestiges of colonization continue with the very clearly demarcated spaces along more class than racial lines. Yet the class-determined spaces are grounded in, and still function as part of, racist structures.

However, the majority of the texts on which this book bases its theorization present more complicated spatial scenarios. Even as the writers considered here depict situations consistent with the kind of split that Fanon outlines, in the majority of these works, the Black and immigrant characters live and work in spaces from which they were previously excluded or in spaces that were not intended for them. Over five decades after Fanon made his observations and during a distinct but similar historical moment, Darko, Foster, James, Smith, Thomas, Unigwe, and the creators of *Call the Midwife*, along with the other authors whose works have been referred to here, depict a diversity of spatial scenarios, and the responses evince the kinds of complications that globalization and increased visibility have created in cities. For example, in *Man Gone Down*, the main character, Ishmael, is a middle-class, educated writer who mostly

moves in circles that do not align neatly with the colonially constructed spatial exclusions that Fanon describes. Yet Ishmael's experiences demonstrate that
while the clearly demarcated lines may not be as prominent, the principles and
structures of exclusion remain. In addition to the Euro-academic spaces in
which Ishmael has spent much of his late teens and adult life, his marriage into
a white, upper-middle-class family exposes him to a different kind of racism, as
he is marked by his wife's aunt as a project for civilization. Similarly, his presence
in the private-school setting, where his children are students, makes Ishmael
susceptible to race- and class-based exclusions: because of the absence of racially
driven ancestral class position, Ishmael lacks the means to fully integrate into a
space in which he is ostensibly allowed to exist. Therefore, while Ishmael is able
to live, work, and learn in the previously "reserved for Europeans only" spaces,
these spaces exemplify the half-open door addressed in previous chapters.[1] With
regard to freedom and to the expression of the fullness of his humanity, Ishmael
is not truly *in* these spaces.

And in an even more complicated example of race- and class-inflected lim-
inality, the main characters in *On Black Sisters Street* and *Beyond the Horizon*
exist in spaces outside what might be deemed the normal sociogeographical
boundaries of the cities where they work. The women in *Black Sisters Street* are
even outside the standard "undocumented" status because of the strategy that
those who are in charge of the trade devise to disempower them: their passports
are seized, and they are forced to seek asylum on bases that are predetermined
to be denied, leaving them disempowered outsiders on multiple levels. Furthermore, the real threat of murder if they decide to leave their jobs or report their
employers adds another (psychological) layer of exclusion to their lives.
Although the "red-light district" in which they work is a known and, to some
degree, legally sanctioned space, as individuals, the women have no legal or even
"illegal" place. Their living space functions as its own kind of district within
the city, with its own (illegal) rules; the space is controlled by the madam, and
she is protected through the complicity of law enforcement officers. Additionally, sex work itself occupies a murky place in the city. The *Brussels Times* reports
on the complicated legal situation: "Sex work in itself is legal. Neither the sex
worker nor the client can be prosecuted" (Maïthé). Yet there are laws, such as
those prohibiting third-party interventions, that still place sex workers at an
(unintended) disadvantage. In addressing such spaces of legal opacity, the article goes on to underscore that although "the aim of this law is mostly to impact
pimps, . . . the law also affects anyone who might provide services to sex workers, such as lawyers or bookkeepers." Therefore, "all third parties are commit-
ting a crime when they get involved" (Maïthé). With this kind of ambiguous
legal position, while sex workers are not officially spatially excluded—in the
way a colonial city, designated for Europeans, such as Antwerp would function
before twentieth- and twenty-first-century globalization—in their lived,

everyday experiences, the women are still outsiders with no official legal status and with none of the protections that citizenship or any related legal status would allow.

Viewed through the prism of Fanon's early characterization of the role of cities in establishing colonial racial-spatial demarcations, the examples I have cited illustrate the continued relevance of postcolonial framings and critical tools in elucidating the way cities have functioned as part of the colonial apparatus. At the same time, in light of the fictional depictions that creatively recover contemporary global-capitalist structures, it is also clear that city boundaries have been disputed in part because of the migrations that have themselves resulted from colonization; the lines have been blurred. While exclusions continue and there are still clear lines of separation within some urban spaces, the actual lines are no longer as defined. This blurring of racial-class lines, then, demands theorizations of cities on the basis of creative renditions of cities as spaces in flux, as sites of opacity. In these representations, we see laid bare a (re)newed global economic order that necessarily renders cities as sites where the colonizers' project of race-based exclusions has been successfully challenged, even as Black and other minoritized citizens still experience the effects of racially determined economic, social, and spatial exclusions.

Small Axe: A Recent Creative Fulcrum

The foregoing discussion illustrates Phillips's aspiration to understand the centrality of creative engagements that enter and explore the interstices of textured global city experiences in a time when inter- and multicultural interactions are inevitable. This need to return to history through a variety of creative modalities in a way that reignites conversations or makes the experiences of minoritized people more visible is again illustrated in Steve McQueen's well-received film anthology series *Small Axe*. As part of the closing analyses in this study, I turn to a brief discussion of McQueen's treatment of some key moments in Black West Indians' ongoing journey toward full inclusion in British cities where West Indians were simultaneously invited into and excluded from mainstream society. *Small Axe* covers events that took place between 1960 and 1980, a two-decade time span; these events overlap with some of the depictions studied here but also provide useful context and expansion. A recent production, *Small Axe* sutures some key themes of the written and audiovisual fictional works with which I have engaged in the foregoing chapters; additionally, the anthology broadens the view of the city. Therefore, while the films are set in London and while they are not uniform, the lived experiences represented in the episodes epitomize immigrant and minoritized people's experiences in Euro-dominated cities. This short docudrama series is especially useful because it brings together historical and contemporary experiences in a way that underscores the central point of this study: cities—as they are depicted in the creative accounts under analysis here—illustrate both the gains and continuing challenges that minoritized peoples confront in a globalized and globalizing world that still bares the scars of colonization. Additionally, the fact that a series of films that creatively recover events that took place decades ago has resonated so well with contemporary experiences in cities and with different audiences illustrates the anthology's relevance as a companion piece to the works analyzed here.

The attentiveness to belonging, addressed in all the primary texts analyzed here, undergirds the episodes in *Small Axe*, which address this theme from a variety of perspectives. Like *Call the Midwife*, *Small Axe* allows viewers access to the city space by way of characters' movements and in a such a way that brings into sharp focus the interactions between Black bodies and the sociomaterial spaces they inhabit and over which they must exercise a modicum of control in order to reshape these locations into homes and places of belonging. In this regard, the opening scene of episode 1 is especially poignant. The action moves from a social space, most likely a bar, where West Indian men are engaged in entertainment that demonstrates the kind of cultural recovery and transplantation that has been such a key area of diasporic studies. The scene that follows is longer, offers more details, and centers on one male character, Frank, who strides along the street of London with confidence and a sense of satisfaction, belonging, and even ownership as Bob Marley's "Try Me" plays in the background. The scenes depicted in the early moments show a London in transition—children of multiple races playing together, a couple (one person Black the other white) standing happily together, buildings being torn down and erected—and the imprints of West Indian presence in the city are palpable. These early moments in the episode, which are mostly without dialogue, also address what the narrator, quoting C. L. R. James, refers to as "new men, new types of human beings. It is in them that are to be found all the traditional virtues of the English nation, not in decay as they are in official society but in full flower because these men have perspective, not particularly that they glory in the struggle. They are not demoralized or defeated or despairing persons. They are leaders but are rooted deep among those they lead" (1:00–2:50).

These new people are in the process of fashioning the imperial city space as a different kind of home, and in the process of staking their claim on the city, they are leaders in a long process toward a heterogeneous London. Yet, as the narrator makes clear, there are two perspectives being held in tandem here: on the one hand, the "new men" (new people) are in "full flower"; on the other hand, this is a flowering that is taking place in the midst of, and despite, their being seen as people "in decay . . . in official society" (2:24–2:28). In this way, *Small Axe* exposes London as a city very much like those portrayed in the fictional works analyzed here: in a way that resonates with Cecil Foster's depiction of Toronto as an increasingly diverse city, the London of the mid-twentieth century is also a door ajar, and as illustrated in the constant face-offs with racist police, the formerly colonized British citizens live under constant surveillance by law enforcement.

Subsequent films in *Small Axe* illustrate the constant pull and push inherent in reconfiguring the city of London as a new home. As evidenced by police officers who target West Indian immigrants, Black West Indians are constantly being engaged in a battle to affirm their personhood and humanity, while segments of white London grapple with the notion of a diverse society that no longer designates a *place* (as articulated by PC Pulley, one of the police officers who targets West Indian immigrants) for Black people.

In chapter 4, I argue that James's characters in *A Brief History* challenge the designated authorities of the cities of Kingston and New York to forge a parallel economic system that undermines the goals of official global neoliberalist configurations. As the chapter argues and as other critics of the novel have suggested, the violence (local and exported) that accompanies this example of the global Western hegemony is destructive and logically creates other problems; perhaps most egregiously, it undermines legitimate and more wholesome responses. While also emphasizing how marginalized groups can subvert the dominant culture, *Small Axe* highlights two key approaches—cultural regeneration and social activism—that successfully contest cities' imperialist paradigms in ways that advance rather than undermine the claims to belonging.

The anthology's official summary describes episode 1, "Mangrove," as "the true story of the Mangrove Nine," who made legal history. In recuperating the infamous Notting Hill protest and the police injustices that spurred it, this episode dramatizes the activism of West Indians in London and highlights one important way in which West Indians have sought to address the social injustices in London and multiple other cities in the post-1950s era.[2] The social activism depicted in "Mangrove" is one clear example of Mike Davis's assertion (quoted in the introduction) that "the new urban poor will not go into this dark night" and that "their resistance . . . becomes the principal condition for the survival of the unity of the human race against the implicit triage of the new global order" (13).

One remarkable component of this episode is the visibility of women activists in this historic demand for inclusion in the city. Althea Jones is a young Black woman, a university student, a Black Panther member, and one of the defendants in the "Mangrove Nine" case. Most importantly, though, all the scenes in which Althea and other women are involved compel viewers to remember that Black resistance (past and present) in London and other cities was and is fierce, sustained, and well organized. Furthermore, the gender disparity in representations of Black activism is not only contested here: female presence, strength, and leadership are foregrounded.

Small Axe offers other insights into the experiences and roles of Black women in cities. In chapter 2 of this book, we observe that when immigrant women or their children achieve social mobility through conventionally sanctioned means, the cost is often their social and psychological well-being, while chapter 3 demonstrates how women are victimized in the global capitalist system through transatlantic sex trafficking. The examples presented in these chapters necessarily configure the female characters as victims, even when the women in *Black Sisters Street* and *Beyond the Horizon* find ways to exercise some control over their lives. In all instances, whatever the women manage to salvage comes at the cost of their connection to community, their freedoms, and their agency. Set in the same city as *NW* and *Call the Midwife*, *Small Axe* offers more extensive and textured depictions of female experience. While *NW*'s Keisha-Natalie and *Call the Midwife*'s Lucille break through racism in social and professional contexts and even though Lucille consistently challenges racial aggression, both women still suffer mostly psychologically and often privately. Conversely, in *Small Axe*, in the presentation of Althea, of the women who chase the police away from The Mangrove restaurant, and of the West Indian women who hold classes for Black West Indian children (see episode 5, "Education"), the series expands, in productive ways, women's involvement in, and responses to, the past and present challenges in global cities, or what Herbert terms "the violence of colonial modernity" (205). Through their involvement in organized resistance and collective action, these women are represented as key players in the quest toward systemic change in the city. In these depictions, the women portrayed in *Small Axe* are seen not only as participants in freedom struggles but also as leaders and sources of inspiration.

The significant visibility of Caribbean culture as a mainstay across the different episodes in *Small Axe* complicates and expands the place of cultural tradition in the journey toward full integration and expression of humanity in today's cities. As I argue in chapter 5, an important intervention that Foster's *Sleep On, Beloved* makes into conversations about Black immigrant experiences in cities is its critical engagement with the limits of cultural regeneration—what I have theorized as an opiate. While West Indian cultural traditions are vibrant and well integrated into the cultural fabric of Toronto, the official power structure of the city places limits on the expression of these cultural practices; that is to say, cultural events are both conveniently mobilized to advance the city's capitalist agenda and also excessively surveilled and contained. Ishmael, Thomas's main character in *Man Gone Down* (chapter 1), ponders the inspirational capacity of African American music, and he and his children privately find inspiration in reggae music. In its treatment of culture, *Small Axe* also presents other useful perspectives on how Black immigrants have harnessed cultural practices in ways that have considerable and lasting impact on the lives of people in these communities. In these depictions, West Indian cultural practices also alter the cultural texture of London beyond seasonal and covert practices. This is not to say that the cultural inroads that West Indians have made have eliminated other problems with racism and integration, because a central conflict that runs through all five episodes is the constant battle over personhood that the immigrant confronts.

McQueen's articulation of the goal and accomplishment of the emphasis on culture provides some useful insights. In an interview with National Public Radio's Michel Martin, McQueen lays out the intervention that the series makes and affirms the duality of immigrant experiences in London that the films engage: McQueen admits that immigrants in the city have some "troubling" experiences. Yet he also points to instances that are "full of love and compassion and triumphs." He highlights the importance of "explor[ing] the whole gambit, to put as much . . . effort into the things which come out organically within Black culture, which is music and how that is used as a healing tool and how that is used to . . . elevate" (3:02–3:44). The healing that McQueen addresses here moves beyond being a mere opiate or temporary relief; healing suggests something more permanent, more profound. Additionally, the visibility that the film series has received because it was broadcast on BBC gives more credence to the historical experiences and broadens the audience base. McQueen observes that "families are watching *Small Axe*. They're looking at it. They're laughing. They're crying. . . . They're embracing. . . . What I'm hearing is that people are sort of opening up and talking about their experiences of living in London during that period to their kids. And kids are asking questions—their grandchildren" (4:12–4:37). McQueen's reflections illustrate some tangible ways in which this artistic account of Black West Indian experiences in London has impacted members of the community being represented as well as their descendants who still must grapple with racism: McQueen's articulation of the on-the-ground, lived impact of the film prompts recourse to Phillips's insistence that artistic representations play a central role in helping communities confront their struggles with racism while also opening up conversations to the broader community in ways that further ignite productive discussions and even policies and practices. Affirming the power of art and the far reaches of artistic accounts, a review of *Small Axe* in the *Guardian* affirms, "Watching *Small Axe* provides viewers of Caribbean descent with the rare thrill of representation, but these histories are national histories—they are for everyone" (Jones 1).

Where Are All the Others?

The title of this section is a riff on Erna Brodber's essay "Where Are All the Others?" In this essay, Brodber calls attention to the fact that Caribbean creole societies are a true hodgepodge of cultures. The aim of the essay is to remind readers of the contribution of Irish and other immigrants whose cultures have been integrated into the new "indigenous" creole culture.[3] Here I activate the question for similar purposes. In the introduction to this book and throughout its chapters, the focus has been on the fictional accounts of Black experiences in "first world" and "third world" cities. The focus on one racial group is due in part to a desire to advance conversation about Black shared experiences by putting in dialogue with each other works depicting Black experiences in a diverse range of urban settings.

Yet, given the grounding of this study in postcolonial-globalization studies, some discussion, even in brief, of the experiences of other minoritized people is warranted. This is important for a number of reasons: At the most basic level, colonization affected almost all indigenous and other groups outside of white or European designation. Relatedly, the waves of immigration that followed in the late colonial and early postcolonial epochs and that continue today included a wide range of racial-ethnic groups that have experienced racism and its concomitant exclusions in similar ways. For example, as Phillips outlines in the introduction to *Color Me English*, he experienced racism alongside the newly arrived Ali, a Muslim teenager from Pakistan—a society that was both created and colonized by the British. This example also illustrates the variegated immigrant experience. Phillips suggests that Ali—who did not have the cover of the English language and Christianity that Phillips, as a West Indian had—experienced more racial-cultural exclusion because, unlike Phillips, "Ali . . . had the worlds of religion and language into which he might retreat and hide from the English which, of course, made him deeply untrustworthy" (7). Phillips's depiction is a useful reminder of the importance of both including and delineating immigrants' experiences of racism across racial, ethnic, and cultural lines.

G. S. Sharat Chandra's short story "Sari of the Gods," which is set in New York City, provides insights into how some Indian writers portray their communities' encounters with foreign city spaces. "Sari of the Gods" relates the experiences of a young couple, Prapulla and Shekar, each of whom approaches life in the city with a different kind of anxiety. And while their responses vary, they both reflect deep concerns about belonging and view themselves as racial-cultural outsiders. Prapulla's anxieties are manifest in her desire to be in an Indian community: "One of the things that Prapulla had insisted on was to have a place waiting for them in New York where other Indian immigrants lived" (13). While clearly on the other end of the spectrum, Shekar's attitude toward New York also betrays concerns about fitting in in a city where he believes his racial-cultural identity will not be validated, where unlike his wife, being identified with other Indians would undermine his efforts to integrate: "It was Shekar who looked distraught at the sight of Indian faces. In the time it took them to travel from the airport to the apartment, he had seen many of his brown brethren in the city streets looking strange and out of place" (14).

The obvious displacement that fellow Indians experience in New York City is the fear that haunts Shekar. This is why "he dreaded being surrounded by his kind, ending up like them building little Indias in the obscure corners of New York" (14). In Shekar's eyes, survival in the city necessitates a disavowal of his Indianness. The mention of "brown brethren" also highlights another layer of racialization beyond Black and white, which serves as a useful reminder of the hegemonic whiteness that still permeates cities and of the imperialist impulses that remain in cities despite the diversity.

When Shekar invites his colleagues to dinner, all his actions are carefully crafted to erase the Indian and perform the Euro-American. He "set the wine glasses next to the handloomed napkins as he had seen in *Good Housekeeping*" (17). He chooses German wine, drinks too much, and provides the cigars he believes befit an "American" dinner. The symbolism of the "Americanized" Shekar's excessive brandy pouring that leads to the ruination of Prapulla's special wedding sari is self-evident: in the eyes of Shekar, whose overreaches to being seen as American are really about professional and economic survival in the city, in respected, successful professional circles, even in a racially and ethnically diverse city such as New York, whiteness and European culture still predominate. For Shekar, to be marked as Indian or to be publicly associated with anything Indian is to be set up for disregard and professional failure, because although Shekar is ostensibly allowed to enter a hallowed professional space, there are many signals that convey to him that his place there is tenuous.

An examination of the experiences of a more racial, ethnic, and cultural diversity in cities also highlights the cross-racial, multiethnic solidarities that have advanced the interest of a wide range of minoritized communities, such as those observed in multiple cities in aftermath of George Floyd's murder by then police officer Derek Chauvin. The dramatization of Black immigrant experience that *Small Axe* offers takes up this important question of cross-racial/cultural solidarities. Althea's leadership extends beyond the British Black community of London. Early in "Mangrove," she addresses a group of South Asian men, a group that, by all appearances, is also ethnically diverse. Althea introduces herself as a "student studying biochemistry" but adds, "Today I am here as a member of the Black Panther movement. I have been invited here by your trade union to talk to you about your workers' rights and your power as a collective force." Althea is clear about the goals and possibilities of cross-racial solidarity. She continues, "We have discovered—discovered and rediscovered— the ways in which *we* can overcome the fragmentation *our* people have suffered throughout our history, and the way is through joining the struggle and being part of an organized struggle. It is the struggle actually which makes us whole" (emphasis mine) (13:05-13:27). It is notable that Althea speaks in the first-person plural: "the ways in which we can overcome the fragmentation our people have suffered" (13:30-13:38) speaks not only to the struggles of Black

West Indian immigrants; as a member of the Black Panthers, she addresses a larger Black diasporic struggle, and her language of collective action as she speaks to a group of South Asian men widens the community even further. Her seemingly joking reference at a more informal meeting with South Asian men addresses the shared struggle more directly: "Well, if colonialism is good for anything it brought us together on this table" (13:43–14:35). This last statement captures the urgent need for joint efforts to combat racism and claim a space in London in a way that reconfigures this city as a genuinely (growing) heterogeneous space. This idea then circles us back to the point of this inclusion: while the scope of this study that centers on artistic renditions of Black experiences in cities does not allow for detailed analyses of representations of other racial and ethnic groups, it is important to draw attention to just a few examples of a large and still-growing body of creative works—literature, film, and other media—that takes up the pressing issues that formerly colonized and minoritized groups continue to face and courageously confront in cities that are almost always intended for Europeans and that maintain a system of domination that manifests itself in old and new ways, despite the rhetoric of the "global village."

The creative works addressed throughout this discussion illustrate and affirm that cities continue to be at the forefront of the ongoing battles over sheer survival and, more importantly, over minoritized people's claims to personhood. While none of the texts—literary or otherwise—offer completely pessimistic outlooks on cities, these creative accounts all support a theorization of cities as incomplete, challenging, dynamic, and sometimes still-daunting spaces of opportunity. Indeed, Fanon's "town cut in two" characterization remains relevant, even as the depictions addressed here show a more layered and complex manifestation of the split that Fanon observed. The vast array of perspectives that each of the texts offers and the on-the-ground confirmation that the response to *Small Axe* shows support Phillips's claim that "writers have a crucial part to play" in the walk toward compassion, plurality, and acceptance of difference. It is my view that, given the offerings we have received from writers and other creative artists whose works have been examined here, cities—where the kinds of challenges that Phillips addresses have been most visible—are also the vanguards in the "imaginative osmosis" (16) that Phillips believes can lead humanity out of its deluge of intolerance. Cities, along with the creative arts, then, can usher in a different kind of globalization, one in which the remnants of imperialist global order will be undermined and erased.

Acknowledgments

Completing a project such as this one challenges the notion that writing is a solitary affair, because successful completion requires the input of so many different people who play diverse roles.

Many of my friends and colleagues supported me by listening to my ideas, helping me to refine them, reading drafts, and offering their insights. For this important contribution, I thank Curdella Forbes, Shirley Wong, Emily Todd, Michelle Stephens, and Denia Fraser. I thank Erold for being the one whose role as a reader, listener, and contributor was ceaseless. My brother Nigel did more reading and research than a younger sibling should be asked to do, and I am grateful to him and my sister-in-law, Letha, who was very much a part of these efforts. My daughters, Nathara and Mandisa, also added reading my drafts to their list of family responsibilities, and for that I am truly grateful.

My colleagues in the English Department at Westfield State University have consistently encouraged me and supported my work. I thank my department chair, Dr. Stephen Adams, for advocating for release time, and interim dean Dr. Emily Todd for her multiyear role in supporting my request for research time. I am also grateful to Dr. Juline Mills, interim provost, for supporting and facilitating release time.

Many thanks to the support from the Black Studies Department at Amherst College, including Robyn Rogers and Desy Williams (Philosophy) for the support.

The year of full-time teaching at Mount Holyoke College was particularly helpful in allowing me time to advance my work on the manuscript. The reduced teaching assignment and smaller classes not only gave me time but also opportunity to test my ideas as I developed courses based on research for this book. I am especially grateful to Professors Kimberly Juanita Brown, Preston

Smith, Nigel Alderman, and Elizabeth Young and the dean of the interim faculty, Dorothy Mosby.

Much of the writing journey includes meticulous editors who walked hand in hand with me. For this supportive company and expertise, I sincerely thank Rosie Pearson, Jordan Trice, and Teri-Ann McDonald.

The confidence and encouragement of so many of my friends have been essential to my motivation to complete this work. For this I thank so many people including Professors Carlene Edie and Keisha-Kahn Perry, Carol B, Carmeneta, Georgia, Sonji, Carolyn Cooper, and Merlene.

I thank my students, who read these texts with me so many times and whose questions and insights have done so much to enrich and challenge my perspectives.

The day-to-day support with the tasks that cannot be put on hold while we read and write has been my baseline of sustenance. For this I thank Erold for all he has done to support me and to stand in for me throughout this process. I am grateful to Kahlia, Miguel, Carolyn, Janet, Letha, Nigel, and Shanice for invaluable roles in this important area. I thank my sisters and all my extended family for their love and support.

I am grateful to Sally and Soji, who offered me a workspace in their home when the COVID-related lockdown kept libraries closed. Similarly, Professor Opal Palmer Adisa and her staff at the Center for Gender and Development at the University of the West Indies Mona kindly offered me workspace, as did Professor Rupika Delgoda and her staff at the Natural Products Institute at the University of the West Indies Mona.

Many thanks to the librarians at Amherst College for their support in making research material readily available to me.

I thank Rutgers University Press, particularly Kimberly Guinta and the editorial and marketing teams, for facilitating this work and the external reviewers for their time and insightful feedback.

Notes

Introduction

1 I place "openness" in quotation marks here because even that mostly accurate characterization of cities is interrogated in later chapters.

2 Rashmi Varma uses the term *postcolonial city* in a very specific way to refer to cities created by the British in areas they colonized to serve colonial purposes. The cities she studies are Bombay, London, and Nairobi. Varma also theorizes "unhomely subjects" to focus particularly on "postcolonial feminist citizenship" (2) through the prism of these imperial and colonial cities.

3 This is not to suggest that Varma's study does not account for the complex and even subversive characteristics of the postcolonial city. See, for example, Varma's insight about the disruptive possibilities of cities (11–13). My point is more one about emphasis.

4 E. Lâle Demirtürk's *The Contemporary African American Novel* is another important work that takes up several concerns germane to those addressed in this book. As evident in its title, *The Contemporary African American Novel* focuses specifically on African American fictions.

5 Smith lays out some of the familiar structural and other features that link cities: in addition to markets and trash, there are "multi-story buildings, long streets, sewer pipes, water mains, and a 'downtown' zone of financial institutions and government offices. There are a thousand varieties of sounds and smells competing with the weather and daylight that frame the skyline of the built environment. There are crowds of people—rich, poor, young, old, female, male, gay, straight, trans, able, disabled, employed, students, jobless, resident and visitors" (3).

6 While Scott wonders "whether postcolonialism has not lost its point and become normalized, as a strategy for the mere accumulation of meaning" (392), Krishna concludes that the "ideas and beliefs of postcolonialism are consequential and important in the struggle against improvising ideational and material effects of neoliberal globalization" (177).

7 Young's essay is a response to one of the most notable conversations about the relevance and future of postcolonial studies, which occurred in a roundtable published in the *PMLA* (2007). There, seven scholars contemplate, with varying

perspectives, the currency of the critical tools that postcolonial studies offer in helping us to understand, explain, and interrogate the ongoing impact of the colonial enterprise. The multiple examples of such inquiries in individual publications, conference panels, anthologies, courses, and even informal conversations illustrate the significant interest in, and extent of interrogation of, both the field of postcolonial studies and the term itself. My goal here is not to rehash these arguments or to align myself to any of the camps. Instead, I want to highlight points of intersection between postcolonial and globalization studies and particularly how the tools they offer continue to help us to make sense of creative accounts that center Black experiences in urban spaces in different formerly colonized locales.

8 These protests voiced concern that the forces of globalization were increasingly bringing the world's economies into a single system. The new technologies, new media, and new political landscape (following the fall of the Soviet Union), protestors said, enabled multi- and transnational companies to enter global markets outside the established markets of the West. This expansion has led to outsourced manufacturing, call centers, and other business deals in any country that is poor and reasonably politically stable. For many of the protestors, then, globalization encouraged dependency, disenfranchisement, and disempowerment deriving from the Coca Cola-ization and McDonaldization that eroded cultural differences. Protestors also expressed outrage that multinational companies based in the West were increasingly controlling the world's natural resources and local economies and regulating spending power (Edwards 161).

9 Edwards's reference to Edward Said's suggestions that imperialism remains a "compellingly important" and significant configuration in the world of power and nations clarifies even further the interconnectedness of these fields. Particularly insightful is the view that imperialism is not about a moment in history; it is about a continuing interdependent discourse between subject peoples and the dominant discourses of those in power (Edwards 161).

10 Nayar presents a justification for the links between colonization and globalization that articulates the rationale for my choice of globalization studies as a guiding frame for this study: globalization, in its economic and cultural form in the twentieth century, is only an *accelerated and newer version* of *imperialism*. Imperialism, a form of globalization, refers to the unification of territories around the world under one imperial power, the use of these territories as sources of raw material and as markets, and the constant mobility—mostly one way—of European goods toward the Asian or African continents. But what links postcolonialism with globalization today is the ethical and intellectual concern with domination, power, and subjugation (Nayar 193).

11 Here I borrow from M. Nourbese Philip's notion of "A Genealogy of Resistance" elaborated in Marlene NourbeSe Philip, *A Genealogy of Resistance: And Other Essays*, 1st edition (Mercury Press, 1997).

12 According to Davis, "Cities . . . are growing by 60 million per year, and 90 percent of the increase in world population over the next generation will be accommodated by the urban areas of less-developed regions. By 2030, two billion more people will struggle for survival in cities, especially in the teeming metropolitan complexes of Africa and Asia" (11).

13 According to Jeremy Seabrook's similar statistics, "In 1950, only 18 per cent of the people in developing countries lived in cities. By 2000, this exceeded 40 per cent" (7).

Additionally, "it is projected that the global share of people living in urban areas will to increase to 70 percent in 2050, compared to 56 percent in 2020" (Szmigiera).

14 In some ways, this suggestion that cities will probably eclipse the nation-state to become new "geographies of centrality" might be similar to the role of cities such as Rome and Constantinople in ancient times.

15 Seabrook also predicts that "by 2020 rural populations will have reached their peak, and almost all subsequent population growth will be absorbed by cities" (12).

16 Seabrook expresses similar expectations for resistance: "People are worn out . . . by work and want and must struggle daily for the necessities of life. . . . This relative quiet should not be read as satisfaction with their lives; but neither should it be taken for granted that they will remain inexhaustible absorbers of humiliations and injustices" (11).

17 James Campbell offers a comprehensive overview of some key moments in the search of diasporic connections, with a particular focus on repatriations attempts.

18 Among the reasons Stephens's study is particularly helpful are (a) its choice of figures who embodied transnational-diasporic experience in their ideology, social activism, and physical location in multiple locations: the Caribbean, Europe, and the Americas; (b) the extensive period, 1914–1962, that it covers; and (c) the range and versions of multi-cross-national areas of interest that the combination of thinkers and historical period addresses. Stephens submits that a key reason for the attempts of James, Garvey, and McKay to pursue transnational Blackness/Black community was to attempt "an oppositional form of Black nationalism" outside the standard colonial, Western, imperial order (3).

19 The value of Stephens's work—which offers a detailed account of the context, value, limits, and challenges of these attempts—is that it offers a thoroughgoing treatment of one of the most influential attempts at diasporic formation, which in turn underscores the usefulness of *diaspora* in current discourses about the representation of transnational experiences.

20 John returns to Negritude, another important moment in the search for understanding of the extent of diasporic connections. Noting two opposing discursive practices, the Afro-centric/African-centered versus the hybrid antiessentialist discourses of scholars such as Stuart Hall and Paul Gilroy, John turns away from fears and misgiving about "essentialism" and devotes her analysis in *Clear Word* to the notion that African diasporic writers are engaged in a search for "cohesion and wholeness" (3). John makes the case for a shared something, which she characterizes as an interior spiritual consciousness that has made its way into the works of multiple African and Caribbean creative writers, including Erna Brodber, Earl Lovelace, and Simone Schwarz-Bart, as well as in the writing of African American writers, including Zora Neale Hurston and Toni Cade Bambara.

21 I also find John's insistence on African diasporic writings as a place in which this sense of a cohesive diasporic sensibility is worked out convincing and relevant to the theorization generated from the works under consideration here. While tantalizing and even plausible, the question of an internal, spiritual consciousness does not factor into the treatment of shared cultural patterns and sensibilities that I take up in this book.

22 See Catherine John's introduction to *Clear Word* for a detailed treatment of the countervailing views of African continuity, Afrocentrism, hybridity, antiessentialism, and other related ideas.

23 Edwards's prologue to *The Practice of Diaspora* begins with a reference to W.E.B. Dubois's speech "To the Nations of the World," delivered at the July 1900 Pan-African Conference. Noting the groundbreaking nature of Dubois's framing that "the problem of the twentieth century is the problem of the color line," Edwards reiterates the critical consensus that this notion of the globally shared color line "is often considered an inauguration for thinking about the significance of race in the modern world" (1); further, he emphasizes the significance of Dubois's framing of this modern world problem along racial lines that transcend the Black-white dialectic of US race relations.

24 Part of what marks Edwards's intervention into this ongoing conversation about diaspora, transnational Black (or of color) relations, and internationalism significant is its recognition of the challenges inherent in such ideological, artistic, and cultural alliances. Edwards draws on the diasporic engagement of Alaine Locke, Edward Said, Kenneth Warren, and others to highlight the way the "boundaries of nation-state," with all the historical and contemporary differences they embody, render any kind of diasporic connection as partial and uneven.

Chapter 1   "Natty Dread Rise Again"

1 Maeve Glass's essay "Theorizing Constitutional History," which details interpretations and enactments of the principles inscribed in the US Constitution over centuries, is an excellent example. Focusing particularly on race and the plantation system, Glass's central argument is that "the paradigm that we have assumed to be a primordial part of the constitutional order only emerged in its current iteration in the late nineteenth-century shift from a plantation mode of production rooted in enslaved labor to a dominant industrial mode of production rooted in wage labor" (334).

2 In an article titled "Trump Wishes We Had More Immigrants from Norway. Turns Out We Once Did," Nurith Aizenman quotes then-President Donald Trump, who reportedly made these comments in the context of a more general conversation about immigration to the United States.

3 Throughout this book, I place "first world" and "third world" in quotation marks to indicate my recognition of the problematic nature of these categorizations and the ongoing challenge to find nomenclature that more accurately makes a distinction between the wealthy and the poor (most formally colonized spaces). When appropriate, I also use the term "Global South" interchangeably with "third world."

4 See for example Staples's "Masculinity and Race."

5 I am borrowing T. S. Eliot's term "tradition and the individual talent" developed in the essay with the same title.

6 For specific reference to police killings of Black males, see Coates 11.

7 See for example Curry's chapter "The Political Economy of Niggerdom" in *The Man-Not* (104–136); Demirtürk's "The (Im)possibilities of Writing Black Interiority in Discursive Terrain" in *The Contemporary African American Novel* (159–182); bell hooks's "Plantation Patriarchy" in *We Real Cool* (1–32).

Chapter 2   "Putting the Best Outside"

1 John Hadlock has also used the term *self-fashioning* in his discussion of the *NW*'s treatment of "self-identity construction" among "city dwellers" as what he describes as "a critical concern in *NW*" (155).

2 For a detailed discussion of the historical and contemporary role of London as an important global city, see Varma.

3 While not a new phenomenon, in the twenty-first century, gentrification has emerged as one of the most visible acts of urban classism and racism in the United States, the United Kingdom, and other Western countries.

4 On April 22, 1993, Stephen Lawrence, the teenage son of Jamaican immigrants, was murdered at a bus stop in Eltham. The racially motivated attack received international attention in large part for the way it revealed the persistence of racism in the United Kingdom.

5 The experienced and accomplished barrister offers Keisha-Natalie this advice on how to navigate the white male legal space when another mentor surmises that Keisha-Natalie is beginning to feel the pinch of racism.

6 The ambivalent relationship between Keisha-Natalie and Leah is one aspect of the novel that has attracted attention. See for example López-Ropero; and Taylor.

7 *The Thing around Your Neck* (2009) is the title of Adichie's short story collection as well as of one of the stories. I use the phrase here to characterize the constricted, suffocating space that the sisters occupy, the class difference that places a wedge between them despite their familial connections.

8 See for example Hadlock; and Wang.

Chapter 3   The Transnational Semicircle and the "Mobile" Female Subject

1 See for example Okolo; Barberán Reinares, *Sex Trafficking* 90–120; and Bastida-Rodriguez.

2 Unigwe uses both "Sisi" and "Chisom-Sisi" in the novel. "Chisom" is the character's birth name, and it is by both names that she is known in Lagos. However, once she leaves for Antwerp and enters the sex trade, her reinvention includes changing her name to "Sisi."

Chapter 4   "Writing the Sprawling City"

1 I refer here to Bennett's poem "Colonization in Reverse" (*Selected Poems*).

2 Given the historical event on which the novel is based, many people assume that this unnamed "Singer" is Bob Marley.

3 Squires notes several mostly negative "spatial and structural" changes that result from urban sprawl within national but beyond metropolitan lines of demarcation in urban sprawl and the uneven development of metropolitan America.

4 For a detailed discussion of the role of dons, see Blake; and for a discussion of clientelism as a subculture within the larger Jamaican democracy, see Edie's *Democracy by Default: Dependency and Clientelism in Jamaica* (L. Rienner, 1991).

5 These critics include Rhone Fraser, Maria Grau Perejoan, and Sheri-Marie Harrison.

6 In "Global Sisyphus," Harrison incorporates two 1960s novels, Orlando Patterson's *The Children of Sisyphus* (1962) and Sylvia Wynter's *The Hills of Hebron* (1962), to locate *A Brief History* within a longer tradition of Caribbean writers' attentiveness to how the experiences of urban citizens illustrate the continuation of colonially rooted inequities.

7 In Fraser's essay "Confronting Neocolonialism: An Evaluation of Marlon James's *A Brief History of Seven Killings*," in which he "examine[s] the 'problem' of racism, imperialism, and neocolonialism" in the novel, he reads the novel as, among other

things, "a cautionary tale . . . about the futility of trying to work within the corrupt neocolonial system in order to change it" (70).

8 This is one way in which *A Brief History* is engaged in a dialogue within James's second novel, *The Book of Night Women*: the representation of area dons mirrors that of the Johnny Jumpers in *Night Women*. Working under the brutality of the nineteenth-century plantation slave system, these Johnny Jumpers, a kind of plantation vigilante police force, depended for their survival not only on the extent to which they did the bidding of the official oppressors but also on the way that they, too, ran their own system of brutality, which included rape, lynching, amputation, beatings, and other violent acts to control other enslaved people and to ensure stability, compliance, and ultimately productivity on eighteenth- and nineteenth-century plantations.

9 Balaclava City is the thinly veiled fictional stand-in for the former Back-O-Wall (the setting of Patterson's *The Children of Sisyphus*), which, through "urban renewal," later became Tivoli Gardens. For a helpful discussion of this important context, see Harrison, "Global Sisyphus."

10 Arthur Jennings is the ghost of a deceased politician. The official narrative records Jennings's death as an accident, but we learn from the ghost and others that his death was in fact a murder orchestrated by a political opponent within the same party. Jennings's appearances serve the important role of connecting events in the novel's present to the past and also explain some of the connections between gang violence and politics that the novel details.

11 Johnny Jumpers appear frequently in James's second novel, *The Book of Night Women*. See note 8.

12 The multiple names here are the various identities that Nina Burgess (her true name) adopts to protect herself from what she believes to be her certain killing, ordered by Wales.

13 Millicent's use of "21" is a reference to the fact that in Kingston, zip codes stop at 20.

Chapter 5   A Door Ajar

1 The nanny job that Ona takes is a fictionalized example of the real-life domestic employment scheme of the 1950s, in which Black women mostly from Caribbean countries were recruited to work in the homes of wealthy or upper-middle-class white Canadian families. Different versions of the employment scheme have continued over the subsequent decades.

2 I use the term "regenerated" to characterize the kinds of Caribbean cultural performances and performance spaces addressed in the chapter to indicate the way these cultures have been both transported to and transformed in the new contexts. These transformations are both inevitable and necessary as the culture, like its immigrant practitioners, adjusts to the needs, resources, and restrictions of the new environment.

3 H. Nigel Thomas isolates race as the primary cause of the representative outsider experiences of Foster's characters. See H. Nigel Thomas, "Cecil Foster's *Sleep On, Beloved*: A Depiction of the Consequences of Racism in Canadian Immigration Policy." *Journal of Black Studies*, vol. 38, no. 3, Jan. 2008, pp. 484–501.

4 "Returning resident" is the official term used in Jamaica for Jamaican nationals who have spent considerable amounts of time overseas and return to live permanently in Jamaica.

5   This is the main point: that Toronto is a metonym, a microcosm of sorts for Canada, where "Blacks feel shut out of Canada's much heralded multiculturalism" (H. Thomas 484).

6   Thomas indicates that Ona was not allowed to immigrate on terms similar to that of European immigrants (491).

7   Orlando Patterson defines "social death" as a set of conditions in which enslaved people are "violently uprooted, . . . dissocialized and depersonalized by slave masters" (*Slavery and Social Death* 38), thus rendering the enslaved person, who has no social existence outside their master, socially dead within the context of slave societies.

8   Being "socially alive" is in contrast to the "social death" that Orlando Patterson theorizes in *Slavery and Social Death*.

9   "School-to-prison pipeline" is a term that has been widely used in recent years decades to characterize both how mostly urban schools are set up in ways that make it difficult for most students of color to succeed and how these schools inaugurate a set of punitive practices that literally usher students into the prison system.

10 In the essay "Color Me English," Phillips recalls the experiences he shared with Ali, a Pakistani immigrant teenager, in a school in Leeds where both children and school officials participated in the abuse and exclusions that Phillips suggests treat these students as outsiders well into adulthood (3–17).

11 In *Transnational Negotiations in Diasporic Caribbean Literature*, Kezia Page discusses two terms, "Kingston 21" and "The Tenth Department," used to refer to Miami and New York, where the presence and impact of Jamaican immigrants are so significant that the cities appear to be extensions of the island.

12 The Hole and its place as a community gathering space hark back to early 1950s immigrant fiction such as Samuel Selvon's *The Lonely Londoners* (1953), in which Moses's home serves a similar purpose as a gathering space. As Foster articulates in *Sleep On*, the Hole is a place where "they met new friends and renewed acquaintances [and] welcomed newcomers" (105).

13 Caribana began as a modest carnival parade down Toronto's Yonge Street on August 5, 1967. It has evolved—over fifty years later—into a worldwide brand. The festival has undergone multiple changes since its inception, the most recent of which occurred in May 2011, when Festival Management Committee (FMC) announced that the name of the 2011 festival was changed to "Scotiabank Caribbean Carnival Toronto."

14 The interest and involvement of government and commercial entities in Caribana date back to the inception of the festival.

15 In 1974, a request to the province to provide funding for the event was denied. In 1976, the province funded another carnival group, the Carnival Band Leaders, which staged a parade at the same time as Caribana, but did not support Caribana. Speaking to the implications of the government's choice, Phillip notes that "the government's decision to grant one group money and not the other put the festival in jeopardy and effectively controlled the interest of both groups" (115).

16 Nangwaya is careful to point out that his goal in this article is not to deny incidents of violence at Caribana but rather to highlight the government's overly (and disproportionate) aggressive responses to them.

17 Cecil Foster's recollection of his own scary encounter with Toronto police in a routine traffic stop provides further support for the perception of police's

unwarranted aggression toward Blacks at Caribana and in the city of Toronto (Foster, *A Placed Called heaven*, 4–6).

Conclusion

1 "Reserved for Europeans only" is an allusion to the visible signs and practices of Apartheid South Africa before the collapse of this racist regime in 1990.
2 The Notting Hill riots took place in that area of London in 1958 as a kind of culmination of ongoing racial tension, motivated in large part by the desire of many white Londoners to keep London white. This was mostly in response to the steady and significant flows of mostly Afro-Caribbean people into London and other cities in the United Kingdom.
3 Here I use *indigenous* to mean created in the Caribbean space, not to refer to the cultures of the first peoples of the region.

Works Cited

Adichie, Chimamanda Ngozi. *The Thing around Your Neck*. Alfred A. Knopf, 2009.

Aidoo, Ama Ata. *No Sweetness Here*. Longman, 1988.

———. *Our Sister Killjoy: or, Reflections from a Black-Eyed Squint*. Longman, 1981.

Aizenman, Nurith. "Trump Wishes We Had More Immigrants from Norway. Turns Out We Once Did." *Goats and Soda: Stories of Life in a Changing World*, 12 Jan. 2018, https://www.npr.org/sections/goatsandsoda. Accessed 3 Aug. 2021.

Agnani, Sunil, et al. "Editor's Column: The End of Postcolonial Theory? A Roundtable with Agnani, Sunil, Fernando Coronil, Gaurav Desai, Mamadou Diouf, Simon Gikandi, Susie Tharu, and Jennifer Wenzel." *PMLA*, vol. 122, no. 3, May 2007, pp. 633–51.

Alexander, Michelle. *The New Jim Crow: Mass Incarceration in the Age of Colorblindness*. New Press, 2012.

Baldwin, James. *The Fire Next Time*. Modern Library, 1995.

———. *Collected Essays*. Library of America, 1998.

Barberán Reinares, Laura. "The Pedagogies of Sex Trafficking Postcolonial Fiction: Consent, Agency, and Neoliberalism in Chika Unigwe's *On Black Sisters' Street*." *Canadian Review of Comparative Literature/Revue Canadienne de Littérature Comparée*, vol. 46, no. 1, 2019, pp. 56–76.

———. *Sex Trafficking in Postcolonial Literature: Transnational Narratives from Joyce to Bolaño*. Routledge, 2014.

Barry, Tom, and Dylan Vernon. *Inside Belize*. Second edition, Resource Center Press, 1995.

Bastida-Rodriguez, Patricia. "The Invisible Flâneuse: European Cities and the African Sex Worker in Chika Unigwe's *On Black Sisters' Street*." *The Journal of Commonwealth Literature*, vol. 49, no. 2, 2014, pp. 203–214.

Bennett, Louise. *Selected Poems*. Sangster's Book Stores, 1983.

Blake, Damion Keith. "Shadowing the State: Violent Control and the Social Power of Jamaican Garrison Dons." *Journal of Ethnographic & Qualitative Research*, vol. 8, no. 1, Fall 2013, pp. 56–75.

Borderless: A Docu-Drama about the Lives of Undocumented Workers. Directed by Min Sook Lee, narrated by Dionne Brand, KAIROS Canadian Ecumenical Justice Initiatives, 2006.

Brand, Dionne. "No Rinsed Blue Sky, No Red Flower Fences." *Sans Souci, and Other Stories*. Firebrand Books, 1989, pp. 85–93.

Brodber, Erna. "Where Are All the Other?" *Caribbean Creolization: Reflections on the Cultural Dynamics of Language, Literature, and Identity*, edited by Kathleen M. Balutansky and Marie-Agnes Sourieau, University Press of Florida, 1998, pp. 68–72.

Brown, Kimberly Juanita. *The Repeating Body: Slavery's Visual Resonance in the Contemporary*. Duke University Press, 2015.

Call the Midwife. Created by Heidi Thomas, directed by Pippa Harris and Caro Newling, Neal Street Productions, 2012.

Campbell, James T. *Middle Passages: African American Journeys to Africa, 1787–2005*. Penguin Press, 2006.

Chamoiseau, Patrick. "Prologue: Globalization, Globality, Globe-Stone." *Caribbean Globalizations, 1492–The Present Day*, edited by Eva Sansavior and Richard Scholar, Liverpool University Press, 2015, pp. 1–15.

Coates, Ta-Nehisi. *Between the World and Me*. Spiegel and Grau, 2015.

Curry, Tommy J. *The Man-Not: Race, Class, Genre, and the Dilemmas of Black Manhood*. Temple University Press, 2017.

Danticat, Edwidge. *Create Dangerously: The Immigrant Artist at Work*. Princeton University Press, 2010.

Darko, Amma. *Beyond the Horizon*. 1988. Heinemann, 1995.

Davies, Carole Boyce. *Black Women, Writing, and Identity: Migrations of the Subject*. Routledge, 1994.

Davis, Mike. "The Urbanization of Empire: Megacities and the Laws of Chaos." *Social Text*, vol. 22, no. 4, 2004, pp. 9–15.

Demirtürk, E. Lâle. *The Contemporary African American Novel: Multiple Cities, Multiple Subjectivities, and Discursive Practices of Whiteness in Everyday Urban Encounters*. Fairleigh Dickinson University Press, 2012.

Dixon, Melvin. "The Black Writer's Use of Memory." *History and Memory in African-American Culture*, edited by Geneviève Fabre and Robert O'Meally, Oxford University Press, 1994, pp. 18–27.

Donnell, Alison. *Twentieth-Century Caribbean Literature: Critical Moments in Anglophone Literary History*. Routledge, 2006.

Doyle, John. "Waking Up to Myths about Multicultural Harmony: Novelist Cecil Foster Asks Reader to See Toronto with New Eyes in *Sleep On, Beloved*." *The Globe and Mail* (Toronto), June 17, 1995.

Du Bois, W.E.B. *The Souls of Black Folk*. Bedford Books, 1997.

Edie, Carlene. *Democracy by Default: Dependency and Clientelism in Jamaica*. L. Rienner, 1991

Edwards, Brent Hayes. *The Practice of Diaspora: Literature, Translation, and the Rise of Black Internationalism*. Harvard University Press, 2003.

Edwards, Justin. "Globalization." *Postcolonial Literature*, edited by Justin D. Edwards and Nicolas Tredell, Palgrave Macmillan, 2008, pp. 160–170.

Edwards, Justin D. *Postcolonial Literature*, Nicolas Tredell, consulting editor Palgrave Macmillan, 2008.

Ellis, Nadia. "Marlon James's Savage Business." *Literary Fiction*, March 3, 2015.

Eliot, T. S. "Tradition and the Individual Talent." *Contemporary Literary Criticism: Literary and Cultural Studies*, edited by Robert Con Davis and Ronald Schleifer, Longman, 1994, pp. 27–33.

Ellison, Ralph. *Invisible Man*. Vintage International, 1995.

Eze, Chielozona. "Feminism with a Big 'F': Ethics and the Rebirth of African Feminism in Chika Unigwe's *On Black Sisters' Street*." *Research in African Literatures*, vol. 45, no. 4, 2014, pp. 89–103.

Fanon, Frantz, et al. *The Wretched of the Earth*. 60th anniversary edition, Grove Press, 2021.

Forbes, Curdella. *From Nation to Diaspora: Samuel Selvon, George Lamming and the Cultural Performance of Gender*. UWI Press, 2005.

Foster, Cecil. *Sleep On, Beloved*. Ballantine Books, 1995.

Foster, Cecil. *A Place Called Heaven: The Meaning of Being Black in Canada*. 1st edition, Harper Collins, 1996.

Fraser, Rhone. "Confronting Neocolonialism: An Evaluation of Marlon James's *A Brief History of Seven Killings*." *Caribbean Quarterly*, vol. 63, no. 1, 2017, pp. 67–82.

Frías, María. "Women on Top: Prostitution and Pornography in Amma Darko's *Beyond the Horizon*." *Wasafiri: The Magazine of International Contemporary Writing*, vol. 37, 2002, pp. 8–13.

Gates, Henry Louis, Jr. *The Signifying Monkey: A Theory of African-American Literary Criticism*. 25th anniversary edition, Oxford University Press, 2014.

Glass, Maeve. "Theorizing Constitutional History." *History and Theory*, vol. 60, no. 2, June 2021, pp. 331–346.

Goldmann, Lucien. *Towards a Sociology of the Novel*. Tavistock Publications, 1975.

Greenblatt, Stephen Jay. *Renaissance Self-Fashioning: From More to Shakespeare*. University of Chicago Press, 1980.

Grau Perejoan, Maria. "Marlon James's 'Dangerous' *A Brief History of Seven Killings*." *Coolabah*, vol. 20, Jan. 2017, pp. 94–97.

Green, Garth L., and Philip W. Scher. "Reading Caribana 1997: Black Youth, Puff Daddy, Style, and Diaspora Transformations." *Trinidad Carnival: The Cultural Politics of a Transnational Festival*, Indiana University Press, 2007, pp. 102–135.

Griffin, Rachel. "Bearing Witness and Paying Mind: (Re)Defining the Meanings of Black Male Success." *Masculinity in the Black Imagination: Politics of Communicating Race and Manhood*, edited by Ronald Jackson and Mark C. Hopson, Peter Lang, 2011, pp. 167–186.

Hadlock, John. "Between Urban Ecology and Social Construction: Environment and the Ethics of Representation in Zadie Smith's *NW*." *Twenty-First-Century British Fiction and the City*, edited by Magali Cornier Michael, Springer, 2018, pp. 155–180.

Harrison, Sheri-Marie. "Excess in *A Brief History of Seven Killings*." *Post45*, Oct. 2015.

———. "Global Sisyphus: Rereading the Jamaican 1960s through *A Brief History of Seven Killings*." *Small Axe: A Caribbean Journal of Criticism*, vol. 54, Nov. 2017, pp. 85–97.

Herbert, Caroline. "Postcolonial Cities." *The Cambridge Companion to the City in Literature*, edited by Kevin R. McNamara, Cambridge University Press, 2014, pp. 200–215.

hooks, bell. *We Real Cool: Black Men and Masculinity*. Routledge, 2004.

Huggins, Nathan Irvin. *Black Odyssey: The Afro-American Ordeal in Slavery*. Pantheon Books, 1977.

Hughes, Evan. *Literary Brooklyn: The Writers of Brooklyn and the Story of American City Life*. Henry Holt, 2011.

James, C. L. R., et al. *Facing Reality*. Bewick, 1974.

James, Marlon. *The Book of Night Women*. Riverhead Books, 2009.

———. *A Brief History of Seven Killings*. Riverhead Books, 2014.

John, Catherine A. *Clear Word and Third Sight: Folk Groundings and Diasporic Consciousness in African Caribbean Writing.* Duke University Press, 2003.

Jones, Ellen. Review of *Small Axe*, directed by Steve McQueen. *The Guardian* (London), 15 Nov. 2020, www.theguardian.com/tv-and-radio/2020/nov/15/small-axe-review-steve-mcqueen-triumphs-with-tales-of-britains-caribbean-history.

Kernicky, Matthew J. "The B-Side of Oblivion: Context and Identity in Michael Thomas's *Man Gone Down.*" *Journal of Men's Studies*, vol. 23, no. 2, June 2015, pp. 212–225.

Krishna, Sankaran. *Globalization and Postcolonialism: Hegemony and Resistance in the Twenty-First Century.* Rowman & Littlefield, 2009.

Life and Debt. Directed by Stephanie Black. Tuff Gong Pictures. 2003.

Lipsitz, George. *How Racism Takes Place.* Temple University Press, 2011.

López-Ropero, Lourdes. "Searching for a 'Different Kind of Freedom': Postcoloniality and Postfeminist Subjecthood in Zadie Smith's *NW.*" *Atlantis*, vol. 38, no. 2, 2016, pp. 123–139.

Maïthé, Chini. "No Man's Land: Belgium's Red-Light District." *The Brussels Times*, 21 Oct. 2020.

Manning, Frank E. "Carnival in Canada: The Politics of Celebration." *Folk Groups and Folklore Genres: A Reader*, edited by Elliott Oring, Utah State University Press, 1989, pp. 78–86.

McClintock, Anne "The Angel of Progress: Pitfalls of the Term 'Post-Colonialism.'" *Social Text*, no. 31/32, 1992, pp. 84–97.

McNamara, Kevin R. "Introduction." *The Cambridge Companion to the City in Literature*, edited by Kevin R. McNamara, Cambridge University Press, 2014, pp. 1–16.

McQueen, Steve. Interview with Michel Martin. *Weekend All Things Considered*, National Public Radio, Washington, DC, 5 Dec. 2020.

Melville, Herman. *Moby-Dick; or, the Whale.* First Avenue Editions, 2014.

Michael, Magali Cornier. "Introduction: Twenty-First-Century British Fiction and the City." *Twenty-First-Century British Fiction and the City*, edited by Magali Cornier Michael, Palgrave Macmillan, 2018, pp. 1–14.

Nangwaya Ajamu. "Policing Caribana like It's a Threat to National Security." *Share*, vol. 38, no. 19, July 2015, p. 5.

Napier, Winston. *African American Literary Theory: A Reader.* New York University Press, 2000.

Nayar, Pramod K. *Postcolonialism: A Guide for the Perplexed.* Continuum, 2010.

Neal, Mark Anthony. *New Black Man.* Routledge, 2005.

Nora, Pierre. "Between Memory and History: Les Lieux de Mémoire." *Representations*, no. 26, Special Issue: Memory and CounterMemory (Spring 1989), pp. 7–24.

Okolo, Ifeyinwa Genevieve. "Unsettled Subjects: Sex Work in Chika Unigwe's *On Black Sisters' Street.*" *English Studies in Africa: A Journal of the Humanities*, vol. 62, no. 2, 2019, pp. 112–123.

Page, Kezia. *Transnational Negotiations in Caribbean Diasporic Literature: Remitting the Text.* Routledge, 2014.

Parham, Marisa. *Haunting and Displacement in African American Literature and Culture.* Routledge, 2009.

Patterson, Orlando. *The Ordeal of Integration: Progress and Resentment in America's "Racial" Crisis.* Basic Civitas, 1998.

———. *Slavery and Social Death: A Comparative Study.* Harvard University Press, 1982.

Philip, Marlene Nourbese. *A Genealogy of Resistance and Other Essays*. Mercury Press, 1997.

Phillips, Caryl. *Color Me English: Migration and Belonging before and after 9/11*. New Press, 2011.

Phillip, Lyndon. "Reading Caribana 1997: Black Youth, Puff Daddy, Style, and Diaspora Transformations." *Trinidad Carnival: The Cultural Politics of a Transnational Festival*, edited by Garth L. Green et al., Indiana University Press, 2007, pp. 102–35.

"Politics with Amy Walter: The Politics of Defund the Police." *The Takeaway*, National Public Radio, New York Public Radio, 12 June 2020.

Pratt, Mary Louise. *Imperial Eyes: Travel Writing and Transculturation*. Second edition. Routledge, 2008.

Rankine, Claudia. *Citizen: An American Lyric*. Graywolf Press, 2014.

Sacks, Marcy. "'To Be a Man and Not a Lackey': Black Men, Work, and the Construction of Manhood in Gilded Age New York City." *American Studies*, vol. 45, no. 1, 2004, pp. 39–63.

Said, Edward W. *Culture and Imperialism*. First Vintage Books edition, Vintage Books, 1994.

Sassen, Saskia. "Introduction." *Global Networks, Linked Cities*, edited by Saskia Sassen, Routledge, 2002, pp. 1–36.

———. "Whose City Is It? Globalization and the Formation of New Claims." *The Urban Sociology Reader*, edited by Jan Lim and Christopher Mele, Routledge, 2013, pp. 308–315.

Scott, David. "The Social Construction of Postcolonial Studies." *Postcolonial Studies and Beyond*, edited by Ania Loomba, et al., Duke University Press 2005, pp. 385–400.

Seabrook, Jeremy. *Cities: Small Guides to Big Issues*. Pluto Press, 2007.

Selvon, Samuel. *The Lonely Londoners*. Longman, 1953.

Sharat Chandra, G. S. "Sari of the Gods." *Sari of the Gods*. Coffee House Press, 1998, pp. 13–22.

Shipley, Joseph T. *Dictionary of Word Origins*. Philosophical Library, 1945.

Small Axe: A Collection of 5 Films from Steve McQueen. Directed by Steve McQueen, BBC, 2020.

Smith, Monica L. *Cities: The First 6,000 Years*. Viking, 2019.

Smith, Zadie. *NW*. Penguin Press, 2012.

Squires, Gregory D. "Urban Sprawl and the Uneven Development of Metropolitan America." *Urban Sprawl: Causes, Consequences and Policy Responses*, edited by Gregory D. Squires, Urban Institute Press, 2002, pp. 1–22.

Staples, Robert. "Masculinity and Race: The Dual Dilemma of Black Men." *Journal of Social Issues*, vol. 34, no. 1, Winter 1978, pp. 169–183.

Stephens, Michelle Ann. *Black Empire: The Masculine Global Imaginary of Caribbean Intellectuals in the United States, 1914–1962*. Duke University Press, 2005.

Stone, Carl. *Democracy and Clientelism in Jamaica*. Transaction Books, 1980.

Szmigiera, M. "Degree of Urbanization 2021, by Continent." Satista, 2 Dec. 2021, www.statista.com/statistics/270860/urbanization-by-continent/.

Taylor, Judith. "Beyond 'Obligatory Camaraderie': Girls' Friendship in Zadie Smith's *NW* and Jillian and Mariko Tamaki's *Skim*." *Feminist Studies*, vol. 42, no. 2, 2016, pp. 445–468.

Thomas, H. Nigel. "Cecil Foster's *Sleep On, Beloved*: A Depiction of the Consequences of Racism in Canadian Immigration Policy." *Journal of Black Studies*, vol. 38, no. 3, Jan. 2008, pp. 484–501.

Thomas, Michael. *Man Gone Down*. Black Cat, 2007.

Unigwe, Chika. *On Black Sisters Street*. Ohio University Press, 2012.

Varma, Rashmi. *The Postcolonial City and Its Subjects: London, Nairobi, Bombay*. Routledge, 2014.

Young, Robert J. C. "Postcolonial Remains." *New Literary History*, vol. 43, no. 1, Jan. 2012, pp. 19–42.

Walonen, Michael K. "Violence, Diasporic Transnationalism, and Neo-Imperialism: *A Brief History of Seven Killings*." *Small Axe: A Caribbean Journal of Criticism*, vol. 57, Nov. 2018, pp. 1–12.

Wang, Hui. "We Are Not Free to Choose: Class Determinism in Zadie Smith's *NW*." *Arcadia: Internationale Zeitschrift Für Literaturwissenschaft*, vol. 51, no. 2, 2016, pp. 385–404.

Waymer, Damion. "A Man: An Autoethnographic Analysis of Black Male Identity Negotiation." *Qualitative Inquiry*, vol. 14, no. 6, Sept. 2008, p. 968.

Wynter, Sylvia. "Novel and History; Plot and Plantation." *Savacou*, vol. 5, 1971, pp. 95–102.

Index

About the Author

CAROL BAILEY teaches in the Black Studies Department at Amherst College, where she offers courses in African American, African diasporic, and Caribbean literatures, as well as in interdisciplinary Black studies. She is the author of *A Poetics of Performance: The Oral-Scribal Aesthetic in Anglophone Caribbean Fiction* and co-editor (with Stephanie McKenzie) of Pamela Mordecai's *A Fierce Green Place*.

Printed and bound by CPI Group (UK) Ltd, Croydon, CR0 4YY

09/06/2025

14685736-0001